Bloom's Modern Critical Views

WILLIAM WORDSWORTH
Updated Edition

Edited and with an introduction by
Harold Bloom
Sterling Professor of the Humanities
Yale University

CHELSEA HOUSE
P U B L I S H E R S
An imprint of Infobase Publishing

Bloom's Modern Critical Views: William Wordsworth—Updated Edition

Copyright ©2007 Infobase Publishing

Introduction © 2007 by Harold Bloom

Chelsea House
An imprint of Infobase Publishing
132 West 31st Street
New York NY 10001

Library of Congress Cataloging-in-Publication Data
William Wordsworth / Harold Bloom, editor. — Updated ed.
     p. cm — (Bloom's moden critical views)
   Includes bibliographical references and index.
   ISBN 0-7910-9318-2
   1. Wordsworth, William, 1770–1850—Criticism and interpretation.
 I. Bloom, Harold.
 PR5881.W46 2006
 821'.7—dc22   2006025337

Contributing Editor: Janyce Marson
Cover design by Takeshi Takahashi
Cover photo © The Granger Collection, New York

Printed in the United States of America

Bang EJB 10 9 8 7 6 5 4 3 2 1

This book is printed on acid-free paper.

Contents

Bloom's Modern Critical Views

African American
 Poets:
 Wheatley–Tolson
African American
 Poets:
 Hayden–Dove
Edward Albee
Dante Alighieri
Isabel Allende
American and
 Canadian Women
 Poets,
 1930–present
American Women
 Poets, 1650–1950
Hans Christian
 Andersen
Maya Angelou
Asian-American
 Writers
Margaret Atwood
Jane Austen
Paul Auster
James Baldwin
Honoré de Balzac
Samuel Beckett
The Bible
William Blake
Jorge Luis Borges
Ray Bradbury
The Brontës
Gwendolyn Brooks
Elizabeth Barrett
 Browning
Robert Browning
Italo Calvino
Albert Camus
Truman Capote
Lewis Carroll
Miguel de Cervantes
Geoffrey Chaucer

Anton Chekhov
G.K. Chesterton
Kate Chopin
Agatha Christie
Samuel Taylor
 Coleridge
Joseph Conrad
Contemporary Poets
Julio Cortázar
Stephen Crane
Daniel Defoe
Don DeLillo
Charles Dickens
Emily Dickinson
E.L. Doctorow
John Donne and the
 17th-Century Poets
Fyodor Dostoevsky
W.E.B. DuBois
George Eliot
T.S. Eliot
Ralph Ellison
Ralph Waldo Emerson
William Faulkner
F. Scott Fitzgerald
Sigmund Freud
Robert Frost
William Gaddis
Johann Wolfgang
 von Goethe
George Gordon,
 Lord Byron
Graham Greene
Thomas Hardy
Nathaniel Hawthorne
Robert Hayden
Ernest Hemingway
Hermann Hesse
Hispanic-American
 Writers
Homer

Langston Hughes
Zora Neale Hurston
Aldous Huxley
Henrik Ibsen
John Irving
Henry James
James Joyce
Franz Kafka
John Keats
Jamaica Kincaid
Stephen King
Rudyard Kipling
Milan Kundera
Tony Kushner
Ursula K. Le Guin
Doris Lessing
C.S. Lewis
Sinclair Lewis
Norman Mailer
Bernard Malamud
David Mamet
Christopher Marlowe
Gabriel García
 Márquez
Cormac McCarthy
Carson McCullers
Herman Melville
Arthur Miller
John Milton
Molière
Toni Morrison
Native-American
 Writers
Joyce Carol Oates
Flannery O'Connor
George Orwell
Octavio Paz
Sylvia Plath
Edgar Allan Poe
Katherine Anne
 Porter

Bloom's Modern Critical Views

Marcel Proust
Thomas Pynchon
Philip Roth
Salman Rushdie
J. D. Salinger
José Saramago
Jean-Paul Sartre
William Shakespeare
William Shakespeare's
 Romances
George Bernard Shaw
Mary Wollstonecraft
 Shelley
Alexander Solzhenitsyn

John Steinbeck
Jonathan Swift
Amy Tan
Alfred, Lord Tennyson
Henry David Thoreau
J.R.R. Tolkien
Leo Tolstoy
Ivan Turgenev
Mark Twain
John Updike
Kurt Vonnegut
Derek Walcott
Alice Walker
Robert Penn Warren

H.G. Wells
Eudora Welty
Edith Wharton
Walt Whitman
Oscar Wilde
Tennessee Williams
Tom Wolfe
Virginia Woolf
William Wordsworth
Jay Wright
Richard Wright
William Butler Yeats
Émile Zola

Editor's Note

My introduction centers upon Wordsworth's exaltation of the natural man, particularly in the sublime poignance of "The Old Cumberland Beggar."

M.H. Abrams, dean of Romantic scholar-critics, contrasts the two traditions of Wordsworth criticism, Matthew Arnold's "Poet of Nature" and A.C. Bradley's Hegelian sense of Wordsworthian Sublimity.

My interpretation of "Tintern Abbey" explores the poem's triumph over its own myth of memory, while Frances Ferguson subtly finds implicit in *The Prelude* a poetically enabling "extensive chain of affections."

The "Intimations of Immortality" Ode is seen by Paul H. Fry as mediating between the Simple Wordsworth (Arnoldian) and the Sublime Wordsworth (Bradleyan).

Thomas Weiskel provides an appropriate Romantic Sublime exegesis of *The Prelude*'s Simplon Pass passage in Book 6, after which Geoffrey Hartman, luminary of twentieth-century Wordsworth criticism, demonstrates the alliance between radical inwardness and expressionistic power in *The Prelude*.

The affinity between Wordsworth and Emerson, despite their different visions of the self, is analyzed by David Bromwich, while Kenneth Johnston examines early poetic influences upon the young Wordsworth.

Something of the complex differences between the separate versions of *The Prelude* is given by Jonathan Wordsworth, after which Dennis Taylor argues for a Catholic element in Wordsworth's achievement.

In this volume's final essay, Sally Bushell traces connections between Wordsworth's drama *The Borderers* and his long narrative poem *The Excursion*.

HAROLD BLOOM

Introduction

There is a human loneliness,
A part of space and solitude,
In which knowledge cannot be denied.
In which nothing of knowledge fails,
The luminous companion, the hand,
The fortifying arm, the profound
Response, the completely answering voice....
—Wallace Stevens

The Prelude was to be only the antechapel to the Gothic church of *The Recluse*, but the poet Wordsworth knew better than the man, and *The Prelude* is a complete and climactic work. The key to *The Prelude* as an internalized epic written in creative competition to Milton is to be found in those lines (754–860) of the *Recluse* fragment that Wordsworth prefaced to *The Excursion* (1814). Wordsworth's invocation, like Blake's to the Daughters of Beulah in his epic *Milton*, is a deliberate address to powers higher than those that inspired *Paradise Lost*:

> Urania, I shall need
> Thy guidance, or a greater Muse, if such

Descend to earth or dwell in highest heaven!
For I must tread on shadowy ground, must sink
Deep—and, aloft ascending, breathe in worlds
To which the heaven of heavens is but a veil.

The shadowy ground, the depths beneath, and the heights aloft are all
in the mind of man, and Milton's heaven is only a veil, separating an
allegorical unreality from the human paradise of the happiest and best
regions of a poet's mind. Awe of the personal Godhead fades before the poet's
reverence for his own imaginative powers:

All strength—all terror, single or in bands,
That ever was put forth in personal form—
Jehovah—with his thunder, and the choir
Of shouting Angels, and the empyreal thrones—
I pass them unalarmed.

Blake, more ultimately unorthodox than Wordsworth as he was, had
yet too strong a sense of the Bible's power to accept this dismissal of Jehovah.
After reading this passage, he remarked sardonically:

Solomon, when he Married Pharaoh's daughter & became a
Convert to the Heathen Mythology, talked exactly in this way of
Jehovah as a Very inferior object of Man's Contemplations; he
also passed him by unalarm'd & was permitted. Jehovah dropped
a tear & follow'd him by his Spirit into the Abstract Void; it is
called the Divine Mercy.

To marry Pharaoh's daughter is to marry Nature, the Goddess of the
Heathen Mythology, and indeed Wordsworth will go on to speak of a
marriage between the Mind of Man and the goodly universe of Nature.
Wordsworth is permitted his effrontery, as Solomon the Wise was before
him, and, like Solomon, Wordsworth wanders into the Ulro or Abstract Void
of general reasoning from Nature, pursued by the ambiguous pity of the
Divine Mercy. But this (though powerful) is a dark view to take of
Wordsworth's reciprocal dealings with Nature. Courageously but calmly
Wordsworth puts himself forward as a renovated spirit, a new Adam upon
whom fear and awe fall as he looks into his own Mind, the Mind of Man. As
befits a new Adam, a new world with a greater beauty waits upon his steps.
The most defiant humanism in Wordsworth salutes the immediate
possibility of this earthly paradise naturalizing itself in the here and now:

> Paradise, and groves
> Elysian, Fortunate Fields—like those of old
> Sought in the Atlantic Main—why should they be
> A history only of departed things,
> Or a mere fiction of what never was?
> For the discerning intellect of Man,
> When wedded to this goodly universe
> In love and holy passion, shall find these
> A simple produce of the common day.

No words are more honorific for Wordsworth than "simple" and "common." The marriage metaphor here has the same Hebraic sources as Blake had for his Beulah, or "married land." The true Eden is the child of the common day, when that day dawns upon the great consummation of the reciprocal passion of Man and Nature. What Wordsworth desires to write is "the spousal verse" in celebration of this fulfillment:

> and, by words
> Which speak of nothing more than what we are,
> Would I arouse the sensual from their sleep
> Of Death, and win the vacant and the vain
> To noble raptures.

This parallels Blake's singing in *Jerusalem*:

> Of the sleep of Ulro! and of the passage through
> Eternal Death! and of the awaking to Eternal Life.

But Wordsworth would arouse us by speaking of nothing more than what we already are; a more naturalistic humanism than Blake could endure. Wordsworth celebrates the *given*—what we already possess, and for him it is as for Wallace Stevens

> As if the air, the mid-day air, was swarming
> With the metaphysical changes that occur,
> Merely in living as and where we live.

For Wordsworth, as for Stevens, the earth is enough; for Blake it was less than that all without which man cannot be satisfied. We need to distinguish this argument between the two greatest of the Romantics from the simplistic dissension with which too many readers have confounded it, that between the doctrines of innate goodness and original sin. Wordsworth is not Rousseau, and Blake is not St. Paul; they have more in common with one another than they have with either the natural religionist or the orthodox Christian.

Wordsworth's Imagination is like Wallace Stevens's *Angel Surrounded by Paysans*: not an angel of heaven, but the necessary angel of earth, as, in its sight, we see the earth again, but cleared; and in its hearing we hear the still sad music of humanity, its tragic drone, rise liquidly, not harsh or grating, but like watery words awash, to chasten and subdue us. But the Imagination of Wordsworth and of Stevens is "a figure half seen, or seen for a moment." It rises with the sudden mountain mists, and as suddenly departs. Blake, a literalist of the Imagination, wished for its more habitual sway. To marry Mind and Nature is to enter Beulah; there Wordsworth and Blake are at one. Blake insisted that a man more fully redeemed by Imagination would not need Nature, would regard the external world as hindrance. The split between Wordsworth and Blake is not theological at all, though Blake expresses it in his deliberately displaced Protestant vocabulary by using the metaphor of the Fall where Wordsworth rejects it. For Wordsworth the individual Mind and the external World are exquisitely fitted, each to the other, even as man and wife, and with blended might they accomplish a creation the meaning of which is fully dependent upon the sexual analogy; they give to us a new heaven and a new earth blended into an apocalyptic unity that is simply the matter of common perception and common sexuality raised to the freedom of its natural power. Wordsworthian Man is Freudian Man, but Blake's Human Form Divine is not. "You shall not bring me down to believe such a fitting & fitted" is his reaction to Wordsworth's exquisite adjustings of the Universe and Mind. To accept Nature as man's equal is for Blake the ineradicable error. Blake's doctrine is that either the Imagination totally destroys Nature and puts a thoroughly Human form in its place, or else Nature destroys the Imagination. Wordsworth says of his task that he is forced to hear "Humanity in fields and groves / Pipe solitary anguish" and Blake reacts with ferocity:

> Does not this Fit, & is not Fitting most Exquisitely too, but to what?—not to Mind, but to the Vile Body only & to its Laws of Good & Evil & its Enmities against Mind.

This is not the comment of an embittered Gnostic. Blake constructs his poetry as a commentary upon Scripture; Wordsworth writes his poetry as a commentary upon Nature. Wordsworth, while not so Bible-haunted as Blake, is himself a poet in the Hebraic prophetic line. The visible body of

Nature is more than an outer testimony of the Spirit of God to him; it is our only way to God. For Blake it is the barrier between us and the God within ourselves. Ordinary perception is then a mode of salvation for Wordsworth, provided that we are awake fully to what we see. The common earth is to be hallowed by the human heart's and mind's holy union with it, and by that union the heart and mind in concert are to receive their bride's gift of phenomenal beauty, a glory in the grass, a splendor in the flower. Until at last the Great Consummation will be achieved, and renovated Man will stand in Eden once again. The human glory of Wordsworth, which he bequeathed to Keats, is in this naturalistic celebration of the possibilities inherent in our condition, here and now. That Wordsworth himself, in the second half of his long life, could not sustain this vision is a criticism of neither the vision nor the man, but merely his loss—and ours.

The Old Cumberland Beggar (1797) is Wordsworth's finest vision of the irreducible natural man, the human stripped to the nakedness of primordial condition and exposed as still powerful in dignity, still infinite in value. The Beggar reminds us of the beggars, solitaries, wanderers throughout Wordsworth's poetry, particularly in The Prelude and Resolution and Independence. He differs from them in that he is not the agency of a revelation; he is not responsible for a sudden release of Wordsworth's imagination. He is not even of visionary utility; he is something finer, beyond use, a vision of reality in himself. I am not suggesting that The Old Cumberland Beggar is the best of Wordsworth's poems outside The Prelude; it is not in the sublime mode, as are Tintern Abbey, the Great Ode, Resolution and Independence. But it is the most Wordsworthian of poems, and profoundly moving.

Nothing could be simpler than the poem's opening: "I saw an aged Beggar in my walk." The Old Man (the capitalization is the poet's) has put down his staff, and takes his scraps and fragments out of a flour bag, one by one. He scans them, fixedly and seriously. The plain beginning yields to a music of love, the beauty of the real:

> In the sun,
> Upon the second step of that small pile,
> Surrounded by those wild unpeopled hills,
> He sat, and ate his food in solitude:
> And ever, scattered from his palsied hand,
> That, still attempting to prevent the waste,
> Was baffled still, the crumbs in little showers
> Fell on the ground; and the small mountain birds,
> Not venturing yet to peck their destined meal,
> Approached within the length of half his staff.

It is difficult to describe *how* this is beautiful, but we can make a start by observing that it is beautiful both because it is so matter of fact, and because the fact is itself a transfiguration. The Old Man is in his own state, and he is radically innocent. The "wild unpeopled hills" complement his own solitude; he is a phenomenon of their kind. And he is no more sentimentalized than they are. His lot is not even miserable; he is too absorbed into Nature for that, as absorbed as he can be and still retain human identity.

He is even past further aging. The poet has known him since his childhood, and even then "he was so old, he seems not older now." The Old Man is so helpless in appearance that everyone—sauntering horseman or toll-gate keeper or post boy—makes way for him, taking special care to keep him from harm. For he cannot be diverted, but moves on like a natural process. "He travels on, a solitary Man," Wordsworth says, and then repeats it, making a refrain for that incessant movement whose only meaning is that it remains human though at the edge of our condition:

> He travels on, a solitary Man;
> His age has no companion. On the ground
> His eyes are turned, and, as he moves along,
> *They* move along the ground; and, evermore,
> Instead of common and habitual sight
> Of fields with rural works, of hill and dale,
> And the blue sky, one little span of earth
> Is all his prospect.

He is bent double, like the Leech Gatherer, and his vision of one little span of earth recalls the wandering old man of Chaucer's *Pardoner's Tale*. But Chaucer's solitary longed for death, and on the ground he called his mother's gate he knocked often with his staff, crying, "Dear mother, let me in." Wordsworth's Old Man sees only the ground, but he is tenaciously alive, and is beyond desire, even that of death. He sees, and yet hardly sees. He moves constantly, but is so still in look and motion that he can hardly be seen to move. He is all process, hardly character, and yet almost stasis.

It is so extreme a picture that we can be tempted to ask, "Is this life? Where is its use?" The temptation dehumanizes us, Wordsworth would have it, and the two questions are radically dissimilar, but his answer to the first is vehemently affirmative and to the second an absolute moral passion. There is

> a spirit and pulse of good,
> A life and soul, to every mode of being
> Inseparably linked.

The Old Man performs many functions. The most important is that of a binding agent for the memories of good impulses in all around him. Wherever he goes,

> The mild necessity of use compels
> To acts of love.

These acts of love, added one to another, at last insensibly dispose their performers to virtue and true goodness. We need to be careful in our reaction to this. Wordsworth is not preaching the vicious and mad doctrine that beggary is good because it makes charity possible. That would properly invoke Blake's blistering reply in *The Human Abstract*:

> Pity would be no more
> If we did not make somebody Poor;
> And Mercy no more could be
> If all were as happy as we.

Wordsworth has no reaction to the Old Man which we can categorize. He does not think of him in social or economic terms, but only as a human life, which necessarily has affected other lives, and always for the better. In particular, the Old Man has given occasions for kindness to the very poorest, who give to him from their scant store, and are the kinder for it. Again, you must read this in its own context. Wordsworth's best poetry has nothing directly to do with social justice, as Blake's or Shelley's frequently does. The old beggar is a free man, at home in the heart of the solitudes he wanders, and he does not intend the humanizing good he passively causes. Nor is his social aspect at the poem's vital center; only his freedom is:

> —Then let him pass, a blessing on his head!
> And, long as he can wander, let him breathe
> The freshness of the valleys; let his blood
> Struggle with frosty air and winter snows;
> And let the chartered wind that sweeps the heath
> Beat his grey locks against his withered face.

Pity for him is inappropriate; he is pathetic only if shut up. He is a "figure of capable imagination," in Stevens's phrase, a Man perfectly complete in Nature, reciprocating its gifts by being himself, a being at one with it:

> Let him be free of mountain solitudes;
> And have around him, whether heard or not,
> The pleasant melody of woodland birds.

Mountain solitudes and sudden winds are what suit him, whether he reacts to them or not. The failure of his senses does not cut him off from Nature; it does not matter whether he can hear the birds, but it is fitting that he have them around him. He has become utterly passive toward Nature. Let it be free, then, to come in upon him:

>   if his eyes have now
> Been doomed so long to settle upon earth
> That not without some effort they behold
> The countenance of the horizontal sun,
> Rising or setting, let the light at least
> Find a free entrance to their languid orbs.

The Old Man is approaching that identity with Nature that the infant at first knows, when an organic continuity seems to exist between Nature and consciousness. Being so naturalized, he must die in the eye of Nature, that he may be absorbed again:

> And let him, *where* and *when* he will, sit down
> Beneath the trees, or on a grassy bank
> Of highway side, and with the little birds
> Share his chance-gathered meal; and, finally,
> As in the eye of Nature he has lived,
> So in the eye of Nature let him die!

The poem abounds in a temper of spirit that Wordsworth shares with Tolstoy, a reverence for the simplicities of *caritas*, the Christian love that is so allied to and yet is not pity. But Tolstoy might have shown the Old Cumberland Beggar as a sufferer; in Wordsworth he bears the mark of "animal tranquillity and decay," the title given by Wordsworth to a fragment closely connected to the longer poem. In the fragment the Old Man travels on and moves not with pain, but with thought:

> He is insensibly subdued
> To settled quiet ...
> He is by nature led
> To peace so perfect that the young behold
> With envy, what the Old Man hardly feels.

We know today, better than his contemporaries could, what led Wordsworth to the subject of human decay, to depictions of idiocy, desertion, beggars, homeless wanderers. He sought images of alienated life, as we might judge them, which he could see and present as images of natural communion. The natural man, free of consciousness in any of our senses, yet demonstrates a mode of consciousness which both intends Nature for its object and at length blends into that object. The hiding places of man's power are in his past, in childhood. Only memory can take him there, but even memory fades, and at length fades away. The poet of naturalism, separated by organic growth from his own past, looks around him and sees the moving emblems of a childlike consciousness in the mad, the outcast, and the dreadfully old. From them he takes his most desperate consolation, intimations of a mortality that almost ceases to afflict.

M.H. ABRAMS

Two Roads to Wordsworth

The first critic of Wordsworth's poetry was Wordsworth himself, and in his criticism, as in his poetry, he speaks with two distinct voices. The first voice is that of the Preface to *Lyrical Ballads*, in which Wordsworth powerfully applies to his poetry some humanistic values of the European Enlightenment. In his Preface the controlling and interrelated norms are the essential, the elementary, the simple, the universal, and the permanent. The great subjects of his poetry, Wordsworth says, are "the essential passions of the heart," "elementary feelings," "the great and simple affections," "the great and universal passions of men," and "characters of which the elements are simple ... such as exist now, and will probably always exist," as these human qualities interact with "the beautiful and permanent forms of nature." His aim is a poetry written in a "naked and simple" style that is "well-adapted to interest mankind permanently." And the poet himself, as "a man speaking to men," both affirms and effects the primal human values: the joy of life, the dignity of life and of its elemental moving force, the pleasure principle, and the primacy of the universal connective, love. The poet "rejoices more than other men in the spirit of life" both within him and without, pays homage "to the grand elementary principle of pleasure, by which he knows, and feels, and lives, and moves," and is "the rock of defence of human nature ... carrying everywhere with him relationship and love."

From *Wordsworth: A Collection of Critical Essays*, pp. 81–91. © 1972 by Prentice Hall.

Wordsworth's second critical voice has been far less heeded by his readers. It speaks out in the "Essay, Supplementary to the Preface" of his Poems of 1815, and reiterates in sober prose the claims he had made, years before, in the verse "Prospectus" to *The Recluse* (first printed with his Preface to *The Excursion*) and in the opening and closing passages of *The Prelude*: claims that it is his task to confront and find consolation in human suffering—whether the "solitary agonies" of rural life or the "fierce confederate storm / Of sorrow" barricaded within the walls of cities—since he is a poet who has been singled out "for holy services" in a secular work of man's "redemption." In his "Essay" of 1815, Wordsworth addresses himself to explain and justify those aspects of novelty and strangeness in his poetry that have evoked from critics "unremitting hostility ... slight ... aversion ... contempt." He does so by asserting that he, like every "truly original poet," has qualities that are "peculiarly his own," and in specifying his innovations, he does not now take his operative concepts from eighteenth-century humanism, but imports them from theology; that is, he deliberately adapts to poetry the idiom hitherto used by Christian apologists to justify the radical novelty, absurdities, and paradoxes of the Christian mysteries. For Wordsworth claims in this essay that there are "affinities between religion and poetry," "a community of nature," so that poetry shares the distinctive quality of Christianity, which is to confound "the calculating understanding" by its contradictions:

> For when Christianity, the religion of humility, is founded upon
> the proudest quality of our nature [the imagination], what can be
> expected but contradictions?

In the "Essay" of 1815, accordingly, Wordsworth does not represent poetry as elemental and simple, but stresses instead its "contradictions"— that is, its radical paradoxicality, its union of antitheses, its fusion of the sensuous and the transcendent, its violation of the customary, and its reversal of status between the highest and lowest. Poetry, for example, imitates the supreme contradiction of the Incarnation itself: it is "ethereal and transcendent, yet incapable to sustain [its] existence without sensuous incarnation." The higher poetry unites the "wisdom of the heart and the grandeur of imagination" and so achieves a "simplicity" that is "Magnificence herself." Wordsworth's own poems manifest "emotions of the pathetic" that are "complex and revolutionary." As for "the sublime"—he is specifically a poet "charged with a new mission to extend its kingdom, and to augment and spread its enjoyments." For as one of the poets who combine the "heroic passions" of pagan antiquity with Christian wisdom he has produced a new synthesis—an "accord of sublimated humanity." And his chief enterprise as a poet is expressed in a Christian paradox—he must cast his readers down in order to raise them up: their spirits "are to be humbled and humanized, in order that they may be purified and exalted."

Wordsworth as primarily the simple, affirmative poet of elementary feelings, essential humanity, and vital joy, and Wordsworth as primarily the complex poet of strangeness, paradox, equivocality, and dark sublimities— these diverse views, adumbrated by Wordsworth himself, were established as persistent alternative ways to the poet by Matthew Arnold and by A. C. Bradley. The cause of Wordsworth's greatness, Arnold said, taking his cue from Wordsworth's Preface to *Lyrical Ballads*, "is simple, and may be told quite simply. Wordsworth's poetry is great because of the extraordinary power" with which he feels and renders and makes us share "the joy offered to us in nature, the joy offered to us in the simple, primary affections and duties." And from the naturalness of his subject and the sincerity of his feeling, his characteristic and matchless style is that of "the most plain, firsthand, almost austere naturalness." Wordsworth's great boon to us in "this iron time," Arnold says in his verses, is that he has restored our lost capacity for spontaneous and uncomplicated responsiveness, "the freshness of the early world." He adds, however, that Wordsworth achieved his "sweet calm" only by the expedient of averting his ken "from half of human fate."

Although Bradley did not publish his great essay on Wordsworth until 1909, thirty years after Arnold's appeared, he set out explicitly to supplement what he regarded as Arnold's valid but incomplete view of the poet by specifying other qualities without which "Wordsworth is not Wordsworth." His challenge to Arnold's way to Wordsworth is direct and uncompromising: "The road into Wordsworth's mind must be through his strangeness and his paradoxes, and not round them." In pursuing this road Bradley follows the lead, not of Wordsworth's Preface, but of his vatic poetic pronouncements, which Arnold had noted only to derogate as the style "more properly ... of eloquent prose." As Bradley's other essays make evident, his critical concepts, and his sensitiveness to negative and paradoxical elements in literature, also owe a great deal to the philosophy of Hegel. As Hegel himself had noted, however, his categories of negation, contradiction, and synthesis are (like Wordsworth's concept of the "contradictions" in the products of the modern poetic imagination) the conceptual equivalents of the paradoxes and the *coincidentia oppositorum* of the Christian mysteries. In the Hegelian cast of his critical concepts, then, Bradley is in broad accord with the spirit of Wordsworth's own "Essay, Supplementary to the Preface" of 1815.

In Bradley's view, that which is most distinctive in Wordsworth's poetry is "peculiar," "audacious," "strange," and Wordsworth's characteristic attitudes are a complex of contraries or contradictions. Although Wordsworth sang of joy and love, "he did not avert his eyes" from anguish or evil, but often represented "a dark world"; and though he undertook to show that suffering and misery can in fact be the conditions of happiness, strength, and glory, he did not pretend that this possibility solved "the riddle of the painful earth"—"the world was to him in the end 'this unintelligible world.'" Wordsworth is "preeminently the poet of solitude," yet "no poet is more emphatically the poet of community." His native bent was not to simplicity, but to "sublimity"; and in this "mystic" or "visionary" strain "there is always traceable a certain hostility to 'sense,'" an intimation of something illimitable, eternal, infinite, that is "in some way a denial" of the limited sensible world, "contradicting or abolishing the fixed limits of our habitual view." As Bradley describes the paradoxical qualities of a Wordsworthian spot of time, using a portentous term, "Everything here is natural, but everything is apocalyptic."

Twentieth-century critics of Wordsworth have tended to follow either Arnold's or Bradley's road to the poet, and the diverse approaches have yielded two Wordsworths. One Wordsworth is simple, elemental, forthright, the other is complex, paradoxical, problematic; one is an affirmative poet of life, love, and joy, the other is an equivocal or self-divided poet whose affirmations are implicitly qualified (if not annulled) by a pervasive sense of mortality and an ever-incipient despair of life; one is the great poet of natural man and the world of all of us, the other is a visionary or "mystic" who is ultimately hostile to temporal man and the world of sense and whose profoundest inclinations are toward another world that transcends biological and temporal limitations; one is the Wordsworth of light, the other the Wordsworth of chiaroscuro, or even darkness. Criticism since mid-century continues to manifest, and often to sharpen, this division, although the commentators who take either the one or the other of the old roads to Wordsworth have introduced new critical concepts that make their work seem, in the 1970s, distinctively "modern." I shall try to identify a few of the more conspicuous innovations within each of the traditional perspectives.

THE SIMPLE WORDSWORTH

In *The Poet Wordsworth* (1950) Helen Darbishire is an unqualified Arnoldian: Wordsworth is a poet whose motive power was "the depth and force of his feeling for humanity," who vindicated "sense-experience as the foundation of knowledge" and represented "simple men and women who are moved by the great emotions." John F. Danby's poet, in a book published a decade later, is also, as his title asserts, *The Simple Wordsworth*; the innovative element is Danby's view that Wordsworth is a craftsman whose simplicity has been achieved by "an alert and conscious artist," who controls the reader's responses by his management of the narrative personae, "tones of voice," and "masks." Danby's critique of *The Idiot Boy* is a belated recognition that Wordsworth is an accomplished comic poet. Its focus is on the interplay of the narrative voice, the voices of the characters, and the poet's own voice in sustaining the fine balance of humor and human warmth in the evolving story.

Danby expressly opposes his treatment of Wordsworth as intentional artificer to the New Critical approach to a poem as a free-standing and autonomous structure of meanings, to be judged without recourse to the artist or his intention. Cleanth Brooks's essay on Wordsworth's *Ode: Intimations of Immortality* demonstrates what can be achieved by such a close reading of the poem "as an independent poetic structure," interrogated for what it "manages to say" entirely "in its own right" as a primarily ironic and paradoxical deployment of thematic imagery. Having assimilated the insights made possible by this strict limitation of perspective in the New Criticism, many critics in the last decade or two have undertaken, like Danby, to rehumanize poetry by viewing the poet, in Wordsworth's phrase in the Preface, as "a man speaking to men," and by exploiting concepts such as "voice," "persona," "tone," and "point of view," which emphasize the poet's own involvement, as well as his management of the reader's participation, in the fictional process.

Such a revitalized rhetoric of poetry is prominent in many recent writings about Wordsworth. In the third chapter of *The Music of Humanity*, for example, Jonathan Wordsworth demonstrates the essential role, in *The Ruined Cottage*, of the interplay between Wordsworth's two "poetic selves," the Pedlar and the Poet, in effecting the reader's imaginative consent to the author's own attitudes toward the tragic story. In an essay that has been much debated, Stephen Parrish reads *The Thorn* not as a quasi-supernatural story, but as an artful dramatic monologue, in which the controlling principle is the revelation of the mental workings of its credulous narrator, the old sea captain. Neil Hertz's essay "Wordsworth and the Tears of Adam"—with a shift of emphasis from Wordsworth's rhetorical artistry to the characteristic disjunction of consciousness in his poetry—discriminates "the transformation of the voice" in a short verse passage, and details the interaction among three "aspects of Wordsworth's self" and a fourth subjectivity, that of the responding reader.

THE PROBLEMATIC WORDSWORTH

In the 1960s there appeared a new mode of criticism in America whose appeal to younger critics presages its growing importance in studies of Romantic literature. The primary terms of this criticism are "consciousness" (or "self-consciousness") and the "dialectic" of its dealings with what is not-consciousness, and its characteristic procedure is to find something "problematic" in the surface meaning of single passages and to regard this as a clue to a deep structure manifesting an unspoken preoccupation of the poet. The proximate sources of this critical procedure are the diverse movements in European thought loosely classified as "phenomenology," "existentialism," and "structuralism," but its central idiom and concerns derive ultimately from Hegel; so that, when applied to Wordsworth, it can be regarded as a revived form of Bradley's neo-Hegelian approach to that poet. The focus, however, is much sharper than Bradley's, and the chief operative concepts are much more restricted. For as Hegel in his *Phenomenology of Spirit* translated the manifold particularities of human and individual history into diverse moments of the transactions between consciousness and its alienated other, so these critics view the manifold surface particularities of Romantic poems as generated primarily by a single submerged plot: the sustained struggle of the poet's consciousness (operating in the mode often called "imagination") to achieve "autonomy," or absolute independence from that adversary which is not itself—namely, "nature," the world of sensible objects.

In his influential essay "Intentional Structure of the Romantic Image," first published in 1960, Paul de Man sets out from the observation that there is a "dialectic" that is "paradoxical"—a "fundamental ambiguity" or "tension" that "never ceases to be problematic"—in Romantic attempts to link the polarities of consciousness, or imagination, and nature. De Man's paradigmatic instance is Mallarmé, who is represented as a revealing point of reference because he is a late Romantic who took over what had hitherto been an implicit tension of polar attitudes, "the alternating feeling of attraction and repulsion that the romantic poet experiences toward nature," and made it explicit as a "conscious dialectic of a reflective poetic consciousness." Mallarmé, unlike earlier Romantic poets, "always remained convinced of the essential priority of the natural object," so that his writings as an extreme "anti-natural poet" are a defiantly hopeless struggle by consciousness (or by the language in which consciousness manifests itself) to annihilate, by reducing to its own self, a nature that Mallarmé knows to be ultimately indefeasible. Wordsworth's poetry, on the other hand, with its "radical contradictions" in the representation of landscape (de Man's example is the passage on crossing the Alps in *The Prelude*, Book VI), puts into question "the ontological priority of the sensory object," by recourse to the faculty he calls "imagination," which "marks ... a possibility for consciousness to exist entirely by and for itself, independently of all relationship with the outside world."

Geoffrey Hartman also finds that Wordsworth's treatment of nature is "problematic," and that a number of passages in *The Prelude* which "overtly celebrate nature" in fact "share a motif opposed to the overt line of argument." Hartman's repeated reference, however, is not to Mallarmé but to Blake, the extreme representative of a deliberate commitment to a visionary and anti-natural imagination. "Blake," says Hartman, "would snap ... that Wordsworth is of his party without knowing it." The difference is that Wordsworth, when he comes face to face with his "autonomous imagination," fears it, shies from it, or veils it. In consequence, his poetry constitutes "a series of evaded recognitions" of imagination and "an avoidance of apocalypse"—where imagination is defined by Hartman as "consciousness of self raised to apocalyptic pitch" and apocalypse signifies "any strong desire to cast out nature and to achieve an unmediated contact with the principle of things," hence as "involving a *death* of nature." It is this "unresolved opposition between Imagination and Nature"—through Wordsworth's "fear of the death of nature"—that "prevents him from becoming a visionary poet."

Two other essays represent an approach to Wordsworth that emphasizes the duplicity and the strain between contradictions in his writings; the major operative concept, however, is not a revived Hegelian opposition between consciousness and an alien other, but the post-Freudian distinction between Manifest and latent, conscious and unconscious content. The basic claim is that Wordsworth's overt or surface meaning often overlies a covert countermeaning that expresses what the poet profoundly felt and believed, as against what he rationalized himself into believing.

David Perkins' *The Quest for Permanence* undertakes to "go beneath the surface" of Wordsworth's poetry in order to explore the "negative implications" that are sometimes "contrary to his overt intentions and obiter dicta"; for any interpretation that concentrates on Wordsworth's obiter dicta "is not touching what is deepest in him." Under Wordsworth's overt claims that certitude and peace attend upon "the union of mind with nature," Perkins finds a contrary sense that there is a "gulf between human nature ... and the rest of nature," and that man is doomed to be an isolated being, estranged from both nature and other men. There are symptoms also of "a kind of schizoid retreat" from situations that threaten the poet's composure, which in its extreme form manifests itself in Wordsworth as an attraction to the ultimate security of the grave.

In *The Limits of Mortality*, published in the same year as Perkins' *Quest for Permanence* (1959), David Ferry's aim is to discover in Wordsworth "ideas and feelings which can in some way be related to our own deepest feelings and ideas." Ferry penetrates to this modern element, as he says, by "a special way of reading his poems." This way to Wordsworth is to strike a sharp dichotomy between the "'surface' of his poems" and the "deeper" and "hidden" meanings which are in "tension" or "conflict" with the surface meanings, and to assert the prepotency of the hidden and antithetic meanings as constituting the "ultimate subject matter" of a poem. As Ferry formulates this semantic peripety:

> [The] apparent subject matter is a kind of cipher or hieroglyph
> for meanings which reject or devaluate the very experiences
> which express them.... The symbolic meanings of [Wordsworth's]
> poems tend to reject their sensuous, dramatic surfaces.

Like A. C. Bradley a half-century earlier, Ferry sets out, as he says, to correct Arnold's "tendency to take Wordsworth's vocabulary of feeling at face value," hence to evaluate him as "the poet of the primary affections and simple feelings." By Ferry's interpretative strategy, however, the paradoxical Wordsworth works free from Bradley's careful qualifications to become the polar opposite of Arnold's Wordsworth. The sophisticated modern reader is now enabled to look right through Wordsworth's surface assertions of reverence for a "sacramental" nature, love for elemental man, and esteem for the simple affections and ordinary experience, in order to discern a countermeaning of which the poet himself remained unaware hat is, a "mystical" yearning for an eternal and unchanging realm of being to which nature and man and even the articulations of poetry itself (since all are alike trapped in the conditions of time, space, and vicissitude) are an intolerable obstruction, an offense against the purity of eternity. Hence to the knowing reader Wordsworth's "sacramentalist" poems, far from being simple and natural in style, often turn out to be "contradictions of themselves" and to express a yearning "for their own destruction," and Wordsworth's "mystical imagination" is recognized to be "a hater of temporal nature" and "the enemy of poetry as of all distinctively human experience." Ferry's closing summation of the Wordsworth of the great decade is that "his genius was his enmity to man, which he mistook for love, and his mistake led him into confusions which he could not bear. But when he banished his confusions, he banished his distinctive greatness as well."

Even the confirmed Arnoldian must admit the plausibility of some of the insights achieved by the recent critics who premise their reading of Wordsworth on the paradoxical strains and equivocal attitudes in his poetry. And it is a measure of the range and magnitude of Wordsworth's achievement that he continues to speak to us and our interests when interpreted by neo-Hegelian concepts, or when viewed as a proto-Mallarmé, or as a Blake manqué, or as, under the brave surface, really one of us in our age of alienation, anguish, and existential absurdity. An inveterate under-reading of the textual surface, however, turns readily into a habitual over-reading. The problem is, to what extent do these recent critical perspectives on Wordsworth simply bring into visibility what was always, although obscurely, there, and to what extent do they project upon his poems the form of their own prepossessions?

This is not the place to argue out the difficult issue. Instead, I shall cite some contemporary critics who, like A. C. Bradley, believe that Arnold described what is really there, but enlarge the scope of their vision to encompass the half of Wordsworth from which Arnold averted his ken. In their work, as in Bradley's essay, Wordsworth stands as a complex but integral poet, rather than as a radically divided one whose deepest inclinations, known to the modern critic but not to the poet himself, undercut or annul his repeated affirmations.

Like the recent explorers of the problematic Wordsworth, Lionel Trilling points to an aspect of his poetry that is strange, remote, even chilling to us. His account of it, however, is not psychoanalytic (Wordsworth's unconscious revulsion from life) but historical—Wordsworth's participation in a persistent strain of Hebrew and Christian culture which, at odds with the modern preoccupation with heroic struggle and apocalyptic violence, is committed to quietism, peace, and a wise passiveness. Wordsworth's quietism, however, "is not in the least a negation of life, but ... an affirmation of life so complete that it needed no saying"; Trilling in fact uses Wordsworth as the positive standard by which to define the negatives of our adversary culture. Wordsworth has an "acute sense of his own being" that sharpens his awareness of other beings, and his intention is "to require us to acknowledge" the being of his narrative personae and so "to bring them within the range of conscience" and of "natural sympathy." It is not Wordsworth but we moderns who "do not imagine being ... that it can be a joy" and who "are in love, at least in our literature, with the fantasy of death." Writing also in the affirmative tradition of Arnold, Jonathan Wordsworth nonetheless identifies in *The Ruined Cottage* a dimension of poetic genius that Arnold had denied to Wordsworth: the power to reconcile us imaginatively with an instance of seemingly pointless suffering, futile courage, and meaningless death in a way that manifests both the poet's artistry and his "humanity"—"an insight into emotions not his own"—and with a success that places him "among the very few great English tragic writers."

The position of Harold Bloom in the critical division about Wordsworth's poetry is a complex one. Citing Geoffrey Hartman, he concurs in the latter's distinction between surface and covert meaning and in the associated claim that, as Bloom puts it, "the inner problem of *The Prelude*, and of all the poetry of Wordsworth's great decade, is that of the autonomy of the poet's creative imagination," hence of a "hidden conflict between Poetry and Nature." But Bloom's reading of Wordsworth, taken overall, is different from Hartman's. He accepts Wordsworth's own statement, most notably in the "Prospectus" to *The Recluse*, that his high argument is the possibility of a union, by means of imagination, between mind and nature, in a reciprocity that redeems the world of ordinary experience. Instead of regarding Wordsworth as an all-but-Blake, he expressly differentiates his poetry from Blake's and parallels it instead to that of Wallace Stevens, as a "naturalistic celebration of the possibilities inherent in our condition here and now." Bloom accordingly reads *Tintern Abbey* as representing the poet in the act of discovering the theme of all his best poetry, a "reciprocity between the external world and his own mind" in which the two agents are equal in initiative and power. The Old Cumberland Beggar, in Bloom's analysis, registers a correlative aspect of Wordsworth's genius, his reverence for essential human life, seemingly alienated and "stripped to the nakedness of primordial condition," yet "still powerful in dignity, still infinite in value." And though he believes that Wordsworth's confidence in an imaginative communion of mind, nature, and man later weakened and failed, Bloom pays tribute to the novelty and magnitude of the enterprise. Wordsworth "personified a heroic mode of naturalism, which even he then proved unable to sustain." "No poet since," he declares, "has given us more." Such a view is consonant with that of the present writer, who has explored *The Prelude*, and the opening book of *The Recluse* into which it leads, as Wordsworth's attempt to save the traditional design and values of human life, inherited from a Christian past, but to translate them to a naturalistic frame of reference—that is, to represent them as generated by a reciprocity between the natural world and the minds of men, "as natural beings in the strength of nature."

Wordsworth criticism is in a flourishing condition these days, and its vigorous internal disputes testify to the poet's continuing vitality and pertinence. We are rediscovering what a number of Wordsworth's major contemporaries acknowledged—that he has done what only the greatest poets do. He has transformed the inherited language of poetry into a medium adequate to express new ways of perceiving the world, new modes of experience, and new relations of the individual consciousness to itself, to its past, and to other men. More than all but a very few English writers, Wordsworth has altered not only our poetry, but our sensibility and our culture.

HAROLD BLOOM

The Scene of Instruction: "Tintern Abbey"

I start with Nietzsche, as perhaps the least Wordsworthian of interpretative theorists. This is one of his notebook jottings, of 1855, urging a revisionary view of "memory":

> One must revise one's ideas about memory: here lies the chief temptation to assume a "soul," which, outside time, reproduces, recognizes, etc. But that which is experienced lives on "in the memory"; I cannot help it if it "comes back," the will is inactive in this case, as in the coming of any thought. Something happens of which I become conscious: now something similar comes— who called it? roused it?

Nietzsche demystifies and desubjectivizes memory; Wordsworth so mystified memory as to make of it the one great myth of his antimythological poetry.

I set against both this demystification and this spiritualization the vast expansion of the concept of memory that took place in Freud. The empirical model for memory, before Freud, was an easy target for Nietzsche's deconstructive energies, since memory was seen as a mechanically causal process, based upon the association of ideas. One idea associated itself with

From *Poetry and Repression: Revisionism from Blake to Stevens*, pp. 52–82. © 1976 by Yale University Press.

another pretty much as the motion of one entity affected another. But here is the philosopher Stuart Hampshire's perceptive brief summary of the conceptual change that Freud accomplished:

> For the simple machinery of the association of ideas, Freud substitutes complex activities of projection, introjection and identification in the solution of conflicts. The importance of this substitution, from the philosophical point of view, is just that these activities are represented as activities; and because they are so represented, the underlying motives of them can be investigated. Within this scheme, the question of "Why?"—the demand for an explanation in any particular case—does not call for a universally valid psychological law and a statement of initial conditions. Since these processes are represented as activities of mind, the question "Why" asks for a description of the situation or situations, and therefore of the given problem, to which these continuing activities were the solution adopted. The effect of the substitution of the active for the passive mood is that the subject is required to search in his memory for the past situation, as it survives in his mind, and to acknowledge or to disclaim its superimposition on the present.

One impulse that rises in me, as I read this lucid philosophical comment on Freud, is to remember Freud's remark that "The poets were there before me," since Hampshire's observation would be a perfectly commonplace and accurate enough description of the difference between a pre-Wordsworthian memory poem, like Gray's Eton Ode, and a poem like *Tintern Abbey*. The difference between Wordsworth and Freud is that while both greatly expanded the concept of memory, Wordsworth very nearly made it into a Kabbalistic hypostasis, a new *sefirah* or magical attribute of Divine Influence, while Freud set it overtly in the context of anxiety, repression, and defense. I revert to my analogical and antithetical principle; a composite trope and a composite defense are different faces of the same ratios of revision. "Memory," for Wordsworth, is a composite trope, and so in Wordsworth what is called memory, or treated as memory, is also a composite defense, a defense against time, decay, the loss of divinating power, and so finally a defense against death, whose other name is John Milton.

In *The Ego and the Id* (1927), Freud suggests as a model of our mental apparatus the vision of an organism floating in water. As the surface of this organism is molded, internally and externally, into differentiation, what results as a difference Freud called the "ego," the "ich." Beneath this surface, and going down to the depth of the organism, is what Freud called the "id," the *it*, a naming in which Freud ultimately followed Nietzsche. The model is complex and subtle, and I cannot give an adequate account of it here. But one feature of it is crucial as part of Freud's concept of memory. The ego is visualized as broadening out from a layer of memory-traces, called the preconscious. These memory-traces are defined as remnants of perceptions, and only through an accumulation of memory-traces is there a growth in consciousness.

A memory-trace is a very tricky notion, one that I myself do not understand, and while Freud doubtless understood it, he never explained it adequately. Freud's word is *Erinnerungsspur*, which could be interpreted psychologically or physiologically. Laplanche and Pontalis, the Lacanian authors of *The Language of Psychoanalysis*, do not help clarify this notion when they say that "memory-traces are deposited in different systems, and subsist permanently, but are only reactivated once they have been cathected," that is, invested with psychic energy. A trace that subsists permanently, while waiting for a heavy psychic investor to come along, is a vision of the mind that all great poetry, including Wordsworth's, refutes. Dr. Samuel Johnson, who darkly knew that the mind is above all a *ceaseless activity*, could have taught these current psychoanalytic linguistifiers a little more respect for the power of the mind over itself, as well as over nature and language. But Freud also, of course, knew what the great moral psychologists from Pascal and Montaigne to Dr. Johnson and Coleridge have known, which is that memory is active mind, always dangerous, always at work misreading the predicaments of consciousness. Here are Laplanche and Pontalis at their most hilarious, reducing Freud to a kind of Chaplin or Buster Keaton of the memory-machine:

> The memory-trace is simply a particular arrangement of facilitations [path-breakings], so organized that one route is followed in preference to another. The functioning of memory in this way might be compared to what is known as "memory" in the theory of cybernetic machines, which are built on the principle of binary oppositions.

Jacques Derrida, as usual, is a much more adequate and perceptive interpreter of the relation of memory to language in Freud. Derrida tells us that the psyche is a kind of text and that this text is constituted of what Derrida calls "written traces." Early Freud (1895) speaks of memory as if it is a composite trope rather like influence; memory is defined as "the capacity to be altered in a lasting way by events which occur only once." Derrida assimilates Freud to Nietzsche by finding "the real origin of memory and thus of the psyche in the difference between path-breakings" or sensory excitations as they encounter resistances in consciousness. What Derrida calls "the trace as memory" is the impalpable and invisible difference between two path-breaking forces impinging upon what becomes the individual mind. With Derrida's more complex and subtle Hiedeggerean notion of the trace proper, as opposed to Freud's memory-trace, I am not concerned here, because I wish to talk only about one text, Wordsworth's *Tintern Abbey*, and the intrusion of a concept of memory into the meaning of that poem. This concept is essentially Wordsworth's own, and can be illuminated by juxtaposition with Freud's, and with Derrida's brilliant exegesis of Freudian memory. But even the Wordsworthian concept of memory is very secondary to my aims in this discourse. I want to offer an antithetical reading of Wordsworth's *Tintern Abbey*, employing my map of misprision and some aspects of a larger scheme of what I have called the Scene of Instruction in chapter 3 of *A Map of Misreading*. In that scheme the study of a poem as misprision or a revisionary text is only the sixth and final phase of a complex attempt at complete interpretation, in which a text is fully related to a precursor text or texts.

I do not believe that Wordsworth meant this poem to be "about" memory; I think he intended what he called "restoration" to be the subject of the poem. He seems to have wanted a far more positive, hopeful, even celebratory poem than the one he actually wrote. As with the *Intimations* Ode, the poet desired to emphasize restitution, compensation, gain rather than loss. But his revisionary genius intended otherwise or, if we want to select Freudian terms, the defensive process of repression gave Wordsworth a very different poem than the one he set out to write. I am going to suggest that the Sublime tropes or, strong hyperboles of *Tintern Abbey* work to repress the still-haunting presence of Milton's texts, particularly of the invocation to Books III and VII of *Paradise Lost*. Because of the preternatural strength of Wordsworth's unconsciously purposeful forgettings of Milton, the true subject of *Tintern Abbey* becomes memory rather than spiritual or imaginative renovation. Indeed, I will go so far as to argue not only that the meaning of *Tintern Abbey* is in its relationship to Milton's invocations, but that the poem becomes, despite itself, an invocation of Milton. Memory deals with absence, and the crucial or felt absence in *Tintern Abbey* is Milton's.

As with my antithetical account of Blake's *London*, which uncovered an opposition in that poem between prophetic voice and demonic writing, *Tintern Abbey* Kabbalized will show some similar patterns of a struggle between voicing and marking, and between hearing and seeing, a struggle in which visible traces usurp the hopeful murmur of prophetic voice. But Blake warred always against the bodily eye, and overtly aspired towards the status and function of the *nabi* or visionary orator. Wordsworth and Coleridge, as their better scholars have shown us, longed for a composite, originary sense that combined rather than opposed seeing and hearing. If memory-traces and their implicit metaphor of script usurp a greater dream in *Tintern Abbey*, then it is not so much the Hebraic dream of divine voice as it is the complex synaesthesia as more culturally mixed idea of the poetic vocation. Thomas McFarland and M. H. Abrams have traced Coleridge's images of "A light in sound, a sound-like power in light" to the theosophist Boehme and the metaphysician Schelling, both of whom were aware of the more ultimate source of these images in Kabbalah. Like most Kabbalist images, these in turn go back to Neoplatonic speculative origins. Wordsworth's source for such images was invariably Coleridge, whose "conversation" poems provided an immediate model for *Tintern Abbey*. Yet we do not feel either Coleridge's presence or absence in the poem, for Coleridge induced in the much stronger Wordsworth no anxieties of poetic influence.

The joy of what they considered to be a fully active imagination expressed itself for both poets in a combined or synaesthetic sense of seeing-hearing. Wordsworth seems to have believed, quite literally, that he had retained this combined sense much later into childhood than most people do. The phenomenon is overtly an element in the *Intimations* Ode, and has little explicitly to do with *Tintern Abbey*. Yet *Tintern Abbey* is at once the most enigmatic and perhaps the most influential of modern poems. Among much else it begins that splendidly dismal tradition in which modern poems intend some merely ostensible subject, yet actually find their true subject in the anxiety of influence.

The most defiantly Wordsworthian of modern critics, Geoffrey Hartman, says that "in Wordsworth, it is always a sound or voice that must 'grow with thought,' as well as a person. As if when voice broke, identity itself were in danger of breaking." Hartman, commenting on the "Boy of Winander" fragment, asserts a remarkable freedom for Wordsworth from the burden of influence-anxiety. Though Hartman, in my judgment, idealizes Wordsworth, his formidable summary here is another antagonist that must be met:

> Now the one kind of echo missing from Wordsworth's poetry, or very carefully used when used at all, is the echo we call a literary allusion. The literary echo, in Wordsworth, is "reduced" to experience by a "cure of the ground"; and when it does occur it is

so internalized that it points to the *phenomenology* of literary allusion. This grounding of allusion in experience—in the personal and mortal experience of time—has an unexpected result. Take away the play of allusion, the comforting ground of literary-historical texture, and you place the burden of responsiveness directly on the reader.

My first response to this is to marvel at the miracle of a cure of the ground so thorough that "literary-historical texture" has disappeared. Hazlitt spoke what he knew to be a relative truth when he said of Wordsworth's poetry that in it we *seem* to begin anew on a *tabula rasa* of poetry. Hazlitt's relativism has become Hartman's absolutism, but then Hartman loves Wordsworth more than Hazlitt did, but then again Hazlitt had the mixed blessing of knowing Wordsworth personally. Hartman's true point is Wordsworth's characteristic *internalization* of allusion. Internalization is at once the great Wordsworthian resource and the great Wordsworthian disaster, and it is never enough to praise Wordsworth for a process in which he was indeed, as Keats saw, the great poetic inventor and, as Keats also saw, the great poetic villain; indeed as much a hero-villain, I would say, as his true precursor, Milton's Satan. In *The Borderers*, Milton's Satan is Oswald, but elsewhere in Wordsworth he becomes a much subtler and finer figure, the Solitary of *The Excursion*, and even finer, the really dangerous element in Wordsworth's own poetic ego, or what Blake would have called Wordsworth's own Spectre of Urthona, the anxiety-principle that usurps voice in all the great poems, and substitutes for voice various memorial inscriptions, various traces of a Miltonic anteriority.

Something richer and more mature in Wordsworth wins out over even this spectral blocking-agent in *The Prelude*, but I am uncertain as to who wins in the greatest and most influential of Wordsworth's shorter poems, the grand triad of *Resolution and Independence*, the *Intimations of Immortality* Ode, and *Tintern Abbey*. I myself love *Tintern Abbey* more than any other poem by Wordsworth, but the love is increasingly an uneasy one. I do not see how any poem could do more or do better; it dwarfs Yeats or Stevens when they write in the same mode. I suspect that *Tintern Abbey* is the modern poem proper, and that most good poems written in English since *Tintern Abbey* inescapably repeat, rewrite, or revise it. If there is something radically wrong with it, something radically self-deceptive, then this radical wrongness at last will not be seen as belonging to *Tintern Abbey* alone.

The language of *Tintern Abbey* centers upon the interplay of hearing and of seeing. To "hear" goes back to an Indo-European root (*ken*) which means to pay attention, watch, observe, beware, guard against, as well as to listen. To "see" goes back to a root (*sekw*) that means to perceive. *To hear is thus also, etymologically, to see, but to see is not necessarily to hear.* This etymological oddity holds, in a Kabbalistic kernel, the deepest anxiety of Wordsworth's poem, which is an anxiety about Wordsworth's relation to his precursor-of-precursors, that mortal god, John Milton. Of all Milton's poetic descendants, including even Blake, Wordsworth was the strongest, so strong indeed that we must face a dark truth. Wordsworth's greatest poem, *The Prelude*, was finished, in its essentials, a hundred and seventy years ago, and no subsequent poetry written in English can sustain a close comparison with it, no matter what fashionable criticism tries to tell us to the contrary. There is an Emersonian law of compensation in literary history as there is in any other history, including the life of each individual. Nietzsche and Emerson, more than any other theorists, understood that other artists must pay the price for too overwhelming an artist. Wordsworth, like Milton, both enriches and destroys his sons and daughters. Wordsworth is a less dramatic destroyer, because of the program of internalization that he carried out, but he may have been the greatest Tamerlane of the two.

Let me reduce my own hyperboles, which seem to have been rather unacceptable to my own profession, the scholars of poetic tradition. The problem of surpassing Wordsworth is the fairly absurd one of going beyond Wordsworth in the process of internalization. But what, in a poem, is internalization? I will compare two passages of poetry, and then ask which of these has gone further in the quest towards internalizing what we still like to call the imagination.

Here is the first:

I am still completely happy.
My resolve to win further I have
Thrown out, and am charged by the thrill
Of the sun coming up. Birds and trees, houses,
These are but the stations for the new sign of being
In me that is to close late, long
After the sun has set and darkness come
To the surrounding fields and hills.
But if breath could kill, then there would not be
Such an easy time of it, with men locked back there
In the smokestacks and corruption of the city.
Now as my questioning but admiring gaze expands
To magnificent outposts, I am not so much at home
With these memorabilia of vision as on a tour
Of my remotest properties, and the eidolon

Sinks into the effective "being" of each thing,
Stump or shrub, and they carry me inside
On motionless explorations of how dense a thing can be,
How light, and these are finished before they have begun
Leaving me refreshed and somehow younger.

This is the opening of John Ashbery's beautiful *Evening in the Country*, one of the most distinguished descendants of *Tintern Abbey*. Contrast it to the ancestral passage:

... that blessed mood
In which the burthen of the mystery,
In which the heavy and the weary weight
Of all this unintelligible world,
Is lightened: that serene and blessed mood,
In which the affections gently lead us on,—
Until, the breath of this corporeal frame
And even the motion of our human blood
Almost suspended, we are laid asleep
In body, and become a living soul:
While with an eye made quiet by the power
Of harmony, and the deep power of joy,
We see into the life of things.

I will revisit these lines later, as I attempt a full reading of the poem. Here I am concerned only with the poetry of the growing inner self. Whose poetic self is more inner, Ashbery's or Wordsworth's? Both poets are experiencing a blessed mood that is at work repairing a previous distress, and both poets are seeing into the life of things. But are there still things for them to see into? Can we distinguish, whether in Wordsworth, or Emerson, or in all of their mixed progeny, between internalization and solipsism? It is palpable, to me, that there is a touch more externality to the world of things in Ashbery's lines than there is in Wordsworth's. In Wordsworth's supreme moments, as in Emerson's, things become transparent, and the inner self expands until it introjects not less than everything, space and time included. At least Ashbery still knows and says "how dense a thing can be," however motionless or quiet the exploring eye of the poet may have become.

No one is going to manage, ever, to accomplish the delightful absurdity of writing the *history* of the perpetually growing inner self. This helps one to see why the phrase "the history of poetry" is, at best, an oxymoron. If a friend came to me and declared that he was about to embark upon a history of consciousness, then I would weep for him. But it is possible to write the more limited history of a few changes in historical psychology, which is what the Dutch psychiatrist J. H. Van den Berg admirably accomplished in a book called *Metabletica*, translated into English under the title of *The Changing Nature of Man*. It is also possible to work out some, at least, of the relationship between philosophy's struggles with the idea of solipsism, and literature's rather more desperate struggles with the same notion. A disputable but provocative book by a British literary scholar, A. D. Nuttall, has attempted just this, quite recently, under the title of *A Common Sky: Philosophy and the Literary Imagination*. Van den Berg does not discuss Wordsworth, but he centers upon Rousseau and upon Freud, both of them relevant to any account of Wordsworthian internalization. Nuttall does not like Wordsworth, whom he oddly compounds with Nietzsche, because to Nuttall the Wordsworthian innerness is essentially a solipsism. Here is a cento of Nuttall on Wordsworth:

> Wordsworth remains a philosophically inarticulate member of the school of Locke....
>
> ... Wordsworth is plainly bewildered. He is afraid that his insights are merely projections, hopes that they are telling him about external reality. But the important thing is that, whatever the final decision ... the categories of his thought are Lockian. But Wordsworth, unlike Locke, has a distinctive psychology, a peculiar cast to his mind, and is therefore afraid, as Locke was not, that his ideas are not truly representative of the world....
>
> ... It was almost inevitable that the slow progress of subjective isolation should have, as one of its psychological consequences, a compensatory obsession with the objective condition. The poet, inhabiting an increasingly mental world, grows hungry for "thinghood." For the Cartesian rationalist, articulate thought is the foundation of or confidence in reality. For Wordsworth one suspects that articulate thought and reality are in some way inimical to one another. This may partly be traced to Wordsworth's own strange spiritual development in which articulateness was attained at the very time when his grip on the object became infirm.

I think that Nuttall, in these comments, has mixed up two closely related but still separate states: highly self-conscious extreme subjectivity, and solipsistic fear that there is nothing beyond the subject. He is correct in observing Wordsworth's curious nostalgia for the object, which after all became the tradition that led from Wordsworth to Ruskin to Pater to Proust to Beckett, and also from Wordsworth to Emerson to Whitman to Stevens to Hart Crane to Ashbery. But this nostalgia for nature, this sense of the estrangement of things, finds a more convincing explanation in Van den Berg's formulations, who distinguishes the historical changes that caused the inner self to expand so alarmingly. Here is a rather full cento of passages from Van den Berg:

> The theory of repression ... is closely related to the thesis that there is sense in everything, which in turn implies that everything is past and there is nothing new....
>
> ... The factualization of our understanding—the impoverishment of things to a uniform substantiality—and the disposal of everything that is not identical with this substantiality into the "inner self" are both parts of one occurrence. The inner self became necessary when contacts were devaluated....
>
> ... A pure landscape, not just a backdrop for human actions: nature, nature as the middle ages did not know it, an exterior nature closed within itself and self-sufficient, an exterior from which the human element has, in principle, been removed entirely. It is things-in-their-farewell, and therefore is as moving as a farewell of our dearest....
>
> ... The inner self, which in Rousseau's time was a simple, soberly filled, airy space, has become ever more crowded. Permanent residents have even been admitted; at first, only the parents, who could not stand being outside any longer, required shelter, finally it was the entire ancestry.... The inner life was like a haunted house. But what else could it be? It contained everything. Everything extraneous had been put into it. The entire history of mankind had to be the history of the individual. Everything that had previously belonged to everybody, everything that had been collective property and had existed in the world in which everyone lived, had to be contained by the individual. It could not be expected that things would be quiet in the inner self.
>
> .. Almost unnoticed—for everybody was watching the inner self—the landscape changed. It became estranged, and consequently it became visible....
>
> ... the estrangement of things ... brought Romanticism to ecstasy.

These passages are the background to Van den Berg's formidable critique of Freud, for Freud is viewed as the prophet of the complete inner self and the completely estranged exterior:

> Ultimately the enigma of grief is the libido's inclination toward exterior things. What prompts the libido to leave the inner self? In 1914 Freud asked himself this question—the essential question of his psychology, and the essential question of the psychology of the twentieth century. His answer ended the process of interiorization. It is: the libido leaves the inner self when the inner self has become too full. In order to prevent it from being torn, the I has to aim itself on objects outside the self; [Freud]: "... ultimately man must begin to love in order not to get ill." So that is what it is. Objects are of importance only in an extreme urgency. Human beings, too. The grief over their death is the sighing of a too-far distended covering, the groaning of an overfilled self.

It is clear to me that Van den Berg's analysis, rather than Nuttall's, is precisely relevant to Wordsworthian internalization, including what Hartman calls the internalizing of the phenomenology of literary allusion. Nuttall sees Wordsworth as another victim of the hidden solipsism inherent in British empiricism from Locke onwards. Thus, the key-formula of British literary solipsism would be the most celebrated sentence in Locke's *Essay Concerning Human Understanding*:

> Since the mind, in all its thoughts and reasonings, hath no other immediate object but its own ideas, which it alone knows or can contemplate, it is evident that our knowledge is only conversant about them.

There are poets who followed Locke, and perhaps an aspect of Wordsworth did, but this is to discount entirely the Coleridgean element in Wordsworth's vision of the imagination. Wordsworth's mind asserted, contra Locke and Nuttall, that it had also an immediate object in nature, or rather an answering subject in nature. But I think it correct nevertheless to say of Wordsworth what Van den Berg says of Rousseau, that the love of that answering subject, nature, is a love that distances and estranges nature. Internalization and estrangement are humanly one and the same process.

I turn to the text of *Tintern Abbey*, and to the interpretation of the poem as a Scene of Instruction. I begin with the last phase of this scene, the application to *Tintern Abbey* of my map of misprision, in order to uncover the pattern of revisionism in the poem, to trace the network of ratios, tropes, defenses, and images that are the final consequences of Wordsworth's struggle with Milton.

Let us map *Tintern Abbey* together. The poem consists of five verse-paragraphs, of which the first three (lines 1–57) form a single movement that alternates the ratios of *clinamen* and *tessera*. The fourth verse-paragraph is the second movement (lines 58–111) and goes from the ratio of *kenosis* to a *daemonization* that brings in the Sublime. The fifth and final verse-paragraph is the third and last movement (lines 112–159), and alternates the ratios of *askesis* and *apophrades*. To abandon my own esoteric shorthand, lines 1–57 shuttle back and forth between dialectical images of presence and absence and representing images of parts and wholes. Lines 58–111 alternate images of fullness and emptiness, of gain and loss, with images of height and depth. Finally lines 112–159 move from inside/outside juxtapositions of the self and nature to an interplay of images of earliness and lateness. This is of course merely a very rough revisionary pattern, but it is there all right, in *Tintern Abbey* as in hundreds of good poems afterwards, down to the present day. What is unique to each poem is the peculiar balance between tropes and defenses in these ratio-structures or patterns-of-images. It will be seen that in *Tintern Abbey* the intricate dance of substitutions between tropes and defenses of limitation and of representation exposes the problematics of the Wordsworthian motives for so thoroughly internalizing literary allusion as to give the effect of the first thoroughly original stylistic breakthrough in British poetry since Milton's *Penseroso*. But the price of this breakthrough is considerable, and can be traced up the interpretative ladder of a scene or scheme of Instruction.

In *A Map of Misreading*, I cited Kierkegaard as the Theorist of the Scene of Instruction, this being the Kierkegaard of the *Philosophical Fragments*. Perhaps I should have cited earlier Kierkegaard, particularly the remarkable brief essay in volume I of *Either/Or* called "The Rotation Method." In some sense, Wordsworth's *Tintern Abbey* is a "rotation method," and it may be illuminating to interpret Wordsworth's opening lines with a few Kierkegaardian excerpts firmly in mind:

> My method does not consist in change of field, but resembles the true rotation method in changing the crop and the mode of cultivation. Here we have at once the principle of limitation, the

only saving principle in the world. The more you limit yourself, the more fertile you become in invention....

The more resourceful in changing the mode of cultivation one can be, the better; but every particular change will always come under the general categories of *remembering* and *forgetting*. Life in its entirety moves in these two currents, and hence it is essential to have them under control. It is impossible to live artistically before one has made up one's mind to abandon hope; for hope precludes self-limitation.... Hope was one of the dubious gifts of Prometheus; instead of giving men the foreknowledge of the immortals, he gave them hope.

To forget—all men wish to forget, and when something unpleasant happens, they always say: Oh, that one might forget! But forgetting is an art that must be practiced beforehand. The ability to forget is conditioned upon the method of remembering.... The more poetically one remembers, the more easily one forgets; for remembering poetically is really only another expression for forgetting....

... Forgetting is the true expression for an ideal process of assimilation by which the experience is reduced to a sounding-board for the soul's own music. Nature is great because it has forgotten that it was chaos; but this thought is subject to revival at any time....

... Forgetting and remembering are thus identical arts.

We cannot apply Kierkegaard to the opening of *Tintern Abbey*, or Van den Berg to its close, without de-idealizing our view of this great poem. Wordsworthian criticism at its best has over-idealized *Tintern Abbey*. To this day I would judge the account of *Tintern Abbey* in Hartman's early book, *The Unmediated Vision*, the strongest reading the poem has received, but it is a canonical reading, and an apocalyptically idealizing one. The experience that Wordsworth had five years before writing *Tintern Abbey* is indeed, as Kierkegaard said, "reduced to a sounding-board for the soul's own music," but Hartman follows Wordsworth's own idealization of his supposed experience. Who is right, Kierkegaard or Wordsworth? Shall we believe the poet in his own self-presentation?

Wordsworth's title for the poem is deceptively casual, or rather this immensely ambitious poem is deceptively left untitled, since the title proper is the throw-away, *Lines*. But the generations of readers who have canonized the poem have given it the mistitle that has stuck, *Tintern Abbey*, which is not even the place of the poem's composition and vision, but gratuitously happens to be the nearest landmark. The place *does* matter, at least to Wordsworth, and so does the time:

> Five years have passed; five summers, with the length
> Of five long winters! and again I hear
> These waters, rolling from their mountain-springs
> With a soft inland murmur.—Once again
> Do I behold these steep and lofty cliffs,
> That on a wild secluded scene impress
> Thoughts of more deep seclusion; and connect
> The landscape with the quiet of the sky.
> The day is come when I again repose
> Here, under this dark sycamore, and view
> These plots of cottage-ground, these orchard-tufts,
> Which at this season, with their unripe fruits,
> Are clad in one green hue, and lose themselves
> 'Mid groves and copses. Once again I see
> These hedge-rows, hardly hedge-rows, little lines
> Of sportive wood run wild: these pastoral farms,
> Green to the very door; and wreaths of smoke
> Sent up, in silence, from among the trees!
> With some uncertain notice, as might seem
> Of vagrant dwellers in the houseless woods,
> Or of some Hermit's cave, where by his fire
> The Hermit sits alone.

That exclamation point in the middle of line 2 indicates surprise that it should have been as long as five years since the poet's last visit, a surprise that must indicate an overwhelming sense of the past recaptured, of everything at first being or at least seeming much the same as it had been. Every interpreter has noted, surely correctly, the importance of the more comprehensive sense, hearing, having the primacy over sight, here at the outset of the poem. Wordsworth does not commence talking about the renewal of vision in any literal sense. Once again he hears *these* waters, with their murmur that to his ears oddly marks them as inland. Wordsworth attached a lame note to this "inland murmur" as to just how many miles in along the Wye you could still hear the sea. But his literalism misinterprets his own figuration, and his "soft murmur" prophesies his own *Intimations* Ode:

> Hence in a season of calm weather
> Though inland far we be,

> Our Souls have sight of that immortal sea
>   Which brought us hither,
>   Can in a moment travel thither,
> And see the children sport upon the shore,
> And hear the mighty waters rolling evermore.

Though twenty-eight years inland from his birth, Wordsworth hears again the particular intimation of his own immortality that he first heard five years before on the banks of the Wye. This is what the opening figuration of *Tintern Abbey* means, but hardly what it says, for the poem's opening *illusio* speaks of an absence in order to image a hoped-for presence. Rhetorically, Wordsworth emphasizes the length of the five years that have gone by, but his meaning is not in how long the absence of the "soft inland murmur" has been felt, but how vividly the presence of the "hearing is revived. Psychologically, the phenomenon is the primary, defense of reaction-formation, the opposition of a particular self-limitation to a repressed desire by manifesting the opposite of the desire. The desire repressed here is the ultimate, divinating desire to live forever and the reaction-formation is the awareness, breaking through repression, of the passage of five long winters, despite the renewal of hearing and subsequently of vision.

Hartman and others have written usefully of the reciprocity that is renewed in the opening passage between Wordsworth's mind and the presence of nature. I want to emphasize instead the transition throughout the poem's first movement, up through line 57, from the initial reaction-formation or rhetorical irony to a psychic turning-against-the-self on Wordsworth's part, which as a figural representation is a remarkable instance of thinking-by-synecdoche. In line 42 of the poem, Wordsworth suddenly switches from "I" and "me" to "us" and "we." He is the part, and all people capable of imaginative experience become the whole. This plural subject is sustained until the magnificent "We see into the life of things" in line 49, after which in lines 50–57, Wordsworth is back to "I" and "me," to being a solitary or mutilated part of a universal whole, and a note of the vicissitudes of instinct, of psychic reversal, enters into the text again. This passage into and out of the universal is determined, in my interpretation, by the poem's largely hidden, revisionary struggle with two great precursor-texts, the invocations to Books III and VII of *Paradise Lost*. I want now to review the first fifty-seven lines of *Tintern Abbey* in the particular context of poetic misprision, of Wordsworth's relation to Milton, which centers upon the curiously placed figuration of the Hermit.

Hartman relates the Hermit of *Tintern Abbey* to the Leech Gatherer of *Resolution and Independence* and both to the vision and voice of St. John in

Revelation. I would use Hartman's own description of the Hermit to suggest a more radical and poetically dangerous identification, in which the Hermit stands, through the fixation of a primal repression, for the blind contemplative Milton of the great invocations. Here is Hartman's account of the Hermit:

> The Hermit of *Tintern Abbey* is an image of transcendence: he sits fixed by his fire, the symbol, probably, for the pure or imageless vision....
>
> ... the Hermit appears, fixed near his fire, freed in his perception from the forms of the external world, a relic of eternity and prophet of the immortal sea's return.

Milton's presentation of himself, in his maturity, is certainly not as a Hermit, I would admit. But the Miltonic Solitary or *Penseroso*, the true start for Wordsworth as Pilgrim and Wanderer, appears at the close of *Il Penseroso* as a Hermit. This Hermit first *hears* an immortal music and only then has a vision of heaven. But the dialectic of Milton's presence and absence begins earlier in *Tintern Abbey* than in the epiphany of the Hermit, and continues long after the vision of the Hermit has faded.

Hartman does not view the traces, hidden and visible, of Milton in *Tintern Abbey* as evidence of Wordsworth's anxiety, but rather of his strength. Hartman does not overestimate the strength, for it is indeed beyond estimation, but he discounts the anxiety that pervades the poem, an anxiety that mixes worries about imaginative priority with more overt worries about the continuity of imagination between the younger and the older Wordsworth. But to discount the anxiety of influence is to commit oneself to the idealizing process that is canonization, and that leads to canonical misreading, so that strong readers become weaker than they need be. Here is Leslie Brisman, very much in Hartman's tradition, writing of the Milton–Wordsworth influence-relation in his sensitive and brilliant book, *Milton's Poetry of Choice and Its Romantic Heirs*:

> Throughout *The Prelude*, Wordsworth labors to create moments where an arrest of time at the "untreated" opens into a sense of the re-created, of imaginative alternatives imagined anew.... But in expressing a longing for a voice like that of nature, Wordsworth achieves a moment of voice: "Spring returns,— / I saw the Spring return." Appealing for poetic voice in the invocation to *Paradise Lost*, Book III, Milton also expressed the failure of voice when he acknowledged that the

seasons return, "but not to me returns / Day." Wordsworth cannot be said to echo Milton—"spring" is just the word for which Milton could not at that moment find voice. But Wordsworth has the power of sight, the power of relationship with nature, and can gather from that relationship the voice with which to proclaim, and rest on the claim, "Spring returns,— / I saw the Spring return." The return of the word "Spring" makes poetry participate in the renewal, taking on the authority of the natural world.

This seems to me a beautiful idealism, but sadly counter to the truths and sorrows of poetic misprision, and particularly to the sorrowful truth of Wordsworth's deep anxieties as to whether his power of relation ship with nature can compensate him for his failures to rise to as much as he could have risen of Milton's more antithetical visionary power. For Wordsworth as well as Milton knows that poetry cannot take on the authority of the natural world, but must assault the supposed priority of the natural object over the trope. The old paradoxes of poetic influence are at work here; Brisman shows us Wordsworth consciously, overtly alluding to the Invocation of Book III. I will proceed now to show Wordsworth unconsciously, repressively alluding to the same invocation in *Tintern Abbey*, with this repression in turn leading to a greater, more daemonic, precisely Sublime repressive alluding to the invocation to Book VII of *Paradise Lost*.

Book III of *Paradise Lost* begins by hailing the Holy Light. Milton speaks of himself as revisiting the Light, and of hearing again the "warbling flow" of Divine waters. But Milton is like the nightingale, and sings darkling. Seasons return, but not to Milton, for the Day does not return. Milton therefore prays to the "Celestial light" to purge and disperse all mist from his mind, that he may see and tell of invisible things. Lines 9–18 of *Tintern Abbey* are a misprision or reversed epiphany of this Miltonic passage, and are resumed in the opening lines of the *Intimations* Ode, where the "Celestial light" is absent though all the glories of nature are present. For Wordsworth, unlike Milton, "the day is come," and the season is seasonally bestowing its fruits to the seeing eyes. The mist that Milton prays be purged from his mind is sent up, to Wordsworth's sight, from the fire of the Hermit's cave. And if all this transposition seems far-fetched, then examine the very strangely phrased opening of the poem's very next verse-paragraph:

> These beauteous forms,
> Through a long absence, have not been to me
> As is a landscape to a blind man's eye:

Need we question who this blind man is?

Let us, for now, pass rapidly over the great second movement of the poem (lines 58–111), concentrating in it only upon the major interplay between tropes and defenses. There are a series of metonymic reductions—thought half-extinguished to gleams, recognitions to dimness and faintness, joys and raptures to aches and dizziness. This emptying-out psychically is less a regression or even an undoing than it is an isolation—the reduction from fullness to emptiness is a loss of context. The enormous restitution for this loss is in the magnificent series of hyperboles that dominate lines 93–111:

> And I have felt
> A presence that disturbs me with the joy
> Of elevated thoughts; a sense sublime
> Of something far more deeply interfused,
> Whose dwelling is the light of setting suns,
> And the round ocean and the living air,
> And the blue sky, and in the mind of man:
> A motion and a spirit, that impels
> All thinking things, all objects of all thought,
> And rolls through all things. Therefore am I still
> A lover of the meadows and the woods,
> And mountains; and of all that we behold
> From this green earth; of all the mighty world
> Of eye, and ear,—both what they half create
> And what perceive; well pleased to recognize
> In nature and the language of the sense
> The anchor of my purest thoughts, the nurse,
> The guide, the guardian of my heart, and soul
> Of all my moral being.

If an antithetical criticism of poetry is in any way useful, then it must illuminate this major instance of the Sublime. If the Sublime depends upon repression, as I insist it does, then where shall we find repression in these remarkably expressive and emphatic lines? How can there be meaningful repression where so much emerges, where it seems surely that Wordsworth must be having his whole say, must be bringing his whole soul into activity?

I would reply to these questions by indicating how problematic this passage is, and how deeply a repressed element is at work in it. Despite the hyperbolic language, Wordsworth makes only a measured assertion of the power of his mind over the universe of sense, and also over language. The hyperboles make it difficult for us to realize, at first, how guarded the passage is. The poet's thoughts are touched to sublimity by a presence that *dwells* in nature and in the mind, but is identified with neither. The monistic presence is clearly more allied to Hebrew than to Greek thought, but this pervasive motion and spirit is not identified with the Hebrew-Christian *ruach*, or breath-of-Jehovah. And though this presence/motion/spirit appears to be monistic in its aims, the poet stops well short of asserting that it reconciles subject and object. It impels both, it rolls both through things and through the poet's mind, but it does not abolish the differences between them. Nor is the poet's reaction to the spirit what we might expect, for instead of declaring his love for or worship of the spirit, he proclaims instead the continuity of his love for natural sights and sounds. Having invoked directly his eye and his ear, he makes, even more surprisingly, a deep reservation about his own perpetual powers, or rather an almost hyperbolical admission of limitation. The mighty world of eye and ear is not a balance of creation and of perception, but of half-creation and full-perception. Having acknowledged such a shading of imagination, it is no surprise that Wordsworth should then be happy to recognize anchor, nurse, guide, and guardian in powers not his own—in nature and the language of the self.

What is being repressed here is Wordsworth's extraordinary pride in the strength of his own imaginings, his preternatural self-reliance, as we find it, say, in the verse "Prospectus" to *The Excursion* or in Book XIV of *The Prelude*. An unconsciously purposeful forgetting is at work in the depths of Wordsworth's own spirit, and what it forgets is a ferocity of autonomy and strength unequalled in British poetry since Milton. Are these the accents of one whose eye and ear only half-create?

> For I must tread on shadowy ground, must sink
> Deep—and, aloft ascending, breathe in worlds
> To which the heaven of heavens is but a veil.
> All strength—all terror, single or in bands,
> That ever was put forth in personal form—
> Jehovah—with his thunder, and the choir
> Of shouting Angels, and the empyreal thrones—
> I pass them unalarmed. Not Chaos, not
> The darkest pit of lowest Erebus,
> Nor aught of blinder vacancy, scooped out
> By help of dreams—can breed such fear and awe
> As fall upon us often when we look
> Into our Minds, into the Mind of Man—
> My haunt, and the main region of my song.

That is Wordsworth, taking on Jehovah and Milton together, only a few months before writing *Tintern Abbey*. That is not a poet whose eye and ear "half-create." *Power* is being repressed in *Tintern Abbey*, a power so antithetical that it could tear the poet loose from nature, and take him into a world of his own, restituting him for the defense of self-isolation by isolating him yet more sublimely. Wordsworth defends himself against his own strength through repression, and like all strong poets he learns to call that repression the Sublime.

What are we to do with the phrase "half-create"? Can we keep memory out of it? I think not. For you cannot have repression without *remembering to forget*, and the price of repression in *Tintern Abbey* is that memory largely usurps the role of subject in the poem. But memory of what? I return to an earlier formula in this discourse there is a struggle in *Tintern Abbey* between voicing and marking, in which Wordsworth wants to rely upon voice and the memory of voice, and somewhat fears relying upon sight and the memory of sight. There is a hidden but quite definite *fear of writing* in *Tintern Abbey*, or perhaps rather a fear of being delivered up to a potential fear of writing.

It is in Dorothy's voice that Wordsworth first recaptures his own former language, and only then does he read his own lost ecstasies in the shooting lights of her wild eyes. All through the poem, the poet says he is being *taught*, indeed he explicitly affirms that he has returned to a Scene of Instruction. But it becomes clearer as the poem proceeds that he wants to be taught or retaught primarily through the ear (as the later Milton was), though he knows that this is not really possible, since the eye is the most despotic of our senses. *And Nature will not stop writing*, though he would prefer her to keep to oral composition. For consider the vocabulary of the poem: it opens with a murmur, but then nature begins to write when the cliffs *impress* thoughts upon the scene, and when they connect landscape and sky. Whatever the source of the Hermit's fire, the silent wreaths of smoke are also a writing, and so are the beauteous forms that have been held as memory-traces. Wordsworth, like his scholarly disciple, Hartman, prefers the after-image to the spoken-trace, but his own poem keeps forcing him to read nature and not just to hear her. The world is not intelligible without writing, not even the natural world, and this is a sorrow to Wordsworth. Though his eye is chastened and made quiet by a power of sound, he still is constrained to say not that he *hears* the life of things, but that he *sees* into them. This pattern persists throughout the poem; the gleams and dim recognitions are visual, and when he does look on nature, in his mature phase, he *hears* loss, however beautifully, in "the still, sad music of humanity." But I have taken us now to the last dialectical movement of the poem, an alternation between metaphor and transumption, and I want to pause to brood on image-patterns before returning to the opposition between sight and sound.

The surprisingly beautiful passage from lines 134 through 146 juxtaposes nature as a benign *outside* force with Dorothy as a benign *inside* presence, but as always with the perspectivism of metaphor, Nature and Dorothy are taken further apart rather than being brought closer together by the juxtaposition. But the remarkable metaleptic reversals of lateness for earliness and earliness for lateness, which follow, give a much more powerful and convincing rhetorical illusion:

> nor, perchance—
> If I should be where I no more can hear
> Thy voice, nor catch from thy wild eyes these gleams
> Of past existence—wilt thou then forget
> That on the banks of this delightful stream
> We stood together

Those gleams are technically the metonymy of a metonymy—they trope upon an earlier trope in the poem, and so work as a trope-reversing trope. This allows Wordsworth a proleptic representation of his own death, and also of a kind of survival through the surrogate of Dorothy. I do not think this is literal death, despite Wordsworth's apparent intention, but the figural and much-feared death of the poetic imagination. The power of Miltonic transumption is worked again; defensively, Wordsworth introjects the past, projects the future except as a world for Dorothy, and utterly destroys the present moment, the living time in which he no longer stands. His gain in all this troping or defending is palpable; it is crucial to consider his loss, which will bring us back to memory, to writing opposing voicing, and at last to Milton again, and with Milton to the poem's full-scale staging of a Scene of Instruction.

Wordsworth's wishful prophecy for his sister would make her mind "a mansion for all lovely forms" and her memory "a dwelling-place / For all sweet sounds and harmonies." Because of the direct contrast the poet enforces between an earlier phase of "wild ecstasies" and a supposedly more "mature" one of "sober coloring" of the close of the *Intimations* Ode, there is something about that "mansion" and that "dwelling-place" that makes the reader a little uneasy. The mansion is a touch like a museum, and the dwelling-place a kind of tape- or record-library. But, setting this uneasiness aside, a curious preference seems to be shown here for "memory" over the "mind," since the preferred sensory impressions are harbored in "memory." Wordsworth of course, unlike Blake, made no sharp distinction between memory and poetry as modes of thought, but we must question still why *Tintern Abbey*, as a poem, ends with so emphatic an emphasis upon memory. Three times Wordsworth repeats his anxious exhortation to his sister, whom he loved and was always to love far more intensely than anyone else (with of course the single exception, always, of himself):

oh! then,

> If solitude, or fear, or pain, or grief,
> Should be thy portion, with what healing thoughts
> Of tender joy wilt thou remember me,
> And these my exhortations! Nor, perchance—
> If I should be where I no more can hear
> Thy voice, nor catch from thy wild eyes these gleams
> Of past existence—wilt thou then forget
> That on the banks of this delightful stream
> We stood together; and that I, so long
> A worshipper of Nature, hither came
> Unwearied in that service: rather say
> With warmer love—oh! with far deeper zeal
> Of holier love. Nor wilt thou then forget,
> That after many wanderings, many years
> Of absence, these steep woods and lofty cliffs,
> And this green pastoral landscape, were to me
> More dear, both for themselves and for thy sake!

I think we learn in time, however much we love this poem, that we must read the last line with four words added: "More dear, both for themselves and for thy sake, and for my sake!" I am not attacking this superb poem, but I wish to acknowledge two very different readings or misreadings of the poem, the powerfully revisionist or deconstructive one implied by Paul de Man, in which the whole poem is an *aporia*, an "uncertain notice" like the smoke sent up among the trees, or the powerfully canonical one, in which Keats pioneered and which culminates in Hartman's *The Unmediated Vision*. Is *Tintern Abbey* an *aporia*, or is it the prolepsis of a dark passage, a major internalization of Milton's *agon* with tradition? Or is it, as an antithetical reading or misreading would seem to tell us, a very great visionary lie, not as much a myth of memory as it is a utilization of memory as a lie against time? Actually or potentially, these are all strong misreadings, and they may not differ from one another as much as they would like to, though clearly they also cannot be reconciled. Which of the three readings/misreadings would cost us too much of the poem's strength? Or to say it in more Nietzschean terms, of these three errors, these three composite tropes, which is the most necessary error?

Why, mine of course, though of the three it is the one I like the least, because it increases the problematics-of-loss in the poem. Memory, in *Tintern Abbey*, attempts to become a trope and/or defense that over comes time, which means that memory, going bad, would fall into the realm of paranoia, but working properly would project or spit-out Wordsworth's fears of the future. I think we must praise Wordsworth, almost always, as a poet so strong that he does make his defenses work, a strength in which we could contrast him, most favorably, to a poet like Eliot, whose *Gerontion* is a curious compound of *Tintern Abbey* gone bad, and one of *Tintern Abbey's* stronger descendants, Tennyson's *Tithonus*. Eliot is a poet whose poems, with some exceptions, tend to become weaker rather than stronger, the more provocatively they trope, defensively, against the burden of anteriority. Wordsworth also deforms himself, or rather his poem-as-self, but in him the deformation has a power so immense that after one hundred and seventy-five years it has not stopped surprising us.

Why is Wordsworth so afraid of time in *Tintern Abbey*? Surely it is time that is the hidden reference in the enigmatic: "more like a man / Flying from something that he dreads than one / Who sought the thing he loved." Yet Wordsworth's dread of mortality impresses us because more than any poet's, at least since the Milton of *Lycidas*, it seems to turn upon the magnificent, primal poetic urge for *divination*, in the complex sense best defined by Vico, the poet's apotropaic concern for his own immortality. Milton and Wordsworth alike feared premature death, "premature" meaning before their great epics had been written.

On an antithetical reading, *Tintern Abbey* is a Scene of Instruction in which the poet brings a Sublime response to a place or state of heightened demand, but the genius of the state counts for more than the genius of place, which means that Milton counts for more than nature does, both here and in *The Prelude*. It is Milton whose hidden presence in the poem makes the heightened demand that forces Wordsworth into the profoundly ambivalent defensive trope of memory. Renovation, or "tranquil restoration" as the text terms it, is only a mystification, a mask for the real concern of the poem. The Hermit is the synecdoche for Milton's hiddenness, and so for Milton's triumphant blindness towards anteriority. To see the writing or marking of nature is to see prophetically one's own absence or imaginative death. To see the "uncertain notice" of the Hermit's presence is to be disturbed into sublimity by way of repressing the mighty force of remembering Milton's sublimity, particularly in the Creation of *Paradise Lost*, Book VII, which haunts every Wordsworthian account of the subject- and object-worlds approaching one another again.

Wordsworth, where he is most self-deceiving, remains so strong that the self-deception finally does not matter. For no other poet since Milton holds Milton off so triumphantly, without even always knowing that he is engaged in a wrestling-match. The greatness of *Tintern Abbey*, no matter what the necessity is or is not of any particular strong misreading of it, is assured by its paradoxical triumph over its own hidden subject of memory. *Our* memory of the poem, any of our memories, is finally not a memory of nature's marking nor of Milton's writing, but of *hearing again*, with Wordsworth, "These waters, rolling from their mountain-springs / With a soft inland murmur." Though he was far inland, too far really from the oceanic autonomy he craved, his literally incredible strength of misprision rescued him, nearly intact, from a Scene of Instruction that had destroyed Collins, and partly malformed Blake. It is the peculiar and extravagant greatness of Wordsworth that only he supplanted Milton as the tutelary genius of the Scene of Instruction, and it is the scandal of modern poetry that no one, not even Yeats or Stevens, in turn has supplanted Wordsworth. The Hermit of *Tintern Abbey* is Milton, but the Hermit in *Notes toward a Supreme Fiction* is William Wordsworth, even if Wallace Stevens repressed his memory of who it was:

> That sends us back to the first idea, the quick
> Of this invention; and yet so poisonous
>
> Are the ravishments of truth, so fatal to
> The truth itself, the first idea becomes
> The hermit in a poet's metaphors,
>
> Who comes and goes and comes and goes all day.

FRANCES FERGUSON

The Prelude *and the Love of Man*

Sometimes it suits me better to invent
A tale from my own heart, more near akin
To my own passions and habitual thoughts;
Some variegated story, in the main
Lofty, but the unsubstantial structure melts
Before the very sun that brightens it,
Mist into air dissolving!
    [I, 221–27]

As in the "Immortality Ode," in which "thought" itself becomes an almost unimaginable subject for contemplation, this passage in *The Prelude* bids farewell to the notion of thought—here, in the form of planning—as a directly constructive, unifying enterprise. For just as the "Immortality Ode" probes the links which bind us to earth—those thoughts and words of perception which seem only initially to be connections which we ourselves have made, so *The Prelude* continually explores the connections between an individual's (Wordsworth's) past and his present. And in that exploration the difficulty of branding one's time, words, and plans as "my own" emerges. The "Blest Babe" passage of Book II (which I shall discuss at greater length later in this chapter) articulates most fully the individual's immersion in a world of perception and language which he "chose" under the delusion that

---

From *Wordsworth: Language as Counter-Spirit*, pp. 126–154. © 1977 by Yale University.

it was merely an extension of an affection which seemed to keep the world whole—and paradisiacal. But just as the "Immortality Ode" tries to imagine the possibility of one's *not* having been educated into an acceptance of this world, so *The Prelude* generally attempts to unravel the web of ties which constrain (and also, in some sense, create) the individual's power to choose and to construct himself. In this sense, *The Prelude*, in its exploration of both memory and the imagination of the future, revolves around issues rather different from the story of one poet's development or the assumption that Nature is a given. For the message of memory—and of the imagination of the future after it has become memory—for Wordsworth is one of the futility of Satan's rhetorical questions and declamation in *Paradise Lost*.

> That we were form'd then say'st thou? and the work
> Of secondary hand, by task transferr'd
> From Father to his Son? strange point and new!
> Doctrine which we would know whence learnt: who saw
> When this creation was? remember'st thou
> Thy making, while the Maker gave thee being?
> We know no time when we were not as now;
> Know none before us, self-begot, self-rais'd
> By our own quick'ning power.
>   [V, 853–61]

Whereas for Satan the inability to remember being created by another is to be taken as proof that one is self-begot, for Wordsworth the gaps and limits of the memory suggest the impossibility of being self-begot. And while neither God nor Milton's God is really at issue for Wordsworth in *The Prelude*, the inadequacy of one's accounts of himself on the basis of memory keeps disclosing the otherness of one's own mind as a force which is divine in its power and persistence. Precisely the individual's inability to construct himself—or even to rationalize the process of his construction—becomes testimony to the thoughts and language of others as an Ur-principle for the individual.

This passage from the "introductory" section of Wordsworth's *Prelude* forms part of the catalogue of the poet's attempts to write "some work of glory." And although the project described sounds a great deal like the project which was to be fulfilled, this account takes its place with a number of discarded plans—plans which seem to have been "tried on" and found ill-fitting. "The discipline / And consummation of a Poet's mind, / In everything that stood most prominent, / Have faithfully be pictured" (XIV, 303–06), says the poet at the end of his poem, yet that early pronouncement about the "unsubstantial structure" of his own most personal memories and thoughts lingers. It has not really ever been completely contradicted, as the notorious gaps and nonsequential turnings of *The Prelude* may indicate.

Moreover, this rejection of a tale invented from the poet's own heart is not simply absorbed into the conclusion, which suggests that he has done precisely what he protested he could not do. For the early rejection of the plan is not simply a "mistake" made at the beginning which is corrected and explained away by the ending of Wordsworth's long poem. Rather, the problems of this passage—and of reconciling it with the bulk of the poem— recapitulate themselves throughout the poem. Wordsworth's autobiography is, as this passage suggests, "invented" from what would seem to be least in need of invention—the habitual. And this process continues in the mode of a rather characteristic Wordsworthian indecision about the process itself, an indecision which is familiar from the strange convolutions of the "Mutability" sonnet ("From low to high doth dissolution climb, / And sink from high to low, along a scale / Of awful notes, whose concord shall not fail") and from the dream vision of the Arab ("He, to my fancy, had become the knight/ Whose tale Cervantes tells; yet not the knight,/ But was an Arab of the desert too; / Of these was neither, and was both at once," V, 122–25). The indecisiveness persists, because in Wordsworth's poetry beginnings are never settled, even by endings.

The crucial indecision of the passage reenacts a dilemma which has remained central in criticism: what is the relationship between the individual mind and nature? The pattern of *The Prelude*, as it develops from the titles and the arguments prefacing the books entitled "Love of Nature Leading to the Love of Man" creates the impression that nature performed a crucial mediatory role between the poet and other men, or as some critics put it, that nature became a support to a solipsistic tendency in Wordsworth to abstract other human beings out of any "real" existence.[1] In this early passage from *The Prelude*, however, nature as an external presence appears strangely locked into an unsatisfactorily symbiotic relationship with the poet's "human nature" as the movement from the internal to the external" begins to be a slippage.

That "very sun" which brightens the "unsubstantial structure" of the poet's passions and habitual thoughts ought to be his own, his recollecting and perceiving eye which irradiates the habitual epic of the past. Yet the drift of the metaphors which would give the structure a substantial and "natural" existence is, however, to subject it to a natural process of disparition. The sun which has been gradually projected from within becomes a counteragent, an intransigent other which dissolves structure into mist into air. This curious drifting of the sun itself becomes emblematic of an analogous movement which Wordsworth discerns in language—its tendency to convert itself into a counter-spirit which seems always to threaten the possibility of the poet's changing his internal story into an external story. The internality, which is possessing his own past, continually implies an externality, which is being possessed by a "mistaken" or "inadequate" version of that past.

This dialectic persists throughout *The Prelude*, repeatedly blurring the boundaries between Nature and (human) nature, so that the boundaries between externality and internality correspondingly blur. Yet perhaps the most interesting aspect of this dialectic in Wordsworth is that he rarely speaks directly of it as a problem exclusive to language. Rather, he continually obtrudes the eye upon his readers, as if to suggest that perception is not so much limited by language as it is worried by the crosscurrents of a similar (or perhaps the same) dialectic.

The familiar view that nature is the primary agent of Wordsworthian perception—the central cause of seeing from which the perception of other humans is deduced—becomes an inadequate and partial account when we consider the vagaries of the internal–external movements in Wordsworth's poetry. For such a view represents an hypostatized assumption that nature is so solidly "out there" that the mind can become simply an internalized landscape, and perception simply a branch of geography. The problem is not that the position is wrong, but rather that it ignores the countermovement in Wordsworth's poetry which erodes the stasis of this position, and lends its strength in eroding it,

As examples of the counter movement against a nature-centered view of perception, it seems appropriate to look to two notable discussions of the eye—the "Blest Babe" passage of Book II and the "Blind Beggar" passage of Book VII. For it is in such excerpts from *The Prelude* that the primacy of the eye (or as Merleau-Ponty would say, "the primacy of perception") becomes more prominent than the perception of nature. And although fitting the eye to nature, or "learning from Nature," remains a principle of narrative movement in *The Prelude*, the very tracklessness of that movement in the "Simplon Pass" or the "Mount Snowdon" episodes suggests that the question of perception (Where does it come from? How does it develop?) operates as a retrograde force which continually draws forward movements back to their unconscious and unknowable beginnings.

The "Blest Babe" passage occurs as a general hymn which is itself a prologue to the poet's description of his particular mother and his particular infancy.

> From early days,
> Beginning not long after that first time

In which, a Babe, by intercourse of touch
I held mute dialogues with my Mother's heart,
I have endeavoured to display the means
Whereby this infant sensibility,
Great birthright of our being, was in me
Augmented and sustained.
     [II, 266–72]

But this prelinguistic recollection open upon a passage which subverts the orderliness of the process of development, as the poet records his mother's death.

                  Yet is a path
More difficult before me; and I fear
That in its broken windings we shall need
The chamois' sinews, and the eagle's wing:
For now a trouble came into my mind
From unknown causes. I was left alone
Seeking the visible world, nor knowing why.
     [II, 272–78]

Like the passage in Book I which registers the disparition of the "Unsubstantial structure" of the poet's plans for a story near his own passions, this developmental narrative eddies into an account of insubstantiality, the lack of content. Yet the "unknown causes" which give rise to the "trouble" are simultaneously the most and the least discernable of processes—the affections.

The props of my affections were removed,
And yet the building stood, as if sustained
By its own spirit!
     [II, 279–81]

Although this account differs from the passage from Book I in leaving the mental edifice "sustained," it recapitulates that earlier sense of the void surrounding the affections. For the description of the poet "alone, / Seeking the visible world, nor knowing why," alternately "explains" Wordsworth's attachment to nature and suggests both the unsatisfactoriness and the satisfactoriness of that substitution. As Wordsworth implies everywhere in his "Poems founded on the Affections" with their radical calculations of loss, the affections are the most literal of human faculties, in that the continued existence of a central beloved figure presents itself as "content"—a substance for the words and the perceptions. Thus, we see the unsatisfactoriness—that the visible world, even in the person of a "Mother Nature" will never yield up the dead loved one to any search—and the satisfactoriness—that the former existence of the content, the beloved for the affections—echoes as an implicit command to research the forms, "Do this in remembrance of me." For even if the disappearance of the "props of the affections" seemingly condemns the poet's search of the visible world to hollowness and makes the mental edifice seem to float without foundation, that very search in visible forms remains the only means of legitimizing the memory of the "content," the corporeal existence of a central loved one. Mediation begins here, where the vanishing of a beloved figure can only, however inadequately, be traced through the neutral forms to which the beloved figure once lent the semblance of value and validity. In that sense, the prominence of the epitaph in Wordsworth's poetry becomes comprehensible: only death destroys the security of the affections in the coincidence of "form" and "content," the appearance and the spirit. Only death thus creates the necessity of the search for meaning in the visible world; only when "something is wrong" can there even begin to be the creation of a myth of the Fall, an explanation and / or a balm for the unhappiness.

If the familiar elegiac lyrics ("I Wandered Lonely as a Cloud," "Tintern Abbey," "Resolution and Independence") record the attempt to recapture past feelings, this passage is an attempt to recover the possibility of feeling itself. But the passions have no memory, which explains why activities like lovemaking and grieving are and must be repeatable, and which also explains why the mediation of memories anchored in the visible world becomes essential. The narrative of the visual, and verbal forms supplants the memorylessness of the passions, creating a time as well as a place where neither time nor place were once felt to exist.

But we have still to seek an understanding of the specific process through which nature—the visible world—becomes a substitute for the mother in particular. A lost object of the affections and the effort to solidify the memory of the affections through the forms of nature may be clear enough, but how was that link established *before* that loved presence became an absence? Wordsworth's general account of the developing infant is particularly important in disclosing the relationship between the affections and nature.

> Blest the infant Babe,
> (For with my best conjecture I would trace
> Our Being's earthly progress,) blest the Babe,

Nursed in his Mother's arms, who sinks to sleep
Rocked on his Mother's breast; who with his soul
Drinks in the feelings of his Mother's eye!
For him, in one dear Presence, there exists
A virtue which irradiates and exalts
Objects through widest intercourse of sense.
No outcast he, bewildered and depressed:
Along his infant veins are interfused
The gravitation and the filial bond
Of nature that connect him with the world.
Is there a flower, to which he points with hand
Too weak to gather it, already love
Drawn from love's purest earthly fount for him
Hath beautified that flower; already shades
Of pity cast from inward tenderness
Do fall around him upon aught that bears
Unsightly marks of violence or harm.
   [II, 232–51]

By contrast with the "Immortality Ode" in which the figure of the mother has already been supplanted by surrogates, Nature as foster-mother in the sixth stanza, mother-as-societal-machine in the seventh stanza, this passage reaches back past memory to an "original" mother. And here the child's rapprochement with the world is far more explicable than in the "Immortality Ode." As Wordsworth puts it in the 1805 *Prelude*, the Babe "when his soul / Claims manifest kindred with an earthly soul, / Doth *gather* passion from his Mother's eye!" (1805, II, 241–43, my emphasis). Whereas Rousseau installs passion (the passion of fear) at the initial stages of language in his myth of the invention of language, for Wordsworth passion is both primary in creating perception and language and always derived, in that it involves a passion for another person who has already received a world of perception and language. "The gravitation and the filial bond / Of nature that connect him [the infant] with the world" are not gravity as a "natural law," not a self-evident belief in animism. Instead, the mother's eye seems to create both the child and the world; and the bond between the infant and nature results from an affection between mother and child so strong as to preclude the possibility of the child's recognizing nature as something alien.

The language of beatitude of the passage appears to reimagine an Edenic world in which that vexing gap between the internal and the external has not yet emerged. For as the infant "with his soul / Drinks in the feelings of his Mother's eye," her eye becomes not only a source of nourishment, a kind of spiritual manna, it also becomes the focal point of both internal feelings and the external world. The pupil of the mother's eye in fact presents itself to her child, her best pupil, as a charmed circle in which his own reflection seems united with all the reflections of the visible world surrounding the mother. Nature does not begin to seem "external" to the infant, because it is always perceived as already internalized by the mother's eye. And the communion between the eyes of mother and child is so intense that it seems never to occur to him that he is external to her. He is "no outcast" in that he seems almost not to have recognized his own birth, his externalization and separation from his mother.

> Such feelings pass into his torpid life
> Like an awakening breeze, and hence his mind
>
> . . . .
>
> Is prompt and watchful, eager to combine
> *In one appearance*, all the elements
> And parts of the same object, else detach'd
> And loth to coalesce.
>   [*The Prelude*, 1805, II, 244–50; my emphasis]

Although Wordsworth deleted these lines from the 1850 *Prelude*, we may see them as a supplement which underscores the intensity of the mother's role in communicating the world to her child. For the child's attempt to combine "all the elements / And parts of the same object" is not so much an acceptance of the world as it is a belief in a kind of internal annexation: the mother herself appears to her child to expand as her eyes seem to draw more of the world of visible forms into themselves. This is, of course, a complicated projection—the projection of love from mother to child, the projection of love and absoluteness from child to mother, and the projection of the world from her eyes to his. But the projection operates by imagining itself as an expansion and consolidation of an internal unity rather than as a relationship between separate entities.

And if Wordsworth portrays the child as an infant—without speech— a related speechlessness, or inability to speak, extends throughout the passage. For even though Wordsworth as an adult is imagining his infancy and remembering his mother's death (which occurred when he was almost eight), the language of the description consistently implies its own inadequacy. How can pronouns like "she" and "he" serve to depict a condition of passion so strong that it was inconceivable that there was any difference between them? Neither the "mute dialogues" of touch nor of sight demanded that recognition of difference, because they carried with them the constant affirmation of ocular and tangible proof; communication was representation in the strongest sense, and all communication represented the affections through direct or indirect bodily contact. By comparison with such communication, language and voice come to seem detached and disembodied, for they carry the burden of appearing as the representatives of the forced recognition of a lack, the missing loved one. Language, thus, is not merely an additional mode of communication to be included in a list with touch and sight; it is essentially different in seeming to be an institutional embodiment of the sudden perception of externality and separation. Language, from this perspective, must always be "second-best," an attempt to communicate across difference where difference was once never felt to exist. When the poet speaks of himself as "left alone / Seeking the visible world nor knowing why," that condition of solitude involves simultaneously the memory of a visual communication which was assured of its own content and the fear that all content—all reason why—in outward forms has permanently disappeared.[2]

Thus it is that the perception of the world and the language which the child acquires come to seem "inadequate." The incorporation of the passion which once constituted the meaningfulness of language and the world has dropped out, and for Wordsworth only the language of undisappointed passion rests secure in its own correlations. For only the language of passion (or the "affections") in Wordsworth is sealed off both from error and from the consciousness of error because it is oblivious to any other possibilities so long as the object of passion endures. Passion, it would appear, does not produce error so much by its existence as by the disappearance of its object. And while Rousseau sees passion generating metaphors, "mistakes" which may be "corrected" over time,[3] Wordsworth sees the loss of the object of passion as the essential mistake, an error never susceptible to correction. If passion is a delusion because it cannot endure, Wordsworth seems to suggest that language deprived of such passionate delusion is inevitably condemned to be an elegy, an attempt to reimagine the certainty which the affections once lent to all perception.

But if the description of Book II links the death of the poet's mother to the trauma of the poet's birth into language and the visible world, the felt inadequacies of language and perception which are deprived of an object of passion appear insignificant after the account of the blind beggar (Book VII, 619–49). In "Residence in London," Book VII of *The Prelude*, the poet speaks with the voice of a spectator, from an externality which almost amounts to condenscension.

As the black storm upon the mountain top
Sets off the sunbeam in the valley, so
That huge fermenting mass of human-kind
Serves as a solemn back-ground, or relief,
To single forms and objects, whence they draw,
For feeling and contemplative regard,
More than inherent liveliness and power.
How oft, amid those overflowing streets,
Have I gone forward with the crowd, and said
Unto myself, 'The face of every one
That passes by me is a mystery!'
Thus have I looked, nor ceased to look, oppressed
By thoughts of what and whither, when and how,
Until the shapes before my eyes became
A second-sight procession, such as glides
Over still mountains, or appears in dreams;
And once, far-travelled in such mood, beyond
The reach of common indication, lost
Amid the moving pageant, I was smitten
Abruptly, with the view (a sight not rare)
Of a blind Beggar, who, with upright face,
Stood, propped against a wall, upon his chest
Wearing a written paper, to explain
His story, whence he came, and who he was.
Caught by the spectacle my mind turned round
As with the might of waters; an apt type
This label seemed of the utmost we can know,
Both of ourselves and of the universe;
And, on the shape of that unmoving man,
His steadfast face and sightless eyes, I gazed,
As if admonished from another world.
     [VII, 619–49]

Perhaps the most curious feature of Wordsworth's description of the entire scene of Bartholomew Fair is that perception is entirely one-sided, so that the observed and the observer are alone. The father watching over his sickly babe becomes an emblem of that fragmentation of human perception; he may be seen, but does not see anything himself except the frail child in his arms:

Of those who passed, and me who looked at him,
He took no heed.
     [VII, 611–12]

By contrast with that father who is separated from the crowd by "love unutterable," the poet is separated not by an excess of affection but by the almost total absence of it. So it is that he presents an almost parodically formalistic aesthetic explanation of the power with which the scene of the father and child moved him: the crowd is merely a foil, which, moreover, makes the mediocre appear the better cause. The judgment that "That huge fermenting mass of humankind / Serves as a solemn background, or relief, / To single forms and objects" not only expresses a spectatorial detachment, it also registers an explicitly disunited perception. Perceiving the scene in terms of its "internal" conflict reverses the pattern of perception which the poet as an infant "learned" from his mother—that tendency to unite all visible forms in one object of love. And the fear that "single forms and objects" may draw "more than *inherent* liveliness and power" (my emphasis) from their contrast with the teeming background represents a dread of being cheated or duped which the affections could not admit.

As Geoffrey Hartman suggests, the poet takes on the role of Aeneas descending to the underworld.[4] But despite the poet's rather magisterial tone, his account does not effectively distinguish him as a living soul in a "universe of death." For with Wordsworth's repeated assertion of the significance of passion for perception, the passionless judgment bespeaks not only the emptiness of the external forms but also a complementary, perhaps primary, emptiness within the perceiving eye. And the exclamation that "The face of every one / That passes by me is a mystery!" denudes the world of visible forms of any possibility of internality, as if it were unimaginable that these faces could be human beings who might take themselves seriously. The poet as an alien thus reduces appearances to their lowest limit by rendering them as externality without any connection with internal existence. The visible becomes, effectively, invisible, because it loses all the force of being thought of as an index to an invisible world of significance. And the poet's facelessness comes to seem a fit Dantean "punishment" for his perception of facelessness; one is what one sees, or else Wordsworth's earliest paean to the infant's development of passion-governed perception is idle:

> For feeling has to him imparted power
> That through the growing faculties of sense
> Doth like an agent of the one great Mind
> Create, creator and receiver both,
> Working but in alliance with the works
> Which it beholds.—Such, verily, is the first
> Poetic spirit of our human life,

By uniform control of after years,
In most, abated or suppressed; in some
Through every change of growth and of decay,
Pre-eminent till death.
    [II, 255–65]

Yet the fascination of looking persists, even in its reduced state, so that the poet entertains, almost unwittingly, the questions of origin and development again—"oppressed / By thoughts of what and whither, when and how." And finally the pressure of his thought upon this scene which is perceived as wholly external seems to render it ghostly, either so external that it appears surreal or so internal that it bears the traces of a haunting memory: "the shapes before my eyes became / A second-sight procession, such as glides / Over still mountains, or appears in dreams."

In the 1805 *Prelude* the poet speaks of this as a moment of desocialization, of estrangement from all humankind:

And all the ballast of familiar life,
The present, and the past; hope, fear, all stays,
All laws of acting, thinking, speaking man
Went from me, neither knowing me, nor known.
    [1805, VII, 603–06]

Yet that phrase, "neither knowing me nor known" prevents us from seeing the poet's condition as the result of pure choice. For that "ballast of familiar life," which is the external dealt with as if it were internal, is precisely what it means for there to be a "me" to know. Here Wordsworth seems to assert, with an intensity rare in such an unpopulous poem as *The Prelude*, the impossibility of a truly self-feeding solipsism. For the sight of other human beings can never be accepted in terms of difference or indifference, in so far as it functions as a reminder of the infant's sense of being created and attached to the world by his mother's sight. Although other humans may seem to be viewed as purely external and alien, they prompt the recollection of the infant's belief in the absolute fusion of the internal and the external.

Instead of being seen, however, the poet is virtually absorbed by sightlessness: "I was smitten / Abruptly, with the view (a sight not rare) / Of a blind Beggar." And here the full ambiguity of Wordsworth's use of the words of vision emerges. Is he merely taking a view of the blind man, or is he responding to the blind man's empty view of him? Is seeing a blind beggar common, or does the blind beggar possess a sight which is not unusual, in being blind among this crowd of people who have eyes and do not see? The poet's notion of the reciprocity of vision issues in this, the earlier sense of a lack of reciprocity being trivialized by being made quite literal in this figure who represents the impossibility of reciprocal vision.

Thus, the description which began with the poet in an apparently aggressive spectatorial role yields an external image which is converted to one of startling internality. For if the poet has been seeing himself as a poor pensioner on outward forms, the blind beggar is the very embodiment of that state. Not merely his perception of the world, his pleasure or displeasure in it, but existence itself is derived and passive for this blind man who "Stood, propped against a wall, upon his chest / Wearing a written paper to explain / His story, whence he came, and who he was." The wall which supports him and the written paper on his chest are so clearly not his own that he offers a rebuke to the fiction of an exclusively internal strength. Outward form presents itself as the blind man's only hold on the world, as "his story" as it has been translated into the external form of writing which he cannot read to affirm or deny. The blind beggar is absolutely a beggar, in having to hope that the words written for him and his sightless face will arouse an imagination of his inward existence, a pity which can only be communicated through the giving of alms, another excursion into outward form.

But Wordsworth's description of the written paper telling the blind beggar's story is especially interesting, in that it goes beyond pity for that individual man. Rather, it issues in an identification which is less self-pity than a universalized lament.

> an apt type
> This label seemed of the utmost we can know,
> Both of ourselves and of the universe;
> And on the shape of that unmoving man,
> His steadfast face and sightless eyes, I gazed,
> As if admonished from another world.
>   [VII, 644–49]

The imagination of the beggar's internal existence develops into a recognition of the dependency of all internal being. For the label is "an apt type" of the limits of human knowledge of the self and of the universe precisely because it is external form pleading for meaning from the reader. In addition to the beggar's need to construct an internal world from the supplemental perceptions and reports of others, the problem—and the power—of the beggar is that external form becomes explicitly a chain of communication. The beggar's internal story has been made voice, which has then been translated into another external form (the writing), which functions both as a reading of the beggar's story and an appeal to other readers.

For Wordsworth here in the middle of his own "story," *The Prelude*, the label and the beggar constitute a return to that early indecision in Book I. The tale from his own heart, the account of his "own passions and habitual thoughts," cannot be written, the description of the beggar would imply. For even the passions which are apparently the most internal of human faculties came to seem dependent, both in their origins and in the external, "final" form of writing. Just as the passions are derived from others for both the poet and the beggar, so also are the external products of their internal existences—their stories—dependent upon their readers for meaningfulness. The self cannot know itself, because it is ineluctably not really a self but rather a composite of selves intertwined through a chain of the affections and continually reaching out in an appeal to additional selves. The admonishment which the poet receives as if "from another world" eludes the mystical and supernatural by carrying its own recognition of the infinitude of human interdependency to an almost mystical pitch. Neither the self nor the story of the self can be consolidated into a fixed external form, because that external form is continually being converted into an imagination of internality, through the inscrutable touch of the affections.

Thus, the "Blind Beggar" episode operates both as an insight into the alienness of external form and as a testimony to the power of external form for creating the very possibility of internality. And, however paradoxical this may appear in connection with Wordsworth's apparent contempt for London and its teeming mobs—the "monstrous ant-hill on the plain / Of a too busy world" (VII, 149–50), the primacy of the human (rather than of nature) begins to assert itself here. For if nature can seem to function as a surrogate mother to replace the mother whom the poet lost, nature also seems an inadequate surrogate, for the simple reason that nature can neither be lost nor gained. Nature can only haunt the poet "*like* a passion" ("Tintern Abbey," my emphasis), because nature is itself passionless, deriving its significance from the poet's passions as they are projected upon it in his perceptions. And because the passions of an individual are neither self-generated nor self-sustaining, there must be a return to other human beings for the self to reexperience the passion upon which all perception subsists. Even in "Tintern Abbey," that celebration of a sense of nature's immediacy which has now been lost, Wordsworth's final, unexpected address to Dorothy points back towards the human passion which has animated Wordsworthian nature. For Dorothy is not simply a mediator between the poet and nature; she can be a mediator because she is Dorothy, his sister. And the almost desperate reiteration of "my dearest Friend, / My dear, dear Friend" and "My dear, dear Sister" emerges as a premonition of her death, the poet's fear of losing yet another human passion which seems to justify his links to earth. If the love of nature leads to a love of man, the love of man also (and first) leads to the love of nature.

Although the pattern of *The Prelude* involves a progressively abstract language of man, so that "man" appears to override individual "men," Book XIV may be seen, with the aid of our previous discussion, as more than a justification and abstract rehearsal of all that has gone before. Here Wordsworth speaks of his story "of lapse and hesitating choice, / And backward wandering along thorny ways" (XIV, 137–38), and love again becomes the explanation for his having escaped the tendency "Of use and custom to bow down the soul / Under a growing weight of vulgar sense, / And substitute a universe of death / For that which moves with light and life informed" (XIV, 158–61):

> To fear and love,
> To love as prime and chief, for there fear ends,
> Be this ascribed; to early intercourse,
> In presence of sublime or beautiful forms,
> With the adverse principles of pain and joy—
> Evil as one is rashly named by men
> Who know not what they speak. By love subsists
> All lasting grandeur, by pervading love;
> That gone, we are as dust.
>   [XIV, 162–70]

Whereas love would appear to be divorced from the possibility of "lasting grandeur," being lodged as it is in perishable human beings, love in fact becomes the unseen agent of imperishability. For the affections not only direct perception, they are the constituents of perception is so far as they lend external forms the semblance of meaningfulness. Wordsworth's avowal that without "pervading love" "we are as dust" registers the latent memory of Ecclesiastes in the service for the "Burial of the Dead," "dust to dust, ashes to ashes," as a recognition that all mortals come from and descend to the earth. And with the framing effect of the dust metaphor, the poet returns to the mystery of the "more than dust" which occupies the space between birth and death.

A curious process of synonymization begins to occur, in which definition rests not on the establishment of boundaries but on the abandonment of them:

> Imagination having been our theme,
> So also hath that intellectual Love,
> For they are each in each, and cannot stand
> Dividually.
>   [XIV, 206–09]

Imagination, reason (imagination being "but another name" for "Reason in her most exalted mood" [XIV, 189–92]), and love become functional equivalents, not because they are the "same" but because Wordsworth describes their operations as inseparable from one another. And, in the light of this synonymization, an imagination purely of and about nature begins to present itself as an impossibility, a delusion based upon a false notion of individuality. For just as the faculties are inextricably implicated in one another, so persons are related as interpenetrating existences rather than as sole and separate individuals. An imagination purely of nature would willingly deprive itself of all attempts to imagine origin and tendency in the only context which makes those notions powerful, the world of mutability.

In the fourteenth book, Wordsworth's narrative resorts to the mode of a sustained address (XIV, 232 ff.). And the poet no longer calls upon nature as if to apostrophize the "spirit in the woods." He speaks to and of Dorothy, Mary (as one who overhears his words to Dorothy), Coleridge, and Calvert. These are the figures to whom he stands indebted, not for any measurable gift (though Calvert left the poet a bequest which enabled him to devote himself to writing) but for their having listened to him and to his song. In spite of the language of teaching in Wordsworth's catalogue of the blessings which each bestowed upon him, these figures educated him through the unconscious doctrine of love rather than any principles of knowledge. For their pedagogy, in the poet's understanding of it, involved primarily the injunction of the affections, "Be like me."

Wordsworth's own plea from the affections, "Be like me," is a conjurer's song; he speaks to the living (Mary) through Dorothy, lingering in a kind of half-life because of debilitating disease, and through Coleridge, a dead man. The poet offers an invitation back into life to these half-dead and dead figures whom he has loved, but he also uses them as mediators—between him and Mary, between him and his readers. And as he reiterates his address to his "friend," Coleridge, throughout the remainder of *The Prelude*, it becomes both a reanimation of Coleridge, by reimagining Coleridge as a reader whose death can somehow be overcome by the living memory of his friend Wordsworth, and an appeal not to Coleridge but to all those who read the poem. Wordsworth speaks to Coleridge not only as the author of *The Friend*, but also as an author of the friend Wordsworth. And just as

Wordsworth refuses to see Coleridge as a dead man so long as he can remember that friendship, so he employs the figure of the dead man as an emblem of the reader who refuses to see the story of "The Growth of a Poet's Mind," the "poem to Coleridge," as merely a collection of dead letters. Through the deeply supplemental processes of the affections, external form—in memory or on the page—becomes a potentiality awaiting the touch from the eye of the friend or the reader which will enable it to have meaning.

Although such an all-inclusive "we" as Wordsworth's may appear to smack of an evangelist's rhetoric, the distance between formulaic evangelism and Wordsworth's gesture may become more clearly perceptible if we recall the stages which have prepared his final enunciation of community. As our starting place in this chapter suggested, the "sun" of one's own mind—and of one's own "wise prospectiveness"—vitiates the solidity of its own thoughts. And this process occurs not simply because an individual changes his mind but rather because the individual mind is not independent of time and of the matrix of thought and language which it shares with other individuals to the point of being unable to achieve more than the illusion of absolute autonomy. Moreover, the particular irony of the passage, that it rejects a plan for *The Prelude* which sounds like an accurate sketch for the completed poem, functions less as a qualification of the poem than of the poet's capacity to bring it forth fully formed as simply the obvious and direct child of his own brain. The individual mind cannot adjudicate its own activities, precisely because Wordsworth's questioning of the processes through which we arrive at thoughts of our own reveals an inescapable underpinning of education, a complex though unstrenuous education which involves nothing more or less than any individual's unwilled assent to the existence of minds other than his own.

Yeats's remark, in the last letter he wrote, that "an individual can embody truth but he cannot know it" is almost an aphoristic summary of Wordsworth's self-education in the futility of autobiography. Yet what is most remarkable about Wordsworth's (and Yeats's) recognition of the impossibility of locating and knowing the self is that such an insight does not become a resting place, a flat and final exposure of the self as a vacuum or as a type of the emperor's new clothes. Rather, the self is an absence primarily in being made up of many beings. In fact, the very faculties of mind which Wordsworth presents in his classification of his poems suggests that an education into selfhood involves disclosing the patterns of internal annexation of others which is the fundamental and inescapable mode of the affections. The imagination of unity and wholeness which the affections delusively assert between the lover and the love object collapses with the

death of the love object, but what remains is a self which is, in the strongest
possible sense, derivative—evolved from a passion which it could not choose
or avoid. And that passion, in which the self is occupied by the existence of
another, not only dictates that the processes of perception and education are
invariably implicated in other beings; it also implies that the closest
approximation to self-recognition is a cataloguing of one's loves.

Wordsworth thus speaks of and to Dorothy, Mary, and Coleridge in the
final lines of his autobiographical poem not simply because he had earlier
omitted the civility of a grateful preface. Instead, his assertion of and his
quest for self have yielded a self which can only be charted through the
illusion of stability and wholeness which is the recurrent product of the
affections. Just as the mother once comprised both the infant self and the
world which he perceived, so here at the end of the poem Dorothy, Mary,
and Coleridge become the strongest testimony to the existence of the poet's
self. Love for them has involved him in that complicated process of the self's
projection of itself upon others and the projection from other selves upon it,
and love for them has committed him both to the illusion of stability which
passion generates and to the terrors of recurrently losing hold of that
illusion. Yet the composite Wordsworth who emerges from "being" Dorothy,
Mary, and Coleridge is, certainly, not the clearest of images of an
autobiographical hero. For the peculiarity of Wordsworth's apostrophes is
that Mary, the only really living one, does not hear but only overhears.
Dorothy in her extreme mental and physical infirmity and Coleridge in death
are the portions of Wordsworth's self whom he addresses directly in the 1850
Prelude. And such otherworldly speech betokens not merely the thoughts of
a man preparing himself for death, but also, and more importantly, the
persistence of the epitaph as Wordsworth's central image of the possibilities
available to language. The substantiality which he seems to amass, in the
closing book of *The Prelude*—the self to which he appears to give an ostensive
definition by pointing to Dorothy, Mary, and Coleridge—is somewhere
between the world of the living and that of the dead, and it speaks of what is
gone.

The summarizing and simultaneously dissolving autobiographer thus
insists upon a strange education for his readers: "What we have loved, /
Others will love, and we will teach them how" (XIV, 446–47). The
confidence of the assertion is not, however, misplaced, because it relies
neither upon the "perfection" of Wordsworth's poetry nor upon the simple
good will of his readers. Rather, the education of which Wordsworth speaks
in the future tense has already occurred, for it is an education like that which
the poet has already sketched in his life. It is a schooling in the affections
which has always been there in the life of any individual, for *The Prelude* is

simply an uncovering of all and any perceptions as dictates of the promptings of the affections. Only that impossibility, a pre-generate Peter Bell, could fail to be taught—and to have been taught all along—because the very act of imagining that the words of the poem have any meaning at all finally returns any reader to the supplemental process of the affections which generated his sense of perceptions and language before he had his own illusions of choice and of individuality, of being capable of distance and detachment.

"Sometimes it suits me better to invent / A tale from my own heart, more near akin / To my own passions and habitual thoughts," Wordsworth had said in his search for a subject in Book 1. But his dalliance with that subject foundered, in attempting to misconstrue the given as the chosen. The "very sun" which brightens the "unsubstantial structure" inevitably dissolves that structure, because the sun—the "light" generated in the affections—subverts the poet's attempt to establish supremacy over such materials. Just as the affections are the human faculty least subject to "invention," so the poet comes to suit the purposes of his affections rather than to presume that a tale from his own heart could suit his fancy.

Sincerity, from this perspective, can be neither chosen nor renounced. For the account of the growth of the poet's mind yields a poet and autobiographer who cannot escape the recognition that he is compounded of nothing but what Keats called "negative capability," because he is nothing more or less than a web of perceptions derived from the sum of his loves (and their loves). For Wordsworth, moreover, "negative capability" appears neither as a choice nor as a specific personality trait but rather as an inevitable and universal faculty; the "egotistical sublime" and "negative capability" for him would seem to be merely different formulations of the same insight—that no self can be created or invented as an isolated entity. Dorothy, Mary, and Coleridge, and before them the mother have partially authored the poem by partially authoring the poet in that interchange of the affections in which no one figure can be independent and originative.

The promptings of the affections and the supplemental relations between lover and love object establish a pattern in which one can neither know oneself fully nor even locate indebtedness with any precision. For not only the notion of sincerity but also the very possibility of any communication whatsoever depends upon a social contract which is silently and unremittingly generated and confirmed by the affections. When any infant accepts the world and also credulously assumes that it is shared (by him and the one central figure of his love), the affections have led to this "mistake" by creating the illusion of certainty about an uncertain and mutable world. But even the disappearance of a central love object cannot really free anyone from the ties which have been forged between him and a world of language and perception. The events of Wordsworth's mother's death, Coleridge's death, and Dorothy's imminent death do not so much disprove the powerful agency of the affections as reaffirm it. Neither Wordsworth's actual life nor theirs any longer matters by the end of *The Prelude*. For both the written words of the poem and the unwritten words of an infinite number of "mute, inglorious Miltons" become implicit testimony to the persistence of the operation of the affections. The very belief that words mean anything—and have a shared meaning—represents a tacit acknowledgment that the only world and self which we can know is a residue of an unfathomably extensive chain of affections which have led us all to imagine the possibility of meaning in the face of all evidence to the contrary.

NOTES

1. See especially Ferry, *The Limits of Mortality*, pp. 51–111, 131–35.
2. For a provocative discussion of the child's acquisition of language see Richard J. Onorato, *The Character of the Poet: Wordsworth in "The Prelude"* (Princeton: Princeton University Press, 1971), pp. 65–66.
3. Rousseau, Essai sur l'origine des langues, pp. 501–05.
4. Hartman, *Wordsworth's Poetry*, p. 234.

PAUL H. FRY

Wordsworth's Severe Intimations

I

Wordsworth's early "Remembrance of Collins" reflects a complex and alert reading of Collins's odes. Beginning as Collins once did with Spenser, Wordsworth's "Glide Gently, thus for ever glide, / O Thames!" recognizes Collins's desire to write the poem of his own chaste marriage. Very possibly, therefore, Wordsworth numbers among the motives of the mad "Poet's sorrows" (20) the epithalamic failure of Collins's odes. Interweaving images from the Death of Thomson Ode and the "Ode to Evening" (and also from Thomson's "Hymn! on Solitude": "Descending angels bless thy train"), Wordsworth tries to purify Collins's typically mysterious haunted moment by arming it with holiness and scattering the daemonic, as did Milton in the Nativity Ode, with a militant poise:

> How calm! how still! the only sound,
> The dripping of the oar suspended!
> —The evening darkness gathers round
> By virtue's holiest powers attended.

Wordsworth's prayer that the "child of song" (19) be attended by a vision that lightens our falling toward darkness, a vision of the high birthplace both

From *The Poet's Calling in the English Ode*, pp. 136–157. © 1980 by Yale University Press.

of ourselves and of our virtue, is offered in order to restore the otherness and innocence of the past to the odes of Collins; and, on a far more difficult occasion, it is also the prayer of the Intimations Ode.

The happier past, as a sign of poetic election and of life after death, can be recovered only through that most ontologically treacherous of faculties, memory. Recollection in "calm weather" can never be facile; indeed, it may be wise to assume, upon careful reading, that recollection in the Intimations Ode is recognized to be an exhilarating but futile exercise. In itself, however, the quality of difference between present and past that is given by memory as a newly refined poetic topic[8]—"and, oh! the difference to me!"—enables the odes of Wordsworth and his major contemporaries to represent change more plausibly than any of Gray's or Collins's resources had permitted. But only *more* plausibly. The Romantic ode writer hopes that one change—from past to present—will imply the coming of another, the redemption of the present. But the disappointment of that hope cannot be avoided, owing to the continued necessity of repetition, which insists upon the immutability of the present. No naturalizing of vocative devices can ever completely suppress this immutability because, after all, the presupposed existence of some indivisible and unchanging power is just what an ode is written to celebrate. The ode bends the quality of difference in all experience to its mono-myth, which is only speciously genealogical.

All the great odes I shall discuss from now on are evening odes.[9] The veils of Gray and Coffins are taken over by the Romantics as a sober coloring of clouds and tropes at sundown that still conceals the "wavy bed" (Wordsworth's "mighty waters") of the sun-poet's origin. That the sense of evening in the Romantic ode is yet more intense than in earlier odes can be shown in a rough way even by comparative biography. Whereas eighteenth-century poets, even Swift, began their careers by assaying the vocational challenge of Pindarism, Wordsworth and Coleridge "began" (if we disregard their school exercises) in the quieter keys of the topographical poem and the slighter lyric modes. M. H. Abrams's inclusion of the Intimations Ode and "Dejection. An Ode" in his persuasively described unifying genre, "the greater Romantic lyric" (encompassing the common themes and structure of the sublime ode and the Conversation Poem), may be questioned simply by appealing to dates. Nearly all the major Conversation Poems of both Wordsworth and Coleridge were written well before the Companion odes that were begun in 1802, begun in response to growing intimations of loss.[10] If the eighteenth-century poet proved himself to be a poet by writing an ode, the Romantic poet proved himself *still* to be a poet by writing an ode, but no longer a poet gifted with unmediated vision. The turning of Wordsworth and Coleridge to the unnatural conventions of ode writing is itself a farewell to the natural holiness of youth.

II

L'ode chante l'éternité, l'épopée sollenise l'histoire, le drame peint la vie. Le caractère de la première poésie est la naïveté, le caractère de la seconde est la simplicité, le caractère de la troisième, la vérité.... Les personnages de l'ode sont des colosses: Adam, Caïn, Noé; ceux de l'épopée sont des géants: Achille, Atrée, Oreste; ceux du drame sont des hommes: Hamlet, Macbeth, Othello. L'ode vit l'idéal....
    —Victor Hugo, *Préface de Cromwell* (1827)

From its publication to the present, the Intimations Ode has had the reputation of being Wordsworth's most confused poem.[11] In this respect it is appropriately an ode or, more precisely, an irregular Pindaric. What Wordsworth dictated to Miss Fenwick, "To the attentive and competent reader the whole sufficiently explains itself" (*Poetical Works* IV. 463), curiously recalls Gray's "vocal to the intelligent alone." As we have seen, from Jonson through Collins, the Pindaric form is a refuge for confusion; it both reflects and deepens uncertainties that will not lend themselves to forthright treatment. As a final preface to the Romantic ode, we may review here, in the form of a summary typology, the confusions that lie beneath the unending hope of the ode to stand purely, through invocation, in the pure presence of what its presentation always stains and darkens.

    Here, then, is the normative course of an ode. Some quality of absolute worth is traced back to its conception, where it appears as a fountainhead, sunrise, or new star. But the landscape of dawning, inescapably twilit, is instinct with regional spirits that misbehave and will not be reduced to order. It is impossible for the compressions of syntax and figure to avoid implicating these dark spirits in the ur-conception of the ode and of its numen alike. Such spirits are "kept aloof" at first, like Collins's "dangerous passions," by the ode's shifting of its etiology from the spiritual to the sublunary plane—from theogony, in other words, to the earliest stages of recorded history or childhood. This descent from the divine is halted and in some measure reversed by the poet's location of a primitive society or early selfhood in a region that he still calls sacred (the magic circle, garland, manger, shrine, or temple). The history of poetry, meanwhile, is imagined as one great ode, sacralized by the analogy between the holy place the ode describes and the circle of its own form. Hence, the transcendent pastness of the past is lost almost completely in the defensive act of exorcizing its false, daemonic, and generically diverse oracles. Once great Pan is pronounced dead, the oracle grows nearly silent, and the vocal occasion of the ode, consecrated to the celebration of the present, is mediated and muted by all the formal defenses that writing ritualizes.

In violent denial of this loss, the ode now loudly reasserts its divine calling: it hazards the frenzied tropes of identification that we call "enthusiastic"[12] and then quickly collapses into self-caricature. This is the brief noontide phase of the ode, envisioned as a Phaeton-myth of flight followed by blindness and a fall into or toward the sea. The sun has been placed once more too squarely in view, so that the excessive bright of its cloudy skirts becomes an ominous darkness, like the darkness of dawn. To avoid the bathos of Phaeton's death, the poet reins in ("Stop, stop, my muse," exclaims Cowley in "The Resurrection," "allay thy vig'rous heat!") and adjusts himself to the light of common day. In the decline of this light toward evening, the ode accepts a diminished calling, often movingly and even cheerfully embraced as the hymning of a favorite name, and never reasserts its enthusiastic mission. Even this dénouement is marred, however, by the regathering and haunting of twilit forces.

We may adapt some of these outlines to the Intimations Ode in order to establish a viewpoint from which its confusion may then be reconsidered more carefully. Wordsworth's ode opens with the recollection of a pastoral dawn[13] when the sun, in place of the poet, had a "glorious birth." This happy scene is peopled by the usual denizens of the vernal ode—songbirds, frolicking animals—from whose jubilee the speaker is excluded. In content the scene is that of the "Sonnet on the Death of West" abused by Wordsworth in his 1800 Preface. In earlier life the speaker's spontaneous vision helped "apparel" the scene he now adorns more conventionally. In order to make himself present to his own childhood, as he attempted to do by evoking the Boy of Winander in *The Prelude*, Wordsworth now invokes and petitions the happy voice of the Shepherd-boy. His identification with a better self, which is wholly fitting in an ode, seems for the moment to yield rewards. The Babe leaps up, as Wordsworth's heart had leapt up the day before, to nestle closer to Mother Nature. But—and here the voice of the original four-stanza ode turns downward after the blindly exclamatory "I hear! I hear!"—but, the poet seems to wonder, does paradise have a mother only? The lost Tree and single Field suggest an Eden that was begotten by a Father, and the adult poet can only partly keep from knowing that his visionary birth, though too noble for pastoral, was nevertheless still erotic. The Pansy at his feet recalls Milton's Pensive Nun, who always keeps her head pointed toward, if not in, the sand. Thus far Wordsworth's expression of loss has simply followed the convention of the amorous vernal ode whereby the speaker looks about frantically for his absent mistress.

Wordsworth does have a glimpse of her, though, and is not pleased, as the fifth stanza reveals. The maternal earth from which he feels alienated has "pleasures of her own," and it is her natural yearning to possess her foster child and make him forget his epic and patriarchal origins, "that imperial palace whence he came." Following exactly the scenario presented by Otto Rank,[14] she interferes, in her lowly role, with the poet's myth of his birth as a hero, and her interference is as erotic as that of the Nurse in *Romeo and Juliet*. Even as we pass the poem thus schematically in review, we should note that there is a degree of voluntarism, even relief, in the adult's alienation from his childhood. The "Child of Joy" is given pause in so designating himself, and feels a hint of Gray's "fearful joy."[15] We shall see in the long run, however, that this impure intimation is vastly preferable to those purer ones that come to replace it. From stanza five onward, the poet will strive to imagine a self-conception that is not an earthy anecdote from the pastoral tradition, to imagine a birth-myth that is not an earth-myth or failed autochthony. At first this seems a good idea. By bringing about a reconciliation of his mortal being with "the light of common day," with the ordinariness of earth, the poet can once more invest with the appearance of dialectical truth the assumption that his immortal being must derive from a region that is *not* common; the animation of the soul seems to depend on the disinspiriting of earth.

The figure of the imperial palace carries the sun's "glorious birth" across the increasingly dualistic chasm of the poet's logic while alienating the sun from the landscape it formerly graced. The poet remembering himself as a bright-haired youth or sun-child now identifies with the Father, through the metalepsis "God, who is our home," in a higher region that is set apart from natural kindness as the sublime is set apart from the beautiful. This brief intimation (his first of immortality) makes up the subsumed epic phase of the ode. In Victor Hugo's terms, Adam has become Orestes. Shaking off the mother, by whose possessive kisses he is fretted (like a brook fretting in its channel [l. 94]), the hero descends from his epic to his dramatic phase, recalling Aristotle's derivation of theatre from child's play in the *Poetics*: "As if his whole vocation / Were endless imitation." Here the Father stands back, the one apart from the many, no longer identified with the son but still tendering the sunlight of his gaze. Now the child becomes the chameleonic Hamlet, trapped in a "prison-house" (68) of nature and changed into a different player by each attention from the mother whose yearnings in her natural kind have caused him so much anxiety. Little actor though he is, however, he is still a solitary and a soliloquist, like John Home in Collins's Scottish Superstitions Ode: "unto this he frames his song." He acts odes.

Hamlet calls the world a "prison" (II. ii); but in *Hamlet* the world is only one of two prisons, the other being identified by the ghost of Hamlet's father: "I am thy father's spirit ..."

> But that I am forbid
> To tell the secrets of my prison-house,
> I could a tale unfold whose lightest word
> Would harrow up thy soul.
>   [I. v. 9, 13–16]

This discordant intimation Wordsworth records in his next stanza:

> Mighty Prophet! Seer blest!
>   On whom these truths do rest,
> Which we are toiling all our lives to find,
> In darkness lost, the darkness of the grave;
> Thou, over whom thy Immortality
> Broods like the Day, a Master o'er a Slave ...

For the child's domination by Mother Earth, then, there is an equivalent master–slave dialectic between son and father.[16] Immortal regions are suddenly as much like prisons as mortal ones; and the ode's noontide, its most high-flown rhetoric, having seen too much reality, falls back to the theme of blindness, which could be an ode's address, thus stated, to its own self blighted celebratory mandate:

> Thou little child, yet glorious in thy might
> Of heaven-born freedom [as a Slave?] on thy being's height,
> Why with such earnest pains dost thou provoke
> The years to bring the inevitable yoke,
> Thus blindly with thy blessedness at strife?

In singling out the main point of repetition in this poem (crucial repetition being typically revealed, as we saw in the "Ode to Duty," by a stutter or gaffe like this one about the slave's heaven-born freedom), we have perhaps come to see why no blessedness is visible that is not in some wise tainted. The child must be admitted to know what he is doing in choosing blinders.

Having absorbed the rival genres in the child's progress toward his earthly prison and then reacted frantically back toward its displaced theme of originary magic, only to discover a different prison in that theme, Wordsworth's ode now lapses into its final, elegiac phase, giving notice of this change with a verbal allusion to "Lycidas": "Not for these I raise / The song of thanks and praise." Here begins Wordsworth's evening retrospect and its attempt to overbalance the heavy weight of custom with the philosophic mind's conversion of remembered joy into "natural piety." The ode becomes a song in praise of sublimation, and it has some sublime moments remaining. It distances the Deluge (into which an ode, like Phaeton, is always falling) from the standpoint of calm weather, thus belatedly justifying the suggestion of a covenant in the rainbow that comes and goes; it returns to the vernal festival of earthy childhood "in thought" only; and finally it returns to the landscape of the first line, adding the word "Fountains" to the initial list because, through the sublimation of dangerous waters, the philosophic mind is now able to recognize a seminal source as well as an Edenic foster mother. All these qualified returns make up Wordsworth's "Stand." The irregularity of all the previous stanzas is reduced to uniformity, with the exception of an odd line out that refuses the eclipse it appears in: "Is lovely yet." Wordsworth's hymnic epode, like Collins's homiletic harvest at the end of the "Ode to Evening," joins the common produce of the common day in an order serviceable. The necessary sacrifice of godlike autochthony for natural piety brings on silence, an unutterable pathos that is vastly different from the shouts of the Child of Joy. The question of immortality is mooted in the end, and we must reconsider it if we are to discover why this is so.

III

          that dubious hour,
That twilight when we first begin to see
This dawning earth....
    —*The Prelude* V. 511–13

Is the Intimations Ode, in Lionel Trilling's deft phrase, about growing old or growing up?[17] It is hard to know how or where to enter this dispute. It seems to me that the poem is about not knowing whether childhood, adulthood, or yet a third state of complete disembodiment is best; that it is, in short, about confusion. In the Fenwick note Wordsworth confesses having experienced the opposite "subjugations" of idealism and materialism in childhood and adulthood, respectively, and seems to imply that the purpose of his poem is to thread its way between prisons, or rather to find a restful expansiveness in their mutual collapse. In this modest aim I think it succeeds, despite serious flaws of coherence that will appear. Deliberately an ode, the poem experiments with presentation, the presentation in this case of an elusive nimbus called a "glory." The experiment fails, but in place of ecstasy the poet gains knowledge, a new awareness of the role played by determinacy in consciousness.

Wordsworth's apology in the Fenwick note for his chosen myth of a prior existence reflects the etiological anxiety of any ode, the fear of dark places, and also recalls the antinomian relation of an ode to orthodoxy. His myth, he says, "is far too shadowy a notion to be recommended to faith." Still, however, as he also clearly implies in the note, he knows no proof of immortality that is not in some way shadowy; this despite the fact that for Wordsworth, as for Coleridge, autonomy of thought cannot be demonstrated without proof of the mind's original participation in an eternal cause. This necessary priority of the spirit is termed by Wordsworth in the note an Archimedean "point whereon to rest" what would be, otherwise, the dreary machine of Associationist psychology.

Although the lack of such proof may cause some anxiousness, it is not really the belief in immortality, however founded, that the ode questions, but rather the nature of immortality. By allusion and repetition, Wordsworth's ode clouds over what in religion are foregone conclusions about the sources of life and death. It is disturbing, for example, that "Nor man nor Boy, / Nor all that is at enmity with joy, / Can utterly destroy ..." alludes to the speech of Moloch in *Paradise Lost* that calls the Creator a destroyer, like Collins's Fancy. Or again, it is difficult to understand what blindness is if the Child is at once "an eye to the blind" and "blindly with his blessedness at strife." As was also apparent in Collins's "Ode on the Poetical Character," a poet cannot merely decree a difference between Vision and vision that his poem fails otherwise to sustain.

To cite another troublesome passage, where is the guilt and on what ground is the misgiving in the following lines?

> Not for these I raise
> The song of thanks and praise;
> But for those obstinate questionings
> Of sense and outward things,
> Fallings from us, vanishings;
> Blank misgivings of a Creature
> Moving about in worlds not realized,
> High instincts before which our mortal Nature
> Did tremble like a guilty thing surprised....

The solipsism of the child is obstinate, and his experience of a lapse is the opposite of Adam's: not a corruption of soul but a falling away of the flesh.

Immortality is intimated by the child as a state of emptiness and vertigo, a Melvilleian blankness that is duplicitous for all its vacancy, since it has more than one habitation ("worlds")—perhaps a true and a false zone of antimatter. The bodily "Creature" would appear to have been created as a companion for the soul's loneliness. The song that is raised, in sum, shows every sign of being a song of thanks for the gift of mortality.[18]

This is not to imply, however, that the entire burden of the song is a foolish critique of immortality. The main point is, rather, that memory harbors phantoms. Whatever immortality may be like, mortal discourse is confined to what a child can know about it, or, yet more mediately, to what an adult can remember of childhood knowledge.[19] The child's recollections are indeed "shadowy," both because adult memory is busy securing the present by darkening the past (in this sense the poem *is* "about growing up" and being happy with the present) and also because, as "be they what they may" rather sheepishly concedes, what the poet remembers is not really the "high instincts" of childhood but the phantom Underworld of the Greeks. The confessed Platonism of Wordsworth's preexistence myth comes chiefly from the Myth of the warrior Er, who "coming to life related what, he said, he had seen in the world beyond" (*Rep.* 614b). Er describes souls struggling to be born between two worlds, governed, like Wordsworth's Slave, by the Spindle of Necessity. But the feeling of Wordsworth's intimations is, in fact, more Homeric than Platonic; it is "impalpable as shadows are, and wavering like a dream" (Fitzgerald's *Odyssey* XI). Wordsworth's ode may be seen as a moving failure of perspective; called forth to be condemned, mortal Nature reasserts its vital strength and beauty.[20]

By comparison, immortality is a dream. In the third stanza there is a crux of remarkable compression, "The Winds come to me from the fields of sleep." Many a hapless recitation of this line has produced "fields of sheep," a slip that is prompted by the surrounding gleeful pastoral in which no creature sleeps during the rites of spring. The fields of sleep belong to an earlier time and place, the threshold of birth which is, later, "but a sleep and a forgetting." Wordsworth's winds bring news of birth, then, yet seem imagistically to recall an even earlier moment, the classical fields of asphodel and poppy.[21] In contrast with the jollity of a child's landscape, the winds of adult memory recollect the stupor of immortality, or what Homer calls the "shores of Dream" (*Od.* XXIV).

In approaching the designedly binding and blinding symbol of the ode, that of the "glory," we must pause over metaphysics a little longer. The prolepsis that the ode never moves beyond is the ambiguous apposition of line 5. Presumably "the glory and the freshness of a dream" modifies "celestial light" in the previous line; but the grammar does not prevent reading the line in apposition to "every common sight." One's total impression of lines 1–5 is that the glory summarily modifies both the common, with which the poem concludes, and the celestial, with which it has begun. Hence either the common itself is glorious, properly viewed (like the cuckoo and the lesser celandine of the 1802 period), or else the glory is a nimbus, a frame of celestial light that leaves the framed common object unilluminated in itself. This sliding apposition looks forward to the confusion of the whole text. The word "dream" belongs to the rhyme group "stream-seem,"[22] and thus its presumptive modifying power over "sight" and "light" is further weakened. Having been spread too thin, the glory is only faintly visible. To parrot the inescapable question of Wordsworth interpretation, does the glory come from without or within?

Since the glory is now absent, and since it is recalled by an *ubi sunt* that is also, at the same time, an indirect invocation, this question is doubly difficult. To disregard for the moment where the glory comes from, even though that is the motivating question of any ode and plainly an important one, it may profit to go on asking what it is. Here an answer is forthcoming. The glory is an "Apparel," a dressy appearance that is Wordsworth's equivalent of Gray's tapestries and Collins's veils.[23] It is worn by every common sight as a covering for nakedness: "not in utter nakedness, / But trailing clouds of glory do we come." The glory screens out the indecent as well as the quotidian commonness of things and poses an obstacle to the kindness of natural yearning. Perhaps it is already clear where the glory comes from. Once more the Fall proves indeed fortunate, as it lends a needful covering to an original state of nakedness. In this poem death is not only the context of intimation, but also, it seems, the context of intimacy. By allusion to Collins's "sallow Autumn fills thy lap with leaves," Wordsworth's imagery of mortality turns autumnal long before his evening ear takes command of the ode. "Earth fills her lap with pleasures of her own" is a covering of Eve's nakedness that unites the pleasures of life and the glory of afterlife in a common veil. Man wears "Earth" even before we are told that he is her inmate, exchanging as he grows up "the glories he hath known" for new apparel.

If we compare the mortally colored imagery of the celestial that the adult remembers from the time of glad animal movement in early childhood with the otherworldliness of the celestial that he remembers from the time of solipsism in later childhood, we can see the distance between two glories, between the festive dress of a young world and the phantom light of interstellar vacancy. Concerning this second glory: Wordsworth could love a clear sky, and in the second stanza we cannot yet feel uneasy about the sky's undress, as "The Moon doth with delight / Look round her when the heavens are bare." But the region of the Moon is absolutely separate from that of man, and her delight cannot be merged with Earth's pleasures. Later, when pleasure has palled, the bare sky will mirror a blank misgiving. In "Dejection," Coleridge will seem to narrow this gulf by giving the moon her own nimbus from the outset, "a swimming phantom light," and he will transfer Wordsworth's earthly pleasure to the sphere of the moon's delight: "I see the old moon in her lap." In "Dejection," as we shall see, it is not the immortal skies that are lonely, but the poet.

Both "Dejection" and the Intimations Ode sometimes touch upon subjects that are too intimate to remain within a shareable sphere of reference. For both poets, but for Wordsworth especially, the daemon of an ode is an unreconstructed and thus far "strong" egoism. What poet before Wordsworth admitted to being relieved and made strong by his own timely utterance? As we have seen, Akenside read Milton for inspiration, Gray Spenser, and so on. Although the position of the sounding cataracts between "I am strong" and "No more shall grief of mine" might indicate that Wordsworth has found his timely utterance in Revelation,[24] one feels that too many more griefs succeed this one to confirm any gospel. Earlier odes have mottoes chosen from the classics; Wordsworth's utterance and his motto (starting in 1815) are all his own. The drawback of this strength is that Wordsworth's allusion to his own uncanonized oeuvre leaves the ordering of his present text in a muddle. It is not possible to say with certainty what Wordsworth's timely utterance was, nor what his thought of grief was. But if a note on the subject in Wordsworth's own hand were discovered, that would be a positive harm. In the text, the grief and the thought are significant because they are unspecified. They remain simply implied presences, emblems of what Coleridge termed the "flux and reflux" of the whole poem. They are impure signifiers—symptoms. Perhaps their presence in the text can be understood, then, as a near-utterance about the idea of repression, about the apparel of the repressed that veils an ode. To refer again to the Fenwick note, what Wordsworth most vividly remembers about writing his ode is frustration. He needed a fulcrum, a prior content without which his form, "the world of his own mind" (*PW* 4. 464), would follow its own irresolute course. The preexistence myth provides inadequate leverage, but the timely utterance, because unspecified, can stand behind and beneath the text as a buried originary voice.

One may wonder about the deference of sound to sight in this ode,[25] noting that elsewhere Wordsworth explored aural areas that have more profound mystical roots than does the (mainly Western) visionary idea. Like Dionysus "disguised as man" in Euripides, this written ode travels daily farther from the East because pure voice would be naked, a too immediate experience of "God, who is our home." This is the experience an ode cannot risk. The prophetic child must be "deaf" in order to read "the eternal deep." The visual blankness of eternity is also an "Eternal Silence," and sound is relegated wholly to "our noisy years": birdsong, the tabor that syncopates the vernal heartbeat,[26] the outer-ance of speech that relieves solitude, the trumpets sounding from the Salvator-fringes of the regenerate landscape, the shouts of happiness. After this outburst, there are no more sounds until the pygmy turns actor; however, even his "song," is not sung but written down, "a little plan or chart."

Sound resonates beyond the setting for pastoral joy only once in the poem, at the end of the ninth stanza, in the song of praise for the adult's recollection of the child's recollections:

> Hence in a season of calm weather,
>   Though inland far we be,
> Our souls have sight of that immortal sea
>   Which brought us hither,
>   Can in a moment travel thither,
> And see the Children sport upon the shore,
> And hear the mighty waters rolling evermore.

This magnificent passage, the pivot (or fulcrum) of the poem, culminates in another unspecified utterance. It is also the key to Wordsworth's version of Milton's resurrected *Lycidas*, the "genius of the shore." It *is* a pivotal passage, yet it is not easy to discover a context for it. It is not clear by what logic the celestial descent has become an aquatic emergence; nor is it clear, though we happily accept the transit, just how we are carried from sight to sound.

I have suggested that the genealogical phase of the ode before Wordsworth leaves out, or tries to leave out, the Deluge, which appears in nearly every scriptural cosmogony in the history of culture and recurs in Jung's belief that the materials of the dream-work are oceanic.[27] Until his personal tragedy concerning a death by water in 1805, Wordsworth, unlike his predecessors in the ode, was a willing voyager in strange seas of thought and loved sonorous waters. The dream-vision of *Prelude* V (88–97) offers up the sort of apocalyptic "Ode" that Wordsworth could have been expected to write:

>   "This," said he,
> "Is something of more worth;" and at the word
> Stretched forth the shell, so beautiful in shape,
> In colour so resplendent, with command

That I should hold it to my ear. I did so,
And heard that instant in an unknown tongue,
Which yet I understood, articulate sounds,
A loud prophetic blast of harmony;
An Ode, in passion uttered, which foretold
Destruction to the children of the earth
By deluge, now at hand.

One might then certainly expect the Intimations Ode, considering its subject, also to leave the shore for deeper waters. But the "Waters" at line 14 are merely lacustrine, and the jolly "sea" of "Land and sea" (30) is, one suspects, only present for the sake of rhyme. For the most part, the movement of this ode is inland and downward, until it comes to rest in a place that is "too deep for tears." Traditionally, the ode takes an aspiring flight but fears Phaeton's plunge, and with partial success avoids the risk of drowning by curbing its flight. Wordsworth's ode bows to this tradition, with the result, however, that this passage, with its seaward direction, seems isolated from the argument of which the passage is meant to be the center.

"Lycidas," not an ode but an elegy, makes room for a drowning. Milton recalls a happy pastoral setting, "by fountain, shade, and rill," to which Wordsworth alludes in lines 1 and 189; but with the death of its pastor, the *locus amoenus* will have fallen silent except for mournful echoes unless Milton can reanimate the strain. Wordsworth's first revision of "Lycidas," then, is to fill his own pastoral site with noise and to locate the noise only there, hoping to imply that the silence of higher places is preferable. However, the errancy of his intimations points to some awareness on his part that Milton was right, as was Sophocles in the *Coloneus*: if the vital and benign genius cannot be given a home within the budding grove, its possible course among the stars can offer little consolation. "Lycidas" announces the return of the genius from water to land through the intercession of one who could not drown. Wordsworth describes the return of memory from land to the shoreline where genius had been left behind.

Or rather, where genius *appears* to have been left behind. Wordsworth's ninth stanza, with its key in "Not for these," begins to look homeward, back toward the starting places of the ode that will be reviewed in stanzas ten and eleven. Wordsworth's journey to the shore begins this review of inland places because, in fact, the journey only seems to have been undertaken. He is and remains inland far; it is only in moments of vacancy, seasons "of calm weather,"[28] that he counteracts his fear of the eternal abyss with memories of "sport" among a community of children who have nothing in common with the solitude of infinite space. The children emerge *from* the "immortal sea," happy to be born, and steadily move inland themselves toward the pleasures of the Shepherd-boy.[29] Immured in our adulthood, our souls seem to want something else, something other than what children want, when they listen to the conch shells of their inner ear. They zoom directly back to the sea itself, and only afterward notice the children playing with their backs to the water. Unlike the ignorant child, the soul of the adult has intimations of death; they are not quite the intimations he was meant to have, but they still induce a state of mind that is preferable, as Jonson's Cary-Morison Ode also insisted, to "listlessness" and "mad endeavour."

The soul's hearing death for the first time, then, is an intimation of voice, of aural immediacy, not as a beginning but as an end. The children's audition, which is permitted by the grammar if not by the parallelism of syntax, is quite different; it is not nostalgic but strains forward, and smooths their passage from the deafening roar of death, which they no longer hear as such, to the companionable shouts of their coming joy. Lycidas our Shepherd-boy is not dead, because the morning star of his return replaces the evening star of his having sunk elsewhere. For Wordsworth's Child we rejoice, as in "Lycidas," because he has been born, not because he was previously drowned:

> The Soul that rises with us, our life's Star,
>   Hath had elsewhere its setting,
>   And cometh from afar:

The child has returned, fortunately, to be Nature's Pastor once more. His "vision splendid" arises from his own glorious birth, when Heaven is no distant bareness of the sky but an immediate environment that "lies about us in our infancy."

"Our birth is but a sleep and a forgetting," the line that precedes those just quoted, wavers uncertainly between two famous counter-statements about life and death in *Measure for Measure*. One of them, Claudio's "Ay, but to die, and go we know not where" (III. i. 118–31), is worth quoting at length, not only because it juxtaposes the two prisons of both *Hamlet* and the Intimations Ode, but also because it expresses the fear that Wordsworth's frostlike weight of life is, in fact, a condition of the afterlife as well:

>   or to reside
> In thrilling region of thick-ribbèd ice,
> To be imprisoned in the viewless winds
> And blown with restless violence round about
> The pendant world....

. . . .
The weariest and most loathéd worldly life
That age, ache, penury, and imprisonment
Can lay on Nature is a paradise
To what we fear of death.

This is the body of imagery that Wordsworth's shadowy recollections cannot dissolve, however much his ode may aspire to the otherworldly viewpoint of the Duke's counsel about sleep and forgetting:

    Thou hast nor youth nor age,
But as it were an after-dinner sleep
Dreaming on both.
    [III. i. 32–34]

The Duke's utterance is not strong enough to be "timely," though; it is merely Stoical, and itself contains the repetition that negates transcendence: "thy best of rest is sleep, / And that thou oft provok'st, yet grossly fear'st / Thy death, which is no more" (III. i. 17–19). Among these less than reassuring attitudes Wordsworth must himself have felt compelled to waver, "when having closed the mighty Shakespeare's page, / I mused, and thought, and felt, in solitude" (*Prelude* VII. 484–85).

    The conclusion seems inescapable that Wordsworth's Intimations are best forgotten; and forgetting is what the last two stanzas in effect achieve. Stanzas ten and eleven seek images for the continuity that was hoped for in "The Rainbow":

The Child is father of the Man;
And I could wish my days to be
Bound each to each by natural piety.

In these lines, the wish for existential continuity is weakened by having been spoken conditionally, and also by the impious bid for autochthonous independence of being that here and elsewhere undercuts Wordsworth's homage to the adult father.[30] Perhaps these slight discords are enough to warn us that an ode for which such a passage is the best available motto will not be smooth going; but they are nothing to the discords that any ambitious presentational ode will engender in itself. In any case, the poet's days are bound each to each at the close of the Great Ode in an altogether "natural" way that is plus if not pious; but his piety is not founded in any visionary or eschatological intimation.

From his and Coleridge's Conversation Poems, perhaps from the Meditative Lyric of the seventeenth century,[31] and certainly from instinct, Wordsworth had formed the habit of concluding with a benediction, which typically, as in "Tintern Abbey" or "Dejection," transmits the boon of gladness in nature to a beloved friend who is less burdened than the poet with the heavy weight of adulthood. The hesitation with which the pronoun "my" is introduced in "The Rainbow" may itself imply the replacement of the self by another in a benediction: my days and perceptions may prove disjointed, but perhaps yours will not. So in stanza ten of his ode, Wordsworth confers his generalized blessing on unself-conscious youth from the detached and newly acquiescent standpoint of "thought." However successful the tone of this blessing may be thought to be, it must still be stressed that there is no scope for benediction in the cult hymns after which odes model themselves. The ending of a hymn leads by nature in quite another direction, toward a petition. In a hymn the petition may possibly involve the blessing of others,[32] but in an ode it is primarily for the self, a request that the poet's egotistically sublime vocation be confirmed. Not just Wordsworth's but nearly all thoughtful odes, however, swerve away from the formula of petition toward benediction and other forms of self-sacrifice that are all essentially vocational disclaimers. At least in this last respect, then, the endings of hymns and odes are similar.

Wordsworth's heart no longer leaps up; rather it goes out, in "primal sympathy," to others, to the whole sphere of those Creatures whom Coleridge's Ancient Mariner learned to "bless" (see the Intimations Ode, 1. 37). Henceforth there is little to be heard of the immortality theme and nothing of substance about the "one delight" (192) of joyous childhood that the poet has now "relinquished"—pretending, with the active verb, to have given it up voluntarily. What now appears, rather, is the severer compassion of the Eton College Ode, the "Ode to Adversity," and Wordsworth's "Ode to Duty": "the soothing thoughts that spring / Out of human suffering." As in the "Ode to Duty," the healing power of Nature is itself now hallowed as routine, as Nature's "more habitual sway," and the sober coloring of the clouds no longer needs to serve as a repressive veil, since the troubled mysticism of the poem is now silenced, apparently by choice. Until the final line of Wordsworth's evening ending there is no hint of immortality, no effort even to carry over or restate the phantom imagery of immortality. Natural piety in these lines is a secular reverence moved by the pathos of mutability:

The clouds that gather round the setting sun
Do take a sober coloring from an eye

That hath kept watch o'er man's mortality;
Another race hath been, and other palms are won.
Thanks to the human heart by which we live,
Thanks to its tenderness, its joys and fears,
To me the meanest flower that blows can give
Thoughts that do often lie too deep for tears.

This is a grave ending, full of allusions to Gray: to the "race" and the "fearful joy" of the Eton College Ode, to the frail blossoms in the Death of a Favorite Cat. Also, as in so many great odes, there is a final "gathering" of the mind's humbled thoughts now rendered as congregational homilies, a gathering that willingly stands far below the cosmic gathering of clouds or twittering swallows. A conclusion of this sort is a service rendered, a graveside hymn to man's mortality, without intimation but with something that would seem to achieve collective intimacy were it not for "To me," a last gift of special knowledge awarded to the self by the odic voice.[33] To the famous question, "Where is it now, the glory and the dream?" we may answer in behalf of Wordsworth's "me": Aye, where is it? Mortality alone has its music.

Intimations apart, then, the question remains, Which is better, childhood or being grown up? It may be of use to measure the Intimations Ode in this respect against a passage from "In Desolation," by a poet whom Wordsworth would have been less than human not to have reperused attentively in the summer of 1803, his new acquaintance Sir George Beaumont's Renaissance ancestor Sir John Beaumont:

If solid vertues dwell not but in paine,
I will not wish that golden age againe,
Because it flowed with sensible delights
Of heavenly things....
    [Chalmers, X. 25]

Like Beaumont, Wordsworth is never quite easy about the glad animal movements of his little pagan selves, though it would be an exaggeration to insist that his nativity ode exorcises them; early childhood, for him, is simply incomplete. The later stages of childhood, however intense, are already projected by present memory toward the double imprisonment of the adult, the state of being shuttled to and fro between the burden and the absence of the flesh; but the difference remains that late childhood lacks the solace of adulthood's deliberative resources. At bottom, as it seems to me, the speaker of the Intimations Ode prefers himself grown up, or just as he is, in fact, at the moment.

Wordsworth's choice of the Pindaric format would mean that he could scarcely have composed the poem on his customary walks, chanting aloud. In attempting the vocality of an ode, Wordsworth would have needed to stay at his desk, weighing meters and blocking stanzas in writing. In facing this paradox, a highly relevant passage may be enlisted from Jacques Derrida: "Writing is that forgetting of the self, that exteriorization, the contrary of the interiorizing memory, or the *Erinnerung* that opens the history of the spirit."[34] Wordsworth's ode is more crucially a forgetting than an attempted reconstitution of any earlier self; it celebrates forgetting in celebrating birth, its own birth ultimately, and does so by entering a poetic shape that imitates the constant discontinuity of being alive and suffering. "Pain," says Nietzsche, "always raises the question about its origin while pleasure is inclined to stop with itself without looking back."[35] Childhood has no myth of childhood, and no fund of suffering to be projected as a benediction. (It goes without saying, I hope, that concerning actual childhood these assertions are probably false; we are speaking here, though, of what the overstrained figures of memory can know about a child's memory in an ode.) The failing powers of adulthood are necessary, like, the fading of Shelley's coal and the secondariness of Coleridge's secondary imagination, for the dissemination of voice in the writing of poetry, which starts, like a mortal stroke, as a severance from the Logos, and then, over that very fissure, takes its stand against the "severing of our loves."

IV

> To the last point of vision, and beyond,
> Mount, daring warbler!—that love-prompted strain
> . . . .
> Thrills not the less the bosom of the plain:
> Yet might'st thou seem, proud privilege! to sing
> All independent of the leafy spring.
> —"A Morning Exercise" (1828)

The Intimations Ode is uncharacteristic of Wordsworth. It is a poem that appears openly to espouse the attitudes that partisans of the sophisticated Wordsworth take to be important but only covertly present in his poetry (longing for apocalypse, hatred of nature), but that actually favors, presumably against the poet's design, the wise naturalism that partisans of the Simple Wordsworth take to be everywhere intended: faith in and through nature without clear revelation, whatever "faith" in this context may mean. The Great Ode loses the power of grounding spiritual knowledge in physical experience, the power which had made "Tintern Abbey" a less confused poem, "well pleased to recognize"

> In nature and the language of the sense
> The anchor of my purest thoughts, the nurse,
> The guide, the guardian of my heart, and soul
> Of all my moral being.

This passage, which redeems even the troublesome foster mother of the Intimations Ode, represents what can with most propriety be called Wordsworth's "unified vision," though needless to say there are rifts in the ground near the Wye as well. Speaking only of "vicious" poetry in his "Essay, Supplementary" (1815) to the 1800 Preface, Wordsworth identifies the quality of "confusion" that Cleanth Brooks was the first to emphasize in the Intimations Ode itself: "the realities of the Muse are but shows, and ... her liveliest excitements are raised by transient shocks of conflicting feeling and successive assemblages of contradictory thoughts."[36] Wordsworth seems to have felt that bad poetry is full of contradictions in terms—oxymorons—yet his own most contradictory poem is his Great Ode. In these concluding remarks I want to reconsider the oxymoron "natural piety" from the standpoint of Wordsworth's lesser odes[37] in order to show that the confusion of all his odes is peculiar to what he would have termed the "mould" in which they are cast (1815 Preface).

It may be remarked, though, before turning to other odes, that Wordsworth could always handle intimations of immortality more positively in poems that were not odes. Unless "The Mad Monk" was written by Wordsworth himself,[38] the clearest forerunner of the Intimations Ode (as of "A Slumber did my spirit seal"), doubtless printed as the first poem in the 1849 edition for this reason, is not an ode but a quieter sort of poem, "Written in Very Early Youth":

> a Slumber seems to steal
> O'er vale, and mountain, and the starless sky.
> Now, in this blank of things, a harmony,
> Home-felt, and home-created, comes to heal
> That grief for which the senses still supply
> Fresh food.

This passage affirms a "blank" vision without being troubled about its blankness; it is quite possibly referred to directly in the compromised affirmation of the Great Ode, lines 145–51, where a blank misgiving condemns the eternally dead to roll round earth's diurnal course with shadows. Another convincingly positive treatment of "this blank of things" appears in an untitled poem of 1800, in which a Solitary forsaken by his beloved exclaims:

> I look—the sky is empty space;
> I know not what I trace;
> But when I cease to look, my hand is on my heart.

This is indeed an intimation, lesser than, but comparable to, the moments of surprised revelation in lassitude that are featured in *The Prelude*. An intimation thus suggestive cannot appear in an ode because its quiet tenor openly founds knowledge in ignorance and avoids afflatus. Perhaps this distinction alone is enough to indicate that an ode can never be characteristic of Wordsworth.

NOTES

8. What is novel is the refinement, not the topic. Memory is a Pindaric topic as early as Congreve's "Daughters of Memory" (1706), and the mid-eighteenth-century lyrists wrote odes to Memory nearly as a matter of course. The association of the lyric with the past (and with childhood) is common to many of the tripartite German *Gattungsunterscheidungen*, most notably those of Heidegger and Emil Staiger. See René Wellek, "Genre Theory, the Lyric, and 'Erlebnis,'" *Festschrift für Richard Alewyn* (Cologne: Böhlau-Verlag, 1967), p. 400. Only Käte Hamburger, in fact, with whom Wellek undertakes to disagree, associates the lyric with the *present* on the grounds that it is the transcribed experience of an "Ich-Origo" ("Die lyrische Gattung," *Die Logik der Dichtung*, 2nd ed. [Stuttgart: Ernst Klett Verlag, 1968], p. 188). I follow Hamburger in proposing my notion of the self-constitution of an ode. (See also her distinction [pp. 192–93] between the "Gemeinde-Ich" of the hymn and the "Ich-Origo" of what I am calling the ode.)

9. This is not to disagree with Thomas McFarland, who says that *all* lyrics are evening lyrics, and that "the ultimate poetic theme is the elegiac theme. Great poems are monuments to our lost selves" ("Poetry and the Poem: The Structure of Poetic Content," *Literary Theory and Structure*, ed. Frank Brady et al. [New Haven: Yale University Press, 1973], p. 104). The past and the past self in the ode, though, are as transparent as shadows.

10. See Abrams, "Structure and Style in the Greater Romantic Lyric," in Hilles and Bloom, *From Sensibility to Romanticism*, p. 527.

11. Cleanth Brooks pioneered this reputation in *The Well-Wrought Urn* (1947; reprint ed., New York: Harvest Books, 1975), p. 125. A. Harris Fairbanks has suggested that "ambiguity is inherent in the form of the Romantic ode" ("The Form of Coleridge's Dejection Ode," *PMLA* 90 [1976]: 881).

12. This most odic of moments is what justifies Leo Spitzer in saying, "According to the pattern fixed by Pindar, an ode must be rhapsodic, since this genre in contrast to others calls for the perpetuation, by the work of art, of the poet's original fervor" (*Linguistics and Literary History* [New York: Russell & Russell, 19621, p. 207).

13. Appropriately identified by Ferguson as "the classical *locus amoenus*" (*Wordsworth*, p. 108).

14. *The Myth of the Birth of the Hero*, pp. 65–96. Several critics have noticed the folkloric material in the fifth stanza; Jared R. Curtis has inferred from the Earth's substitute status that she is probably to be imagined as an old nurse (*Wordsworth's Experiments with Tradition: The Lyric Poems of 1802* [Ithaca: Cornell University Press, 1971], p. 131).

15. See Lionel Trilling, "Wordsworth and the Iron Time," in *Wordsworth: A Collection of Critical Essays*, ed. M. H. Abrams (Englewood Cliffs, N.J.: Prentice-Hall, 1972), on the consequences of the sexual repression effected by Wordsworth's logic of the "unitary reality." Barbara Garlitz explains the appeal of the ode as an appeal to an age-old cultural belief that conception is a divine gift ("The Immortality Ode: Its Cultural Progeny," *SEL* 6 [1966] 648).

16. See the remarks on this anomaly by Abbie F. Potts, "The Spenserian and Miltonic Influences in the Immortality Ode and The Rainbow," *SP* (1932): 221, and Ferguson, *Wordsworth*, p. 119.

17. Lionel Trilling, *The Liberal Imagination: Essays on Literature and Society* (Garden City, N.Y.: Anchor Books, 1953), p. 127.

18. In an argument strongly opposed to my own, Florence G. Marsh takes this passage for a transcendentally affirmative point of departure: "Wordsworth's *Ode*: Obstinate Questionings," *SiR* 5 (1965–67): 219–30. As Curtis points out (*Wordsworth's Experiments*, p. 133), the appositions in the passage were heaped on sometime between 1804 and 1807, thus only deepening its ambivalence (I would say) in underlining its importance. For troubled readings of the passage that are related to mine, see: Helen Regueiro, *The Limits of Imagination: Wordsworth, Yeats, and Stevens* (Ithaca: Cornell University Press, 1976); p. 69; Ferguson, *Wordsworth*, p. 123; Hartman, *Wordsworth's Poetry*, p. 276; G. Wilson Knight, *The Starlit Dome: Studies in the Poetry of Vision* (New York: Barnes & Noble, 1960), p. 41.

19. There are two fine articles on memory's loss of immediacy in this poem; Stuart M. Sperry, Jr., "From 'Tintern Abbey' to the 'Intimations Ode': Wordsworth and the Function of Memory," *WC* 1, no. 2 (1970): 40–49; and Kenneth R. Johnston, "Recollecting Forgetting: Forcing Paradox to the Limit in the 'Immortality Ode,'" *WC* 2, no. 2 (1971): 59–64. I am surprised, however, to find Johnston (pp. 61–62) reading the "obstinate questionings" as a forgetting not of sensation but of immortality. Elsewhere Johnston himself quotes a passage from *The Recluse* (1. ll. 781–83) that could gloss this one against his own reading ("The Idiom of Vision," *New Perspectives on Coleridge and Wordsworth*, ed. Geoffrey Hartman [New York: Columbia University Press, 1972], p. 2). Paul de Man puts the relation of memory and absence dialectically in saying, "nostalgia can only exist when the transcendental presence is forgotten" ("Intentional Structure of the Romantic Image," in Bloom, *Romanticism and Consciousness*, p. 69).

20. Cf. E. D. Hirsch, *Wordsworth and Schelling: A Typological Study of Romanticism* (New Haven: Yale University Press, 1960), p. 161.

21. Mario D'Avanzo plausibly suggests *Aeneid* 6. 739–45, in "Immortality's Winds and Fields of Sleep. A Virgilian Elysium," *WC* 3, no. 3 (1972): 169. See the conclusion of the present discussion.

22. This is pointed out by Brooks, *The Well-Wrought Urn*, p. 127.

23. Brooks was, I believe, the first to define the "glory" thus precisely. See ibid., pp. 127–28.

24. This is the suggestion of Hartman, in *The Unmediated Vision: An Interpretation of Wordsworth, Hopkins, Rilke, and Valéry* (New York: Harbinger Books, 1966), p. 41; and in *Wordsworth's Poetry*, p. 275.

25. Wordsworth's epigraph for the 1807 Intimations Ode, *paulo maiora canamus*, was also used as an epigraph in several MSS of the later ode "On the Power of Sound" (see John Hollander, "Wordsworth and the Music of Sound," in Hartman, *New Perspectives*, p. 67); the Virgilian phrase, thus conceived, would deepen the irony of the silence that pervades the present in the Intimations Ode.

26. I suspect that Wordsworth's pastoral scene owes something to a poet who shares his grounding in the Psalms, Giles Fletcher, in *Christ's Victory in Heaven*, where after Easter, with immortality now guaranteed, the lambs hear the birds "piping grief away," and begin to "dance and play" (Chalmers, 10:76). See Ferguson on "the ancient instruments provoking the lambs' dance" (*Wordsworth*, p. 110).

27. The prominence of the rainbow may suggest that it is a talisman to keep off future floods. See Kenneth R. Lincoln, "Wordsworth's Mortality Ode," *JEGP* 71 (1972): 217. On the immanence of the Flood and its Miltonic provenance in Wordsworth, see Neil Hertz, "Wordsworth and the Tears of Adam," in Abrams, *Wordsworth*, p. 122. The Flood is still more prominent in the argument of Hartman, *The Unmediated Vision*, esp. p. 30.

28. F. W. Bateson compares Wordsworth's "calm weather" to the tranquility with which, in the "Preface," emotion is recollected, in *Wordsworth: A Re-interpretation* (London: Longmans, 1965), p. 162.

29. See John Jones's fine evocation of this passage, differing from mine, in *The Egotistical Sublime: A History of Wordsworth's Imagination* (London: Chatto & Windus, 1954), p. 96; and the equally fine discussion by W. K. Wimsatt, "The Structure of the Romantic Nature Image," *The Verbal Icon: Studies in the Meaning of Poetry* (New York: Noonday Press, 1964), pp. 114–15.

30. See Ferguson on what she calls the "heuristic language" of the poem (*Wordsworth*, p. 99); and William Heath, *Wordsworth and Coleridge: A Study of Their Literary Relations in 1801–02* (Oxford: Clarendon Press, 1970), pp. 64–65.

31. On the use of meditative formats in the Romantic Period, see Reeve Parker, *Coleridge's Meditative Art* (Ithaca: Cornell University Press, 1975).

32. See the conclusion of "To the Small Celandine" (a Poem of Fancy written in the spring of 1802) quoted later in the body of my text: "I will sing, as doth behove, / Hymns in praise of what I love!"

33. In *The Starlit Dome* (p. 38), Knight has argued that since "immortality" can simply mean "death negated," Wordsworth's ode is "a vision of life victorious," which "need have nothing to say about life-after-death."

34. *Of Grammatology*, p. 2f. Later in this work, Derrida understands the evil of writing for both Rousseau and Lévi-Strauss as the rupture of the self-presence of childhood innocence.

35. *The Gay Science*, trans. Walter Kaufmann (New York: Vintage Books), p. 86.

36. *The Prose Works of William Wordsworth*, 3 vols., ed. W. J. B. Owen and J. W. Smyser (Oxford: Clarendon Press, 1974), 3:63.

37. I shall have nothing to say of the pseudo-laureate odes of 1814–16 that crow over the fall of Napoleon; the reader is referred to Byron's immensely superior and more genuinely ode-like ode on the same subject.

38. For the fullest discussion of this possibility, see Thomas McFarland, "The Symbiosis of Coleridge and Wordsworth," *SiR* 11 (1972); 267–68.

THOMAS WEISKEL

Wordsworth and the Defile of the Word

—Does Mr. Wordsworth think his mind can surpass Jehovah?
  Blake to Henry Crabb Robinson

Nearing the end of the first book of the poem on his own life, Wordsworth confesses to some uncertainty. He fears that already he may have been misled "By an infirmity of love for day / Disowned by memory," and he counts on Coleridge's sympathy to see him through (*P* 1.612 ff.). His project in this loving reclamation of childhood had been frankly therapeutic:

> ... my hope has been, that I might fetch
> Invigorating thoughts from former years;
> Might fix the wavering balance of my mind,
> And haply meet reproaches too, whose power
> May spur me on, in manhood now mature,
> To honorable toil.
>   [1.620–25]

Yet his original project is fast receding before an enterprise more tentative and promising. Even if his hope should be "but an impotent desire,"[1] he has made a discovery, which now solicits him with the charm of the visionary and displaces the reproaches he had anticipated to a new quarter:

From *The Romantic Sublime: Studies in the Structure and Psychology of Transcendence*, pp. 167–204.
© 1976 and 1986 by The Johns Hopkins University Press.

> Yet should these hopes
> Prove vain, and thus should neither I be taught
> To understand myself, nor thou to know
> With better knowledge how the heart was framed
> Of him thou lovest; need I dread from thee
> Harsh judgments, if the song be loth to quit
> Those recollected hours that have the charm
> Of visionary things, those lovely forms
> And sweet sensations that throw back our life,
> And almost make remotest infancy
> A visible scene, on which the sun is shining?
>   [1.625–35]

It is difficult to know how open is this question addressed to Coleridge. For Coleridge, we feel, is not the real addressee; he stands, like a neutral alienist, sympathetic but mute, for an agent or element in Wordsworth himself that would judge harshly the enterprise now in view. As if an answer to his question scarcely mattered—he is picking up confidence—Wordsworth continues:

> One end at least hath been attained; my mind
> Hath been revived, and if this genial mood
> Desert me not, forthwith shall be brought down
> Through later years the story of my life.
> The road lies plain before me;—'tis a theme
> Single and of determined bounds; and hence
> I choose it rather at this time, than work
> Of ampler or more varied argument,
> Where I might be discomfited and lost....
>   [1.636–44]

We note that Wordsworth's "genial mood" depends upon neither his own self-understanding nor the successful communication of his history in the terms of "knowledge." This cure, if such it is, comes about almost incidentally, as a side effect in his rehearsal of the past. By settling for less in the way of theme and argument, he gains more, a genial state of mind which cannot be sought directly, only received gratuitously.

It is true that Wordsworth will later seem to be educated by the visible scenes of childhood, as if their rememoration indeed constituted a kind of knowledge. Certain episodes seem especially instructive, imbued with a latent message now to be decoded:

> There are in our existence spots of time,
> That with distinct pre-eminence retain
> A renovating virtue, whence, depressed
> By false opinion and contentious thought,
> Or aught of heavier or more deadly weight,
> In trivial occupations, and the round
> Of ordinary intercourse, our minds
> Are nourished and invisibly repaired;
> A virtue, by which pleasure is enhanced,
> That penetrates, enables us to mount,
> When high, more high, and lifts us up when fallen.
> This efficacious spirit chiefly lurks
> Among those passages of life that give
> Profoundest knowledge to what point, and how,
> The mind is lord and master—outward sense
> The obedient servant of her will.
>   [12.208–23]

One can have much of Wordsworth by heart and still be surprised, notably by the submerged metaphors. Here, "lurks," with its suggestion of the hidden and even the sinister, makes one pause only to find that resonance picked up by "passages": a spirit lurks in a passage. "Passages" refers presumably to events that involved a passing from one state to another and also to the passing back and through of retrospection; in this sense, "passages of life" are equivalent to "spots of time." But a "passage" is also a text; one reads these texts or signifiers by passing into and through them. Such passages "give" knowledge but conceal the efficacious spirit; at the very least this spirit, lying as is were in ambush, is to be distinguished from knowledge of the mind's sovereignty. (Actually, "knowledge" is a late idea here; Wordsworth first wrote that the spirit lurks among passages "in which / We have had deepest feeling that the mind / Is lord and master" (1805, 11.270–71), and this phrase evolved through "Profoundest feeling" to become "Profoundest knowledge."[2]) The knowledge or feeling of the mind's great power is often given to Wordsworth, but the spirit comes not as a consequence of this insight but as if in response to it. If *The Prelude* is an indirect quest for the efficacious spirit or genial mood, that quest is fulfilled in a hidden and somewhat unpredictable concomitance.

What then was Wordsworth's discovery? His undeniable claim to originality can be advanced in many directions—he aggrandized the everyday; he virtually destroyed the-poem-which-is-*about*-something by taking the subject out of poetry; he naturalized the archaic, daemonic, and divine sources of power. What must orient us here is his discovery of a mode of conversation, now most easily recognized outside of poetry in the domains of the authentic psychoanalyst and a certain kind of expert teacher too tentative to know or say for sure what he "really" thinks. This conversation is not a "communication" (the cant word of our social world); its aim is not the transmission of knowledge or a message but the springing loose of an efficacious spirit which haunts the passages of self-knowledge, however shallow or deep. Yet to describe *The Prelude* as any kind of conversation seems perverse. Its apparent form is closer to monolithic monologue; it drifts, gets lost, peters out now and then, and generally proceeds without the dramatic constraints a stricter form or a genuine auditor would compel. The ostensible interlocutor has no chance to reply, and indeed it might be said that Coleridge's assumption of this role presupposed his own subsidence as a poet. Worst of all, this "conversation" has for its exclusive theme the inner history of the speaker, and it is thus a discourse apparently exempt from the veridical testing conversation normally entails.

Nevertheless, in its deeper lineaments *The Prelude* has the shape and structure of a dialogue. Wordsworth's real interlocutor is not Coleridge but himself, a part of himself, archaic or prospective but in any case alienated from his present, who beckons to him across a "vacancy." "Often do I seem," he says, "Two consciousnesses, conscious of myself / And of some other Being" (2.31–33). That "other Being" is in part a remembered state of mind, a previous consciousness, and in part the inferred protagonist of visible scenes of whom he is now conscious for the first time. For the first time because that other Being did not exist in the past; though he now exists there, he is a creation of the present. Freud regarded the appearance of a subject as an active character in his own memory as decisive evidence that the original experience had been worked over.

> It may indeed be questioned whether we have any memories at all *from* our childhood: memories *relating to* our childhood may be all that we possess. Our childhood memories show us our earliest years not as they were but as they appeared at the later periods when the memories were revived. In these periods of revival, the childhood memories did not, as people are accustomed to say, *emerge*; they were *formed* at that time.[3]

The radical reading of *The Prelude* must begin with this insight, which no one who has tried the experiment of recollection needs an analyst to confirm. So Wordsworth is to be found forming his significant other Being even as he searches for his signature in recollected hours, perhaps finding him truly only "in that silence while he hung / Listening" like the boy at Winander in conversation with the owls (5.364–88).

In general, the other Being or consciousness implied by Wordsworth's speech remains inaccessible except through the immensely mediated languages of memory and desire. The whole series of representations— images, thoughts, ideas, words—function as the signifiers in this dialogue, and they cannot be short-circuited in an unmediated intuition because that Other is defined, as locus or possibility, only by these signifiers. Insofar as Wordsworth is a speaker, that Other is the being to whom his speech is unconsciously directed; but the Other is also the one to whom he listens, and it is in fact mainly as a listener that Wordsworth overtly construes his identity in *The Prelude*. For there is and has been an evident continuity in his listening. Even as a child, he says, amid "fits of vulgar joy" and "giddy bliss,"

> ... even then I felt
> Gleams like the flashing of a shield;—the earth
> And common face of Nature spake to me
> Rememberable things ...
>   [1.581–88]

and they are still so speaking because "The scenes which were a witness of that joy / Remained in their substantial lineaments / Depicted on the brain" (1.599–601). If he fails to understand this speech, and he often does, sometimes egregiously, the fact of being spoken to remains, and its aim and value depend in no way on the accurate reception of a message. It may even be that Wordsworth's misconstructions, his significant *méconnaissances*, are the essential pivots of this dialogue, for they enable him to change from listener to speaker; they enable him to be cured. We appreciate in any case that these failures are not the result of a faulty archeology, as if the past could indeed be unearthed by consciousness. They are liberating evasions, obscurities which preserve both the mystery (and hence the power) of his interlocutor and the authenticity of his own speech, which otherwise might slide toward the vain repetition or imitation of an alienated self. We might even suppose, as the point of an ideal cure no doubt hypothetical, a moment of pure speech in which the Other is so entirely obscured as not to exist, and Wordsworth knows only a presence uncompounded by the absence which makes speech necessary.

We may have the vague impression that it is Nature with whom Wordsworth is speaking. In one sense this is true, for "the earth / And common face of Nature" is the predominant locus of the signifier. But Nature herself exhibits a paradoxically fugitive omnipresence in *The Prelude*.

Wordsworth rarely speaks directly to Nature, more often of or about her; we find a more or less consistent differentiation between Nature and "the language of the sense":

> Ye Presences of Nature in the sky
> And on the earth! Ye Visions of the hills!
> And Souls of lonely places! can I think
> A vulgar hope was yours when ye employed
> Such ministry, when ye through many a year
> Haunting me thus among my boyish sports,
> On caves and trees, upon the woods and hills,
> Impressed upon all forms the characters
> Of danger or desire; and thus did make
> The surface of the universal earth
> With triumph and delight, with hope and fear,
> Work like a sea?
>   [1.464–75]

Nature is generally two or more ontological degrees removed from the "characters" that can be perceived or intended, listened to or read. Nature hovers in the background as the sum or ground of the intermediary personifications ("Powers," "genii," "Presences," "Visions," "Souls") who are supposed as actual agents of articulation. Nature is thus the guarantor of the dialogue, at once the principle assumed to cover and redeem its discontinuities and a kind of screen on which the multiplicity of representations is projected. When "forms" begin to assume the shape and function of "characters," Nature's significant absence (or "negative presence") is already presupposed, for characters are symbols standing in for something no longer immediately there. Behind every symbol is an absence, the death of the thing (form or image) whose place the symbol takes. Hence speech itself is founded on the withdrawal of the primordial object, in which we find as well the essential formula of anxiety.

It is in this passage from forms to characters, from image to symbol, that the efficacious spirit lurks, and it is the intricate turnings of this passage that I propose to follow and hope to map. We may conceive two domains, an order of imagination or memory and an order of symbol or speech, though the content of these opposed domains ought to be educed from the analysis and not out of an hypothesis. *The Prelude* as a whole is an attempt to negotiate the strait leading from remembered images, and from the power of mind to which these images continue to testify, to capable speech. "I have seen such things—I see them still (memory)—and see moreover deeper into them, as if anew (imagination)—I therefore was and am a favored being (identity)—and I can speak (be a poet)." This argument, here abstractly reduced and overemphasized, presides over each rememoration in the poem, as if this poem were in fact a prelude, achieving its unforeseen finalities only under propaedeutic pretense. In a way the argument serves as "profoundest knowledge" to orient and occasion the "efficacious spirit" which is the poem itself. Moreover, the passage discernible in the project of *The Prelude* emerges with strange and almost literal insistence in the poem's crucial episodes and at the heart of its recurrent figures.

We use the notion of poetic imagination loosely to gloss over the mysterious gap between a power of perception and a power of articulation or composition. Keats says that "every man whose soul is not a clod / Hath visions, and would speak, if he had loved / And been well nurtured in his mother's tongue,"[4] but that can't possibly be true; a mute inglorious Milton is no Milton at all. At times it seems as if the Romantic poets (Blake, of course, apart) were engaged in a conspiracy of occultation concerning the Word, as if to acknowledge that its enjoining power involved the betrayal of a dangerous secret.

The fact is that the passage from imagination to symbol was occluded for Wordsworth, and yet the essential moment of his greatest poetry is right in the midst of this occlusion. He halts or is halted right at the point where the image is eclipsed—where it is on the verge of turning into a "character" in a higher, nonvisual discourse. This moment—and it is an experience as well as a dialectical locus—is the sole province of what he calls "visionary power," and it is the very type of the sublime moment. Here is one of Wordsworth's first attempts to formulate its liminal significance:

> ... for I would walk alone,
> Under the quiet stars, and at that time
> Have felt whate'er there is of power in sound
> To breathe an elevated mood, by form
> Or image unprofaned; and I would stand,
> If the night blackened with a coming storm,
> Beneath some rock, listening to notes that are
> The ghostly language of the ancient earth,
> Or make their dim abode in distant winds.
> Thence did I drink the visionary power;
> And deem not profitless those fleeting moods
> Of shadowy exultation: not for this,
> That they are kindred to our purer mind
> And intellectual life; but that the soul,

Remembering how she felt, but what she felt
Remembering not, retains an obscure sense
Of possible sublimity, whereto
With growing faculties she doth aspire,
With faculties still growing, feeling still
That whatsoever point they gain, they yet
Have something to pursue.
   [2.302–22]

The mood of shadowy exultation lies beyond the profane domain of form or image, and yet the subject is here not quite integrated into the order of symbolic sound. The notes to which he listens remain a "ghostly language," a pattern of signifiers without signifiers, a language without semantic dimension. The signifier precedes the signified, which may indeed never arrive; or in terms closer to Wordsworth's, the subject is initiated into the *how* of the discourse but not the *what*, and the affective exaltation depends precisely on this halting at a threshold. The "power in sound / To breathe an elevated mood" is here being listened to, but that slight personification ("breathe") refers us obliquely to Wordsworth's situation as a speaker who knows how he wants to sound but not quite what he has to say.

Wordsworth was not a symbolic poet and not a descriptive poet either, if indeed a poet can be descriptive. His landscapes hover on the edge of revelation without revealing anything, and so the very moment of hovering, of glimpsed entry into the beyond, when "the light of sense / Goes out, but with a flash that has revealed / The invisible world" (6.600–602), usurps the missing climax of symbolic revelation. In the Snowdon vision, for example, the salient elements of that magnificent scene—the suspended moon, the sea of hoary mist, the blue chasm in the vapor—refuse to harden into symbolic equation with the imagination or anything else, as Geoffrey Hartman has observed.[5] And this is so despite the fact that Wordsworth is there working explicitly with notions of analogy, type, and emblem. So too with that spot of time when the young boy, having lost his way while riding near Penrith, sees a naked pool, the beacon on the summit, and the girl with a pitcher forcing her way against the wind-salient images which are less than symbols and all the more powerful for that. Or the schoolboy in his mountain lookout, waiting to be fetched home for a holiday that turned into a funeral, who later finds himself returning to certain "kindred spectacles and sounds"—

     ... the wind and sleety rain,
And all the business of the elements,
The single sheep, and the one blasted tree,

And the bleak music from that old stone wall,
The noise of wood and water, and the mist
That on the line of each of those two roads
Advanced in such indisputable shapes ...
    [12.317–23]

—thence to drink as at a fountain. Many instances of such salience could be adduced, but this feature of Wordsworth's landscapes is widely appreciated and is here evoked only to suggest the scope of the moment we wish to isolate. If the images so projected into the field of Wordsworth's past were to lose their opacity and become the transparent signifiers of an invisible world, the soul would "remember" what she felt and have nothing left to pursue. The conversation, propelled as it is by the baffled misconstruction of the signifier, would be over; Wordsworth would understand himself. Indeed, as the poem goes on Wordsworth is less and less disposed to interrogate the images that rise upon him. The gestures of self-inquisition become the mere feinting of a mind learning how knowledge is opposed to efficacious power.

Visionary power is associated with the transcendence of the image and in particular with the "power in sound"; yet it depends upon a resistance within that transcendence of sight for sound. In the Wordsworthian moment two events appear to coalesce: the withdrawal or the occultation of the image and the epiphany of the character or signifier proper. A form or image may be installed in either the imaginative or symbolic domains. There is a world of difference between the two, but the differentiation can never be found within the image itself. If an image is symbolic, that fact is signaled by what we loosely call "context"—its inscription in an order or language whose structure is prior to its meaning (signifieds) and so determines it. On the other hand, an image (fantasy or perception) may fall short of the symbolic, in which, case it remains opaque and meaningless in itself. Earlier we spoke of rememoration as a confrontation with a signifier, but strictly speaking, an image becomes a signifier only when it is recognized as such, and this may involve imputing an intentionality to the image. (A homely example: a child responds to pictures or the type in a book only as colors and shapes until the magical moment when he discerns that they are representations; it is the displaced recapitulation of this moment that is in question here.) There is implicit in the passage from imagination to symbol a confrontation with symbolicity—the very fact of structure in its priority and independent of its actual organization. Hence the signifier may be misconstrued in two possible ways. It may be simply misread, or—and this is in point with Wordsworth—there may be a resistance or a barrier to its recognition as a signifier, a resistance to reading itself as opposed to seeing. I think the resistance may be identified with what Wordsworth calls imagination.

DEATH AND THE WORD

The spots of time give to the mind the knowledge or feeling of its own sovereignty and occasion the gift of efficacious spirit as well. "Life with me," says Wordsworth, "As far as memory can look back, is full / Of this beneficent influence" (1805, 11.277–79). It is curious that these remembered events should have therapeutic power, since the two memories Wordsworth goes on to present are of a kind we should normally call traumatic, and they each contain intimations of death.

In fact, however, the whole idea of spots of time is installed in a line of associations concerning death. In the first manuscripts containing the bulk of books 1 and 2 (MSS. V, U), the passage "There are in our existence spots of time ..." follows Wordsworth's account of the drowned man at Esthwaite, later assigned to book 5 (42.6–59). He had seen a heap of garments on the shore and watched for half an hour to see if a bather would emerge. But no one did, and the next day—"(Those unclaimed garments telling a plain Tale)"—the body was recovered:

> At length, the dead Man, 'mid that beauteous scene
> Of trees, and hills and water, bolt upright
> Rose with his ghastly face....
>   [1805, 5.470–72]

Why Wordsworth hadn't run for help the night before. isn't clear, since surely the "Tale"—or at least the suspicion of something wrong—would have been plain enough to a boy of eight. In any case, MS. V continues with a meditation on disasters that later proved full of beneficent influence:

>   ... bolt upright
> Rose with his ghastly face. I might advert
> To numerous accidents in flood or field
> Quarry or moor, or 'mid the winter snows
> Distresses and disasters, tragic facts
> Of rural history that impressed my mind
> With images to which in following years
> Far other feelings were attached; with forms
> That yet exist with independent life
> And, like their archetypes, know no decay.[6]

And then follows "There are in our existence spots of time...." The sequence suggests that the spots of time were in their origin "tragic facts" for which time has provided a kind of redemption, permitting their association with "Far other feelings." We might find the tragic (or deathly or traumatic) associations clustering around "spots," whereas "of time" suggests the curative efficacy of a supervening continuity. Here the misconstruction of a memory-representation—entering, we must always assume, into the representation itself—and in particular the poet's indifference to the role of death in his most valuable memories, would seem to lie at the heart of the cure.

In the first spot of time Wordsworth is a very young boy of five or so riding with a trusted family servant on the moors near Penrith.

> We had not travelled long, ere some mischance
> Disjoined me from my comrade; and, through fear
> Dismounting, down the rough and stony moor
> I led my horse, and, stumbling on, at length
> Came to a bottom, where in former times
> A murderer had been hung in iron chains.
> The gibbet-mast had mouldered down, the bones
> And iron case were gone; but on the turf,
> Hard by, soon after that fell deed was wrought,
> Some unknown hand had carved the murderers name.
> The monumental letters were inscribed
> In times long past; but still, from year to year,
> By superstition of the neighbourhood,
> The grass is cleared away, and to this hour
> The characters are fresh and visible:
> A casual glance had shown them, and I fled,
> Faltering and faint, and ignorant of the road:
> Then, reascending the bare common, saw
> A naked pool that lay beneath the hills,
> The beacon on the summit, and, more near,
> A girl, who bore a pitcher on her head,
> And seemed with difficult steps to force her way
> Against the blowing wind.
>   [12.231–53]

The emotional pivot of this episode is a word, a name, a group of characters suddenly glimpsed. One kind of fear, not knowing where one is, is violently superseded by the virtual panic of another kind of fear, being in a terrible

place or spot. Losing its way, the ego is exposed involuntarily to a death, for
the characters mean "a murderer was executed at this spot": death for a
death, the law of sacrifice which is the simplest formula of justice. The
custom in the background here is the execution of a murderer at the spot of
the crime, so that the spot become charged with the ritual significance of
atonement. It is a place in nature but not of it, the very point of contiguity
between the natural order and the order of law; hence "By superstition of the
neighbourhood, / The grass is cleared away" lest the stark exigencies of the
law should be mitigated by natural process. The centrality of spot-ness
here—migrating, subliminally, into the idea of spots of time—is even clearer
in the 1805 version:

> Faltering, and ignorant where I was, at length
> I chanced to espy those characters inscribed
> On the green sod: forthwith I left the spot....
>   [1805, 11.300–302]

In one sense the spot is an image within a continuum of images, just as
the spots of time are salient memory representations within the vaguer
continuum structured by a linear idea of time. But the text insists, with an
emphasis as extraordinary as it is literal, on this spot as a signifier: characters,
"monumental letters," or "writing" (1805). This it is which mediates the
meaning of the spot, turning faltering confusion "forthwith" into panic and
headlong flight. The order of law is inserted into the order of nature by
means of writing. Precisely parallel to the point of contiguity between law
and nature—that is, the idea of death and the logic of death for death—is the
point of contiguity between image and signifier or symbol. We arrive, by no
doubt too great a jump as yet, at the equation writing = death, or more
exactly, the recognition of a signifier = the intimation of death.

Here we are greeted by a curious fact. In the first manuscript version
we have, the characters that were to be given such prominence are
unmentioned:

> A man, the murderer of his wife, was hung
> In irons, moulder'd was the gibbet mast,
> The bones were gone, the iron and the wood,
> Only a long green ridge of turf remained
> Whose shape was like a grave. I left the spot....[7]

Evidently in revision (between 1802 and 1805) Wordsworth brushed up on
the facts. He would have learned that the victim was a man and learned too,

possibly for the first time, of the characters, and that they were still extant. (This is the kind of genetic detail that renders unacceptably naive that reading of *The Prelude* which would accept Wordsworth's myth of memory at face value and evade the origination of the memories in the present tense of a grown man.) In revision, the "long green ridge of turf ... Whose shape was like a grave" turns into the portentous characters, which suggests that the representations of a secondary anxiety were being retrospectively superimposed upon the memory trace of a grave. If this is "association," it is deeper than what we usually mean by association, for the revision enables the poet Wordsworth to concentrate and perhaps to discover the emotional center of the memory. The element of panic enters the text with the appearance of the characters, as if they constituted the deep meaning of the grave, and not vice versa. At any rate, we have underlined in the very genesis of the passage a deep connection between death and the word.

Yet the point of the episode and its justification as a spot of time lies not in the epiphany of characters but in the subsequent vision:

> It was, in truth,
> An ordinary sight; but I should need
> Colours and words that are unknown to man,
> To paint the visionary dreariness
> Which, while I looked all round for my lost guide,
> Invested moorland waste, and naked pool,
> The beacon crowning the lone eminence,
> The female and her garments vexed and tossed
> By the strong wind.
>   [12.253–61]

Things are invested with a "visionary" aspect as if in recompense for the prior fear; though for the boy it is a dubious consolation, for he must contend with "dreariness," an involuntary perceptional alienation from the "ordinary" (hence he doesn't think to hail the girl). This is a liminal state in which mediations have fallen away. The common that he ascends is "bare," the pool "naked," the moorland a "waste," and even the beacon crowns a "lonely Eminence" (1805). The features of the landscape by which he might expect to orient himself are remote, withdrawn in an unapproachable stasis. The girl, however, "more near" in more ways than one, is an image not of stasis but of difficulty, of forces locked in contrariety. There is a play on clothing beneath the surface: dreariness invests the landscape by divesting it until it is naked, just as the wind whips at the girl's garments. The girl proceeds "with difficult steps to force her way" against the visionary

divestment which threatens her with the fate of the denuded, static
landscape. As object ("outward sense") to the boy's mind she yet retains her
motion and her humanizing garments against the involuntary, dehumanizing
strength of that mind, and she thereby images the boy's own difficult struggle
against his imagination.

How should the imagination—that is; the literal, perceptional
imagination—come to have such withering strength? Both the intensity and the
alienating effect of the imagination in its phase of lordship and mastery seem to
derive from the terror that has gone before. We need to put the two halves of
the spot of time back together. Vision occurs in flight from the characters and
appears to realize the deathly intimations read in the characters. But the
proportions of seeing to reading, of image to symbol, have been reversed. "A
casual glance had shown them, and I fled": the briefest sight, surcharged with
meaning, while visionary dreariness is drawn out seeing, twice rendered by the
poet—as if there were indeed a hidden message threatening to emerge in the
pool, the beacon, and the girl—which yet falls short of symbolic revelation. An
extended seeing replaces reading in this flight; it is a "backward" displacement
or regression from the order of symbol to that of image, and it functions to
defend the ego against the death which has been signified. That death is
displaced or projected (and thereby diffused) into the denuded landscape where
the fixating spot is doubled as the naked pool and the beacon on the summit.
The wind against which the girl—and by extension the boy—are struggling
represents not death but the obscure power we have found inextricably
associated with death, a power for which we have as yet no name. For in truth,
as strange and indeed academic as it sounds, it is against the fact that things may
come to signify that the boy is forcing his difficult way.

The uncontrollable intensity of the imagination is often rendered as a
strong wind in *The Prelude*, as M. H. Abrams showed long ago.[8] In the
preamble, for example, the inner breeze is creative up to a certain point:

> For I, methought, while the sweet breath of Heaven
> Was blowing on my body, felt within
> A corresponding mild creative breeze,
> A vital breeze which travell'd gently on
> O'er things which it had made, and is become
> A tempest, a redundant energy
> Vexing its own creation.
>   [1805, 1.41–47]

Here too is evidently a threshold after which the wind becomes de-creative,
"vexing" (as with the garments of the girl) what has been brought to birth in

perception. In composition as in reading, winds attend the threshold of the word, for wind is the image of the invisible, the representation of the peculiar power of signifying within the perceptional order of the imagination. In book 5 Wordsworth brings the liminal concept of the visionary into connection with the works of mighty poets:

> Visionary power
> Attends the motions of the viewless winds,
> Embodied in the mystery of words:
> There, darkness makes abode, and all the host
> Of shadowy things work endless changes,—there,
> As in a mansion like their proper home,
> Even forms and substances are circumfused
> By that transparent veil with light divine,
> And, through the turnings intricate of verse,
> Present themselves as objects recognised,
> In flashes, and with glory not their own.
>   [5.595–605]

Wordsworth had a gift for phrasing that defies analysis. Power attends motions of winds which are embodied in a mystery: a series of quasi-metaphorical displacements away from words, compounded by indefinite reference ("there," "that transparent veil"). The passage is evoking the penumbra of words, the power inherent not in what they mean but in that they mean; or, in what they are, independent of their meaning—in an earlier language, the *how* and not the *what* of sublimity. When a "form" or a "substance" is taken up by a signifier, it receives a super-added power and a divine glory immanent in the circumfusing veil of the signifier. Power inheres not in the perceptional form but in language or symbolicity itself; we remember that the boy drank the visionary power listening to a language devoid of forms and substances ("by form / Or image unprofaned"),

> ... notes that are
> The ghostly language of the ancient earth,
> Or make their dim abode in distant winds.
>   [2.308–10]

But there is in "ghostly language" a ghost to be confronted; our spot of time has shown us that in the passage to the visionary power of signification lurks the thought of death. There, "darkness makes abode," and "shadowy things" as well as "light divine." In order to arrive "As in a mansion like their proper home," forms and substances must die out of the imaginary or perceptional order and into the symbolic order of verse. For the speaker or poet this passage appears to involve the intimation of sacrifice and the assumption of guilt.

In the next spot of time, the fact of guilt is explicitly focused in relation to the visionary moment. Wordsworth is remembering his vigil on a crag where he waited for a pair of horses to bear him home from school for the Christmas holidays:

> ... 'twas a day
> Tempestuous, dark, and wild, and on the grass
> I sate half-sheltered by a naked wall;
> Upon my right hand couched a single sheep,
> Upon my left a blasted hawthorn stood;
> With those companions at my side, I watched,
> Straining my eyes intensely, as the mist
> Gave intermitting prospect of the copse
> And plain beneath.
>   [12.297–305]

Before the holidays were over, his father was dead:

> The event,
> With all the sorrow that it brought, appeared
> A chastisement; and when I called to mind
> That day so lately past, when from the crag
> I looked in such anxiety of hope;
> With trite reflections of morality,
> Yet in the deepest passion, I bowed low
> To God, Who thus corrected my desires;
> And, afterwards, the wind and sleety rain,
> And all the business of the elements,
> The single sheep, and the one blasted tree,
> And the bleak music from that old stone wall,
> The noise of wood and water; and the mist
> That on the line of each of those two roads
> Advanced in such indisputable shapes;
> All these were kindred spectacles and sounds
> To which I oft repaired, and thence would drink,
> As at a fountain.
>   [12.309–26]

There are several suggestions of dissonance in this retrospection. The salient features of the landscape are rehearsed twice, as in the Penrith passage, and the secondary emphasis is upon the features themselves rather than upon their incidental discovery in an ulterior seeing, a looking for a lost guide or a pair of horses. The mist, for example, is at first an interposed obstacle, giving "intermitting prospect of the copse / And plain beneath" on which the boy's expectant eyes are focused; when the memory is re-formed, the mist advances in "indisputable shapes," itself a signifier. More striking, however, is the dissonance surrounding the matter of guilt. If the "desires" corrected by God were simply the boy's eagerness to go home, it is at least odd that his father's death should be felt as a chastisement of that most natural and filial wish. For a boy of thirteen to feel ambivalent upon the occasion of his father's death is perfectly normal, and the ambivalence that may be presumed to be original has made its way into the phrasing—in the "anxiety of hope" and that curious uncertainty about the decorum of grief: "With trite reflections of morality, / Yet in the deepest passion, I bowed low / To God...." We begin to suspect that there is more to those desires than the boy's wish to go home for Christmas.

Editor de Selincourt finds in the "indisputable shapes" of the mist an echo of Hamlet's confrontation with his father's ghost: "Thou com'st in such a questionable shape / That I will speak to thee."[9] Hamlet means "a shape that can be questioned" as well as "an uncertain shape": in contrast on both counts, the shapes of Wordsworth's ghost-mist are "indisputable." Again we have the *how*—in a way that can't be questioned—but not the *what*: the liminal moment when the signifier appears, *apparently* without a signified. But could it be that Wordsworth on the crag had a premonition of his father's death, that this is the signified of those signifying shapes? In fact, he could not have known of his father's fatal illness while waiting to go home,[10] but the first formation of this memory, in the very early *Vale of Esthwaite*,[11] makes this very premonition explicit:

> Long, long, upon yon naked rock
> Alone, I bore the bitter shock;
> Long, long, my swimming eyes did roam
> For little Horse to bear me home,
> To bear me—what avails my tear?
> To sorrow o'er a Father's bier.
>   [422–27]

Of course, we have no way of knowing what the boy on the crag felt, and I might add, no need to know. We have insisted all along that it is a question of "creative" retrospection, of memories formed at the time they seem merely to emerge. The whole theme of guilt may well be a "later" addition, a reworking of the original impression, as indeed the Vale text goes on to imply:

> Flow on, in vain thou hast not flow'd,
> But eased me of a heavy load;
> For much it gives my heart relief
> To pay the mighty debt of grief,
> With sighs repeated o'er and o'er,
> I mourn because I mourned no more.
>   [428–33]

The ground of our speculation is but the firmer if we assume that the guilt—incurred by an unconscious desire for his father's death—is retrospectively associated, through the premonition, with visionary salience. It is as if that "indisputable" premonition, like the characters on the turf, were the cost of vision, the price of salience. At first, when he "called to mind / That day so lately past," he experienced not renovating power, but a feeling of guilt, so that he bowed low to God. It is only "afterwards" that the kindred spectacles and sounds" come to be a source of power—after, that is, the power has been paid for by the ritual gestures of expiation and correction.

For what is striking about this spot of time is not the presence in it of a commonplace oedipal ambivalence but the deeper evasion of the oedipal "correction." God ironically corrects the filial desire for reunion (to go home) by fulfilling the unconscious desire signified in the premonitory "indisputable shapes." Hence the guilt. More important, however, is the question, In what sense does Wordsworth stand corrected? Far from repenting—or repressing—the spectacles and sounds which are linked to his desires, Wordsworth repairs often to them, "and thence would drink / As at a fountain":

>   ... and on winter nights,
> Down to this very time, when storm and rain
> Beat on my roof, or, haply, at noon-day,
> While in a grove I walk, whose lofty trees,
> Laden with summer's thickest foliage, rock
> In a strong wind, some working of the spirit,
> Some inward agitations thence are brought....
>   [12.326–32]

The inner or correspondent breeze has its source in a deep affiliation with a visionary moment whose ambivalent burden or message of death has been unconsciously repudiated even as it is consciously expiated. Hence the importance of his ritual chastisement; it covers (from himself) a deeper refusal to bow low. Hence, too, the division in his mind, which intends on the one hand "deepest passion" in its bowing low and yet is aware of the triteness and the ritual conventionality of the gesture. "I mourn *because* I mourned no more": as in the Vale text, grief is a "mighty debt"—something owed, not felt, or felt only because it is owed. Lest it seem too schematic to speak here of conscious and unconscious, we have in a draft Wordsworth's own intuitive attribution of the "working of the spirit" to an inner conflict, unconscious and unresolved:

> When in a grove I walk whose lofty trees
> Laden with all their summer foliage, rock
> High over head those workings of the mind
> Of source and tendency to me unknown,
> Some inward agitations thence are brought
> Efforts and struggles tempered and restrained
> By melancholy, awe or pleasing fear.[12]

The last line of the draft employs the very diction of the negative sublime in its third, or resolution, phase. But the "inward agitations" derive from a source, the locus of visionary power, which is prior to that resolution and in fact resists it, so that these agitations must be "tempered and restrained" as by a God who awes and corrects.

We are now perhaps in need of drawing back and assuming a perspective from which the pattern exhibited in the spots of time can be seen in relief. Both spots of time locate the visionary—the phase in which the mind is lord and master—just "this side" of the order of the signifier ("characters," "indisputable shapes") in the liminal space where the signifier appears but is not yet fully—consciously—read. Yet the spatial metaphor may distract us; in so crucial a matter it is wise to guard against being traduced by the specious simplicity of a diagram. For the liminal space of the visionary is also a liminal moment, and a moment not before but *after* the threshold has been repressed in retreat. In the first case, the flight from the word and the extraordinary seeing attending it are represented quite literally, though it is the figurative flight which we have now in view. (According to Freud, flight is the prototype of repression.[13]) The signified of those characters—death—is repressed in this flight, but it thereupon reappears in the imaginary order, in the landscape as invested by "visionary dreariness." In the case of the holiday vigil, the flight is much subtler: it is both revealed and covered by the acceptance of a guilt for which the cause remains obscured and unacknowledged. This permits a return to the "kindred spectacles and sounds," as if the intimations of death with which they were imbued could be detached and exorcised through a ritualized guilt.

We may now return to our initial perplexity with some chance of enhanced understanding. How is it that the spots of time retain a "renovating virtue," a therapeutic efficacy? Not, it would appear, because they "give / Profoundest knowledge" of the mind's great power—that feature of them merely marks those "passages of life" in which the spirit is likely to be found lurking. The spots of time revive the mind because through them the ego returns, in retrospection, to the liminal place where "some working of the spirit, / Some inward agitations" still are active. It is true that the liminal place is the very locus of the visionary, but we have seen that visionary salience is itself a dialectical response to the order of symbol. The symbol— the image as symbol or signifier—is glimpsed, and the power of the subsequent visionary state depends upon the repression of the signified, which reappears, as by a profound logic or economy, in the protective domain of things seen. It follows that the reviving of the imaginative power which the spots of time effect depends upon the continued repression of the signified. If the "source and tendency" of those "workings of the mind" were to become known to Wordsworth, no "inward agitations," no "Efforts and struggles" could thence be brought; there would be no correspondent breeze answering the "strong wind" without. Both within themselves, as coherent memory-fantasies, and within the poem, as episodes in the project of recollection, the spots of time dramatize a saving resistance to the passage from image to symbol. This resistance is the imagination—a higher, "visionary" seeing whose very intensity, either as salience or as "redundant energy," occludes the symbol.

INTERLUDE: THE WORDSWORTHIAN DARKNESS

It is tempting to retreat from the complexity of this structure to texts outside *The Prelude*, wherein the threshold between image and symbol is more simply manifested. In "Tintern Abbey," for example, we recognize the crossing of that threshold "With some uncertain notice" when the image of "wreaths of smoke / Sent up, in silence, from among the trees!" becomes a sign. As a sign it demands not merely to be seen but to be read, and reading it involves imputing an intentionality "behind" the sign,

> ... as might seem
> Of vagrant dwellers in the houseless woods,

Or of some Hermit's cave, where by his fire
The Hermit sits alone.
     [19–22]

The rhythm of seeing ("Once again I see") is broken in this simple surmise, which nevertheless moves Wordsworth uncertainly beyond the security of the visible, so that the poem comes to a dead halt. The saving externality of things depends upon their remaining images, and the "abyss of idealism" Wordsworth feared may often be recognized at the point, the fixating spot, where things come to signify.

Yet it is the main drama of *The Prelude* which necessarily solicits us, for we have rendered only a few of its episodes. That death somehow embodied in the mystery of words still remains opaque to our effort of elucidation. It is not that we cannot find evidence at what is called the "thematic" level of the connection between death and the word: there is a range of intriguing evidence in book 5, the book on "Books," alone. If we approach that book as fundamentalists—and we must always, I think, begin as literalists in reading Wordsworth—we will soon be baffled by the very explicitness of the opening theme: Poetry versus apocalypse. And it is Poetry literalized—the very book-ness, the pages and print of it, the frail shrines, "Poor earthly casket of immortal verse" (5.164)—which is threatened by a very literal Apocalypse. The actual man Wordsworth wept to read in Milton of the destruction of paradise by the flood;[14] the Wordsworth of this book contemplates "in soberness the approach / Of an event so dire, by signs in earth / Or heaven made manifest" (5.157–59). The violent fate of Nature and implicitly of natural man causes him no apparent anxiety:

A thought is with me sometimes, and I say,—
Should the whole frame of earth by inward throes
Be wrenched, or fire come down from far to scorch
Her pleasant habitations, and dry up
Old Ocean, in his bed left singed and bare,
Yet would the living Presence still subsist
Victorious, and composure would ensue,
And kindlings like the morning—presage sure
Of day returning and of life revived.
     [5.29–37]

How out of line is the indifference—or the confidence—with the Wordsworth of the other books! I put this impressionistically, but as fundamentalists our attention will be caught by dissonance more precise and

yet more strange within the dream of the Arab itself. The Arab says the shell
of poetry

> ... was a god, yea many gods,
> Had voices more than all the winds, with power
> To exhilarate the spirit, and to soothe,
> Through every clime, the heart of human kind.
>   [5.106–9]

But what does the shell of poetry actually say? When Wordsworth held it to
his ear, he "heard that instant in an unknown tongue," which yet he
understood,

> ... articulate sounds,
> A loud prophetic blast of harmony;
> An Ode, in passion uttered, which foretold
> Destruction to the children of the earth
> By deluge, now at hand....
>   [5.93–98]

Where is the power, claimed by the Arab, to exhilarate and to soothe? In
truth, one cannot read a dream as a literalist because the first thing one learns
about dreams is that they distort, sometimes unrecognizably, the thoughts,
wishes, and fears that are their motive or cause. Wordsworth the dreamer
and Wordsworth the teller of the dream would like to cleave unto the Arab's
view of poetry, but the deeper truth of the dream is that poetry is allied to
apocalyptic destruction—a connection clearly signified as prophecy. Poetry
is not threatened by Apocalypse: poetry threatens Apocalypse, at least insofar
as it is prophetic poetry. In this light, Wordsworth's odd solicitude for print
and pages—as his friend says, "in truth / 'Twas going far to seek disquietude"
(5.52–53)—begins to look like a reversal masking his fear of poetry itself.

A fear of poetry itself—this surely requires explanation. Poetry, in the
opening of book 5, is specifically the poetry of great precursors
("Shakespeare or Milton, labourers divine!" [5.165]). Wordsworth's
interpretation of the dream neatly reverses his fear of being annihilated by
this poetry into a concern, a "fond anxiety" (5.160), for its survival and
continued power. The very literalness of the Apocalypse here envisaged
locates the source of his real anxiety with respect to the great poets of the
past. The mystery embodied in their words is still a literal one; their archaic
power comes from the fact that their prophecy points to a literal fulfillment,
just as what the shell utters is even "now at hand." Their word is, or is in

touch with, the Word. More than the enlightened conditions of belief, more than the general and gregarious advance of intellect makes this impossible for Wordsworth. It is a question, not of scepticism, which can be (as in Keats) generous and liberal, but of fear. As the first great humanizer of the mystery, Wordsworth has priority, but his very priority exposes him to the terror and the literalness of the archaic sublime. (Hence he can become, as it were, Keats's stalking horse, shielding the later poet from the baleful radiance of Milton's awful certainties.) As post-Enlightenment poets, Wordsworth and Keats have come to the same point, but not at the same time:

> This Chamber of Maiden Thought becomes gradually darken'd and at the same time on all sides of it many doors are set open— but all dark—all leading to dark passages—We see not the ballance of good and evil. We are in a Mist—*We* are now in that state—*We* feel the "burden of the Mystery," To this Point was Wordsworth come, as far as I can conceive when he wrote 'Tintern Abbey' and it seems to me that his Genius is explorative of those dark Passages. Now if we live, and go on thinking, we too shall explore them. He is a Genius and superior [to] us, in so far as he can, more than we, make discoveries, and shed a light in them—Here I must think Wordsworth is deeper than Milton.[15]

Wordsworth can make discoveries in those dark passages, but they are discoveries of depth, of thinking into the human heart, not of power. When Keats in *The Fall of Hyperion* finds himself in the terrain of mystery, the meal has already been tasted and discarded, the apparatus of the sacred lies "All in a mingled heap confus'd," and he learns from Moneta that the major event, the disenthronement of the archaic Titans, has long been over; tragedy for her, the event for him is already the nostalgia of wonder. He comes to witness, not to struggle—or if to struggle, it is only in order to be allowed to witness a superannuated sublime, beside "forlorn divinity, / The pale Omega of a wither'd race."[16]

Keats's situation is worth sketching, however briefly, for it enables us to plot in yet another (historical) register Wordsworth's liminal confrontation with the mystery in those dark passages. Wordsworth's fear of the word is quite specifically, though not exclusively, fear of the Word. The epiphany of the signifier intimates death (the apocalyptic destruction of nature and the natural man) because that showing forth is charged with the only creative power that is absolute—the power to create literally and the power of the literal. For what, displacements aside, is the manner of the Word? *God said, Let there be light: and there was light*: the most remembered of Longinus's examples, marked for its simplicity by Boileau. In a change of mood, from subjunctive to indicative, reality is born. That is the "Omnific Word," identified by Milton and tradition with the Son, the filial Godhead.[17] Losing just this power, Keats's fallen Saturn is pathetic:

> ... and there shall be
> Beautiful things made new for the surprise
> Of the sky-children—" So he feebly ceas'd,
> With such a poor and sickly-sounding pause,
> Methought I heard some old man of the earth
> Bewailing earthly loss; nor could my eyes
> And ears act with that pleasant unison of sense
> Which marries sweet sound with the grace of form,
> And dolorous accent from a tragic harp
> With large-limb'd visions....
> [*The Fall of Hyperion* 1. 436–45]

What Saturn says is beautiful in thought and phrase, but there is no fulfillment; hence, for Keats, he is a bad poet, depending as he does upon a power no longer there. Saturn's literal sublime is now superannuated; he lacks the subjunctive self-consciousness of the new regime, of Apollo or whoever is to succeed him, of the poetry that creates of mind and in mind alone.

The poetry of mind, reflective poetry, is always subjunctive; before every such poem there is an implicit *Let there be*. No doubt even Wordsworth was content with second place to the Godhead, if not to Milton. The terror that invests the poetry of the past with an apocalyptic aspect is not born of an obsession with priority, for Wordsworth's ambition—as well as his achievement, as Keats helps us to see—is consciously identified with his sublimation or displacement of the high argument into the mind and heart of man. There are in Wordsworth many old men of the earth bewailing earthly loss, but they are not viewed ironically or pathetically. They speak a stately speech, choice word and measured phrase, though the burden of their speech is far more humble and banal than Saturn's lament. Hence it seems to me not the necessary secondariness of either the earthly or the humanizing mind which threatens Wordsworth. It is instead the fact that the mystery still lays claim to him; it is still in the mist that he finds the power, and the power is still, as it was for Collins, "dark power." Knowledge and power are opposed in Wordsworth in a way that to Keats will seem itself archaic and rugged, superstitiously egotistical. Not only is knowledge purchased by the loss of power, but power is purchased by terror, and terror assaults the possibility of perception or insight. Here in ampler lineaments is the very structure of the negative sublime, which exists in Keats only as affectation or as a stage of the mind to be recapitulated in wonder.

Power is "dark" because it requires the assumption of an archaic guilt. In an earlier chapter we considered this accession to guilt in terms of the classical psychoanalysis of the individual, and we noted that the identification in which it is performed is always in excess. Culture is very largely constituted by this crucial supererogation, and hence it is the measure by which the merely personal history of poet or man is exceeded by his sense of destiny—what he *must* do. The inevitable symbol for the initiatory identification which founds and empowers the culture-ego is the profoundly ambivalent symbolic image of the sacrifice. This is no place to review the fascinating speculation on the founding symbol of the sacrifice which has followed in the wake of *Totem and Taboo*; nor am I competent to conduct such a review with any rigor. It is enough to note that the sacrifice, posited, no doubt mythically, as the founding moment of culture, is also the first symbolic act and thereby the origin of the symbolic order, of language in the wider sense. In any case, there is no mistaking the presence and associations of the sacrifice in Wordsworth. We have already glimpsed its aspect behind the ambivalent fixation of what Hartman calls the spot syndrome, and we have observed the alignment it suggests between the advent of the word and the ambivalent annunciation of death. But there is evidence less oblique.

In the penultimate book of *The Prelude* we find a sequence which puts back to back Wordsworth's hope, his own conception of his originality, and his fear, in all its archaic resonance. Wordsworth is celebrating, in the way that is so reassuring to him, the coincidence of Nature's humanizing project with the task of the poet; and so he comes to treat of his own special mission:

> Dearest Friend,
> Forgive me if I say that I, who long
> Had harbour'd reverentially a thought
> That Poets, even as Prophets, each with each
> Connected in a mighty scheme of truth,
> Have each for his peculiar dower, a sense
> By which he is enabled to perceive
> Something unseen before; forgive me, Friend,
> If I, the meanest of this Band, had hope
> That unto me had also been vouchsafed
> An influx, that in some sort I possess'd
> A privilege, and that a work of mine,
> Proceeding from the depth of untaught things,

Enduring and creative, might become
A power like one of Nature's.
    [1805, 12.298–312]

This is the hope: first, that there is no discontinuity between the poets, past
or present, since they are "Connected in a mighty scheme of truth"; second,
that the "influx" conveys a power not opposed to Nature but allied to her
benevolent pedagogy. And this is the astonishing sequel, which proceeds
without interval:

A power like one of Nature's. To such mood,
Once above all, a Traveller at that time
Upon the Plain of Sarum was I raised;
There on the pastoral Downs without a track
To guide me, or along the bare white roads
Lengthening in solitude their dreary line,
While through those vestiges of ancient times
I ranged, and by the solitude o'ercome,
I had a reverie and saw the past,
Saw multitudes of men, and here and there,
A single Briton in his wolf-skin vest
With shield and stone-axe, stride across the Wold;
The voice of spears was heard, the rattling spear
Shaken by arms of mighty bone, in strength
Long moulder'd of barbaric majesty.
I called upon the darkness; and it took,
A midnight darkness seem'd to come and take
All objects from my sight; and lo! again
The desart visible by dismal flames!
It is the sacrificial Altar, fed
With living men, how deep the groans, the voice
Of those in the gigantic wicker thrills
Throughout the region far and near, pervades
The monumental hillocks; and the pomp
Is for both worlds, the living and the dead.
    [1805, 12.312–36]

This is the fear. The mere entertaining of the hope (1850: "To a hope / Not
less ambitious once among the wilds / Of Sarum's Plain, my youthful spirit
was raised ..." [13.312–14]) brings as its mental consequence a vision of
archaic sacrifice. The features of the spot syndrome are here—losing the

guide ("without a track / To guide me"), the bare dreariness of the roads. But no properly visionary salience intervenes to discharge the coming intimations of death in perception or to keep Wordsworth from being overwhelmed by solitude. First, "reverie," which yields the past in its utter, archaic discontinuity ("Our dim ancestral Past in vision clear" [13.320]). Following hard on this, the very gesture of the Druid-magus:

> I called on Darkness—but before the word
> Was uttered, midnight darkness seemed to take
> All objects from my sight; and lo! again
> The Desert visible by dismal flames;
> It is the sacrificial altar....
>   [13.327–31]

Wordsworth *summons* Darkness; *he* performs the incantation, and he is moved to it by a vision of the absolute past, in which power is alienated in time ("Long moulder'd") and different in kind ("of barbaric majesty") from the "power like one of Nature's" he had just hoped for. His word is omnific, fulfilled even before it is uttered, and its fulfillment is the sacrifice, the universal, propitiatory symbol which unites "both worlds, the living and the dead."

The Salisbury vision exhibits with stunning clarity Wordsworth's ambivalent relation to the archaic power of the Word. He is in part the victim of the vision; there is naiveté in his incantation; he doesn't know what will follow. But he also participates in the power, assuming the ancient role as if it were his inevitable due. That the vision presents such a contrast to his self-conception as a poet serves to expose the partiality of that conception, though not its sincerity. The repeated plea to Coleridge ("Dearest Friend, / Forgive me") and the self-abnegation, nervous and overdone ("forgive me, Friend, / If I, the meanest of this Band, had hope ... that in some sort I possess'd / A privilege"), signal not false modesty, but fear of his own strong claim to power—and of its terrifying claim on him. After all, in such passages Coleridge stands for something within Wordsworth, who needs his own forgiveness. But it is the sequence rather than the tone which argues for Wordsworth's doubled perception of the "influx" and its cost. His ambition, consecrated to a grateful imitation of Nature's power, is betrayed by the very *idea* of power into darkness, the nonnatural or supernatural locus of power. Part of Wordsworth's greatness as a poet is the way he consistently realizes as literal episode the unconscious, figurative structure of his thought.

We associate the Wordsworthian darkness with the early work and the crisis of the poet's twenties. *The Borderers*, for example, turn; elaborately if

somewhat unconvincingly upon an expiatory sacrifice and the assumption of
guilt, which are supposed to be an initiation into power. Marmaduke is
betrayed, but clearly the program of Oswald's dark sublime engages obscure
compulsions and deep inevitabilities within him. "Power," says Wallace of
Oswald, "is life to him / And breath and being" (3.1432–33), and it is power
that Marmaduke involuntarily seeks in his acquiescence to Oswald. What he
finds is overwhelming guilt, which he, unlike Oswald, is learning to bear at
the close of the play. The crisis richly sounded in this play and in the work,
like *Guilt and Sorrow*, of the same period seems to have a generic status.

Even Wordsworth's descents to gothic claptrap are charged with the
resonance of his mediate historical position, and this is so from the
beginning. Twenty-five lines into *The Vale of Esthwaite* the essential pattern
appears:

> At noon I hied to gloomy glades,
> Religious woods and midnight shades,
> Where brooding Superstition frown'd
> A cold and awful horror round,
> While with black arm and bending head
> She wove a stole of sable thread.
> And hark! the ringing harp I hear
> And lo! her druid sons appear.
> Why roll on me your glaring eyes?
> Why fix on me for sacrifice?
>   [25–34][18]

The poet initiates a movement to the darkness specifically of superstition,
and this search for a chilling thrill coincides with a quest for the source of
poetic power. (The terrifying harps of *The Vale* are eventually named as "the
poet's harp of yore" [l. 335].) He finds the power all right, and its immediate
aspect of sacrifice. Observe, in the continuation, the mode of his saving
enlightenment:

> But he, the stream's loud genius, seen
> The black arch'd boughs and rocks between
> That brood o'er one eternal night,
> Shoots from the cliff in robe of white.
>   [35–38]

"*But* he": the threatening, archaic druids are naturalized, *seen* (eventually as a
stream) through the mediate idea of the *genius loci*; in another manuscript the

transition from sound to sight, from ghost to landscape, is less secure, for "the stream's loud genius" is "the torrent's yelling spectre." The venturing into terror followed by a saving sharpness of sight (prototype of the imagination's salience) already dominates the structure of *The Vale*, as a kind of systole and diastole. At such moments Wordsworth seems to recapitulate and perform the Enlightenment all on his own.

The early Wordsworth can here only be invoked, not responsibly reviewed. The material is far too rich and extensive for an interlude. Moreover, our central subject is not the themes of the Wordsworthian darkness but the dialectical role of that darkness in occasioning and charging the recoil of extraordinary seeing which Wordsworth names "Imagination." Our structure invites us to consider two movements, as it were, within it; these movements correspond to two phases of a quest, as well as to the opposed directions taken by the argument of *The Prelude* and its implicit therapy, its search for efficacious spirit. First, there is a movement *toward* power, from image to symbol, from ordinary seeing, through self-consciousness (ambition), to the locus or spot of power, manifested in a symbol of sacrifice and guilt. Second, there is a movement, the Imagination's proper movement, *away* from power, from symbol back to image: this is the humanizing direction Wordsworth consciously celebrates in his claim that the Imagination is redemptive.

Wordsworth wants to persuade himself and us that the second movement is the genuine one for mind, for the mind so conceived will feed on power without being threatened or annihilated by it. In the climax of this movement at Snowdon we are given

> ... the emblem of a mind
> That feeds upon infinity, that broods
> Over the dark abyss, intent to hear
> Its voices issuing forth to silent light
> In one continuous stream....
>   [14.70–74]

The mind with this intent will hear the astounding roar of "torrents, streams / Innumerable" mounting through the "fixed, abysmal, gloomy, breathing-place" to be converted into sight (14.58–60). In 1805 the emblem was

> The perfect image of a mighty Mind,
> Of one that feeds upon infinity,
> That is exalted by an under-presence,
> The sense of God, or whatso'er is dim

>   Or vast in its own being....
>   [1805, 13.69–73]

The Godhead and the unconscious depths are here significantly allied as the "under-presence," of source and tendency unknown, which powers the mind into its exaltation. The search for power enters the abyss, the "deep and gloomy breathing-place" or "dark deep thoroughfare" (1805, 13.57, 64), from the opposite direction and with the intent not of converting power into exaltation but of finding the voice absolutely strong, the archaic voice of the Godhead.

No doubt Wordsworth does persuade himself and us. But we remain haunted by what still haunts him, and we know that the dark passage leads in both directions. If Wordsworth could, as Keats said, "shed a light" in those dark passages, he was also strong enough to call on Darkness. The paradox thus roughly thrust into view is that Wordsworth's search for efficacious power was opposed to the humanizing originality which was his historical opportunity and necessity. The Snowdon vision does not cancel the opposite motion of the spots of time. We read poetry both for the exaltation of wisdom and for the renovation of power, and I, for one, would not know how to choose between the two.

CROSSING THE THRESHOLD

Of all the "passages of life" recorded and explored in *The Prelude*, the Simplon Pass passage in book 6 is the most spectacular.[19] It looms up in the middle of the poem, unforeseen but somehow inevitable, a paradigm of the Wordsworthian threshold and hence the very type of Romantic transcendence. And yet within this passage lurks perplexity which seems to resist the light of interpretation.

Wordsworth's recollection approaches his memory of the Simplon Pass with some foreboding. He comes to it naturally enough in the course of retracing the walking tour he and Robert Jones had taken through the Alps in the summer of 1790. In what he calls "the eye and progress of my Song" (1805, 6.526), his day in the Simplon Pass (August 16) follows the Grande Chartreuse, Mont Blanc, and Chamounix, as it had on the tour, but something distinguishes it in his recollection, a "dejection," a "deep and genuine sadness" (1805, 6.491–92). In lines (6.562 ff.) conspicuously matter-of-fact (considering what is to follow), he describes how he and Jones had mounted up the rugged road of Simplon and stopped for lunch. Here they were rather hastily abandoned by their muleteer guides, and when they resumed their hike the path led downward to a stream and seemed to go no

further. Deliberating awhile, they crossed the stream and took a path that
pointed upward, but after climbing for an hour and a half or so "anxious
fears" beset them, and they began to realize that they were lost. They met a
peasant who confirmed their fears and worse: he told them they had to return
to the perplexing spot and then go downwards, following the stream.
Without knowing it, they had already crossed the summit; evidently it was a
cloudy, rainy day, and the heights were obscured. Their immense
disappointment at this news is the "sadness" still alive in the mind of the poet
as he remembers and writes fourteen years later.

> Loth to believe what we so grieved to hear,
> For still we had hopes that pointed to the clouds,
> We questioned him again, and yet again;
> But every word that from the peasant's lips
> Came in reply, translated by our feelings,
> Ended in this,—that *we had crossed the Alps.*
>   [6.586–91]

But they hadn't really "crossed" the Alps; the most difficult stretch, the
treacherous defile of Gondo Gorge, lay just ahead, though downwards. The
tidings of the peasant had depressed them, but "The dull and heavy
slackening ... Was soon dislodg'd" (1805, 6.549–61): in the mixed metaphor,
power or energy emigrates from their suddenly relaxed will and acts as if
from without upon their mental state, which is now an obstacle to be
"dislodg'd." Yet at first the power seems still theirs, for they act precipitously:

> ... downwards we hurried fast,
> And enter'd with the road which we had miss'd
> Into a narrow chasm; the brook and road
> Were fellow-travellers in this gloomy Pass,
> And with them did we journey several hours
> At a slow step.
>   [1805, 6.551–56]

Their hurrying downward is checked; they must submit to the pace of brook
and road, their new guides. Losing their former guides, they had "paced the
beaten downward way" (l. 568) and had come to a perplexing spot (l. 580)
where "After little scruple, and short pause" (1805, l. 507) they had made an
error. They had failed to read the perplexing spot correctly—to recognize
their new "fellow-travellers"—choosing instead to follow "hopes that
pointed to the clouds," a kind of impulse toward origins and ultimates in

contrast to the possibility of the stream intercepted in mid course. Their "crossing" of the "unbridged stream" was premature—an unwitting evasion, under the aegis of hope, of the larger crossing (of the Alps) in which they were engaged.

The text that follows has become such a set piece of the sublime that a special effort is required to recover its contextual or experiential dimension. Max Wildi's photographic reconstruction of the fateful hours spent in the Gorge of Gondo makes the travelers' lack of anticipation or forewarning plausible enough.[20] What is less clear is how, with the memory of the spectacular ravine in mind, Wordsworth in 1804 could have approached the Simplon adventure possessed by the "deep and genuine sadness" of his disappointment. There is a genuine problem here, the tip of an iceberg, I think; but even apart from perplexities of sequence the passages offers a difficult grandeur. This is simply not the way Wordsworth writes or thinks, not his kind of greatness:

> The immeasurable height
> Of woods decaying, never to be decayed,
> The stationary blasts of waterfalls,
> And in the narrow rent at every turn
> Winds thwarting winds, bewildered and forlorn,
> The torrents shooting from the clear blue sky,
> The rocks that muttered close upon our ears,
> Black drizzling crags that spake by the way-side
> As if a voice were in them, the sick sight
> And giddy prospect of the raving stream,
> The unfettered clouds and region of the Heavens,
> Tumult and peace, the darkness and the light—
> Were all like workings of one mind, the features
> Of the same face, blossoms upon one tree;
> Characters of the great Apocalypse,
> The types and symbols of Eternity,
> Of first, and last, and midst, and without end.
>   [6.624–40]

The aspect of Eternity checks and supersedes the evidence of things seen, so that the image of process, change, or motion evokes and indeed signifies its supratemporal contrary. The woods themselves are decaying, but decay itself is eternal: in the aspect of Eternity there is no past or future tense. Water itself falls, but falling itself is "stationary." The elements of nature come and go, passing through the *order* of nature which, abstracted, is Eternity.

The order of Eternity is synchronic, and what Wordsworth earlier calls "the speaking face of earth and heaven" (5.13) participates in that order not substantially, but typologically or symbolically—insofar as, image becoming symbol, phenomena are *read*. At the "level" of perception—at once the human, the imaginative, and the natural domain—things confound themselves ("Winds thwarting winds, bewildered and forlorn"), confusing the perceiver. But this very confusion signifies oneness ("one mind ... the same face ... one tree"). Signification here, as always, is not "natural" in the sense that the image participates its meaning: nothing in the self-thwarting winds or in "Tumult and peace, the darkness and the light" conduces perceptionally to oneness. Hence the passage cannot be read phenomenologically, as we nearly always read Wordsworth. We are oddly closer to the Mutability Cantos than to the Snowdon vision. In any case, we are outside the precincts of Imagination, whose conferring, abstracting, and modifying powers—"alternations proceeding from, and governed by, a sublime consciousness of the soul in her own mighty and almost divine powers"[21]—are always transitive operations upon the initially visible, though they may lead to infinitude. The structure of the passage is not immanence but double vision, with the leap of signification between its two terms. This massive sentence pivots rhetorically upon a highly deliberate simile, which itself subverts the metaphoric potentialities of perception.

For the one mind, face, tree, signified in the landscape is not in any meaningful sense human, not is it here claimed as human possibility. The allusions to the Godhead, biblical and Miltonic, are unusually direct: this is the only occurrence of the word "Apocalypse" in Wordsworth's poetry, and he ends the passage by aligning it conspicuously with Adam and Eve's morning hymn to the Creator, "Him first, him last, him midst, and without end" (*PL* 5.165). Perhaps an aggressive humanism such as Hegel's could here claim the Godhead as its own archaic aspect, but that is just the claim the poet himself foregoes. In a letter to Dorothy three weeks after his experience of the Gorge, Wordsworth comes in his narrative to the Simplon Pass and remarks that "the impressions of three hours of our walk among the Alps will never be effaced." At the lake of Como, he goes on to say, he felt "complacency of Spirit ... a thousand dreams of happiness" associated with the "social affections," and it was impossible not to contrast this mood "with the sensations I had experienced two or three days before, in passing the Alps.... Among the more awful scenes of the Alps, I had not a thought of man, or a single created being; my whole soul was turned to him who produced the terrible majesty before me."[22] Nothing in *The Prelude* text suggests that his soul is not still so turned toward the Godhead as he remembers the event and writes some years later.

The passage may strike us as archaic not only in its embrace of traditional ontology but also in its surprising lack of self-consciousness. In the style, for example: the Shakespearean doublets ("the sick sight / And giddy prospect of the raving stream, / The unfettered clouds and region of the Heavens") suggest an amplitude which retards the progress toward climax by detemporalizing it, so that the order of description already subtly leaves the chronicle of experience for the reflective order of Eternity. The climax itself—

Tumult and peace, the darkness and the light—
Were all like ...

—is not revelation, a lifting of the mask, but the merest sliding over the threshold into interpretation. The mounting rhythm of perception is then discharged in the subsequent phrases and the very variety of alternatives they enlist: "workings ... features ... blossoms ... Characters ... types and symbols." In a sense, however, the perceptional *gradatio* is illusory, for the interpretative (symbolic) order has already been the aspect of these images: "were all along like" rather than "now suddenly became." In style as well as in thought the "I"—with its characteristic effect of making the progress of the verse the very dramatic progress of a consciousness—has disappeared. Not Wordsworth's kind of greatness.

We wonder, in fact, where the "I" has gone. What kind of experience, after all, is it for the travelers? The strait is "gloomy" (622); in the night to come, "innocent sleep" will "Lie melancholy among weary bones" (6.647–48). De Selincourt finds here an echo of the horror of the regicide Macbeth ("Methought, I heard a voice cry, 'Sleep no more! / Macbeth does murder Sleep,'—the innocent Sleep;"[23]), but that dark suggestion seems to me dubious. Evidently something terrible did happen on that day or night. In 1820, with Dorothy and Mary in tow, Wordsworth revisited the "dreary mansion" where he and Jones had spent that night. Dorothy refers in her journal to the "awful night" of thirty years before and adds mysteriously that the two travelers were "unable to sleep from other causes" than the deafening roar to which *The Prelude* account ascribes their insomnia. She felt a strong desire to know this place, but Wordsworth could not be persuaded to accompany her within. He refused to enter.[24] Wildi concludes that the youth had suffered "some kind of traumatic experience"[25]—which is to say that we don't know and no doubt never will. But the biographical mystery need not distract us from what *may* be its refraction in the bland of soul, the absence of self-consciousness, that the passage about types and symbols exhibits.

It is difficult to see in any case how the three hours spent in the ravine—gloomy, terrifying, and spectacular as we know it to have been—could have slipped Wordsworth's mind in his preoccupation, fourteen years later, with the "dejection," the "deep and genuine sadness," of his disappointment at Simplon. We hear, nothing of this disappointment in the contemporary letter to Dorothy, which twice verbally associates the *passing of the Alps* with the sensations and impressions, never to be effaced, of Gondo Gorge. Wildi's reconstruction of the fateful afternoon shows how immediately the gorge follows the actual summit of the pass—a matter of a few minutes, if they hadn't taken the wrong path; the two halves of the total crossing could not have been disjoined in a memory fourteen years later without a powerful secondary motive.

I propose, therefore, that the remembered disappointment—"*that we had crossed the Alps*"—is in fact a screen memory drastically inflated (if not created) in order to block the emergence of the deeper, more terrifying and traumatic memory of Gondo Gorge. The structure of the remembered disappointment and its details—pacing the downward way, crossing the unbridged stream, attempting to translate and interpret the speech of the peasant—suggest that it is a wishful parody of the larger actual crossing, the passing through the gorge itself. Hence the phrase, *that we had crossed the Alps*, with its signal emphasis, fulfills a wish under the mask of a disappointment—the wish to have already passed or crossed the defile looming subliminally before the "eye and progress" of the retrospective song. Probably Wordsworth did meet a peasant and was disappointed, but the experience has been retrospectively augmented and seems to be attracting to itself the emotional valence ("anxious fears") we might have expected to be associated with the gorge. Indeed, if we are prepared to read Wordsworth with the psychological sophistication he invites, we should have to view somewhat sceptically the very matter-of-fact clarity in his memory of getting lost. Not merely the significance of the memory emerged as he was writing in 1804. The memory itself *may* have been formed at this time—to what degree we certainly cannot tell, though we can speculate with more assurance that the affective quality of the event, the deep sadness, came into being retrospectively.

Yet this hypothesis must be cleared of several apparent objections. That the very "impressions" the traveler Wordsworth said would "never be effaced" should much later have been temporarily blocked ought to cause us no difficulty unless we insist absurdly that a man of thirty-four remain consistent to the predictions of his twenty-first year; moreover, those impressions were not in any sense effaced, but displaced and momentarily repressed. (In this connection it is curious that the Ravine of Gondo is conspicuously absent from *Descriptive Sketches* [composed 1791–92], which covers nearly everything else on the Alpine tour: perhaps the "blocking" began thus early.) A second difficulty has a more substantial aspect. In 1845 Wordsworth published the "Characters of the great Apocalypse" passage (6.621–40) under the title "The Simplon Pass," and gave 1799 as the date of its composition.[26] By 1845, however, Wordsworth was notoriously unreliable about dates. De Selincourt was justly sceptical, and Wordsworth's most exact chronologist has since concluded that the passage was probably composed in 1804, in sequence with the rest of book 6.[27] The passage is entirely unlike anything Wordsworth wrote in 1799, and there is no evidence to corroborate the guess of the poet nearly half a century later.[28] Moreover, if "The Simplon Pass" was composed in 1799, the deep disappointment remembered by the poet as his song approached the pass becomes still harder to explain, and in a sense the hypothesis of a screen memory would be plausible *a fortiori*.

A third objection is indeed substantial, for it has been dramatized by the very course of our analysis. We found in the "Characters" passage a notable absence of self-consciousness, a soul turned wholly toward the original Maker and the terrible majesty of his signifying creation. Yet we have argued that the poet's actual impressions of Gondo Gorge were traumatic enough to have caused their threatened emergence to be blocked by a memory of disappointment. Can these two readings possibly be reconciled? We should have to suppose that for Wordsworth the greatest threat was the experience which denied him the possibility of self-consciousness.

We have already come to such a supposition following the path of theory through the negative sublime. We may recall that the sensible imagination (here the mental eye of retrospection) is checked in an experience of exhaustion or terror as it attempts to comprehend the relative infinity of phenomena. An "identification" with the higher power—ultimately with the Godhead—is required in order to cross the threshold into the domain of the supersensible, and this identification requires the suppression or turning against the narcissistic self-consciousness associated with perception. Hence the sensible imagination is depressed; it feels a sacrifice or deprivation of its "hopes that pointed to the clouds." Such, at any rate, was Kant's theory, and it helped us to locate the terror precisely at the threshold of the supersensible—*sublimen*, as the etymology oddly (and no doubt fortuitously) confirms: the ego is terrified into annihilating its sensible portion. In Burke and elsewhere we found the structure of the negative sublime converging with the drama of poetic influence, which finds its archetype in the relation of the human imagination to the "Omnific Word," the absolute originality, of the Godhead. In the light of this theory, here too roughly reprised, we can speculate about the grounds of Wordsworth's terror. To reenter Gondo Gorge in memory would have exposed him to the extinction of the self-consciousness with which he identified imagination and originality. To remember a disappointment, however, enabled this threat to be usurped and displaced and had as well the advantage, as we must now proceed to appreciate, of confirming his consciousness of self.

Yet the objection still points to two readings of the event, and still carries force. It has merely been reformulated, not answered. For evidently, Wordsworth was *not* halted at the threshold of the symbolic order, even by his own screen memory. He did cross the passage through the types and symbols of eternity. It is no longer possible to suppress what may be the most important element of the whole sequence, the astonishing intervention between "*that we had cross'd the Alps*" (1805, 6.524) and "The dull and heavy slackening that ensued / Upon those tidings by the Peasant given / Was soon dislog'd" (1805, 6.549–51). As he remembers and writes in 1804 Wordsworth is suddenly interrupted:

> Imagination! lifting up itself
> Before the eye and progress of my Song
> Like an unfather'd vapour; here that Power,
> In all the might of its endowments, came
> Athwart me; I was lost as in a cloud,
> Halted, without a struggle to break through.
> And now recovering, to my Soul I say
> I recognise thy glory....
>   [1805, 6.525–32]

The "eye and progress" of the song is nothing more or less than the mental journey of retrospection which we know is just on the verge of coming to Gondo Gorge. The Imagination rises athwart this progress: this can only be a moment, how long we do not know, of amnesia. The memory of the next steps, the fateful hours in Gondo Gorge, is blocked again, more directly and violently. It is as if the screen memory of disappointment were not enough, as if it did not work: the Imagination operates first *through* memory, and then, this failing, *against* memory, and with such intensity as to occlude sight. The Imagination rises in flight from the Word; or (in another metaphor) in resistance to the showing forth of the Word. We have seen the pattern before, in the spots of time passages and in particular in the boy's flight from the "Characters ... fresh and visible" (12.245) which signified a death and a sacrifice.

What then is this "awful Power" which Wordsworth names "Imagination"? In the late version, Wordsworth will tell us that the power is "so called / Through sad incompetence of human speech" (6.592–93), but the name is of course entirely right, for the power of sight does rise in intensity from memory through salience to the occlusion of the visible. The Imagination may be structurally defined as a power of resistance to the Word, and in this sense it coincides exactly with the psychological necessity of originality. But a structural definition merely locates an experience; as an experience or moment the Imagination is an extreme consciousness of self mounting in dialectical recoil from the extinguishing of the self which an imminent identification with the symbolic order enjoins. Hence the Imagination rises "Like an unfather'd vapour": it is at once the ego's need and its attempt to be *unfathered*, to originate itself and thereby refuse acknowledgment to a superior power. The Imagination is not an evasion of the oedipus complex but a rejection of it. From a certain perspective (such perspective, for example, as is implied by the history of poetic influence) that rejection is purely illusory, a fiction. To reject the oedipus complex is not, after all, to dispel it. But the fiction is a necessary and saving one; it founds the self and secures the possibility—the chance for a self-conviction—of originality. And so Wordsworth can turn to his "conscious soul" (1850) and say, "I recognise thy glory."

We might speculate along lines suggested by Harold Bloom in *The Anxiety of Influence* that something like the distortion evident in the construction of a screen memory characterizes the poet's first line of defense against the identification which would absorb him into his precursor. But the Imagination as it is defined dramatically in the Simplon sequence is the poet's ultimate defense, the final foundation of his individuality. Hence it is the expression of a wish deeper than anxiety, an answer, therefore, to terror. Wordsworth was "Halted, without a struggle to break through" (1805, 6.530): he made no "effort" (1850) to break through because the usurpation answered a need deeper than the rhythm of his retrospective progress; such defenses are final. In life, it is our defenses that enable us to exist and therefore to create; so in poetry, the fiction of originality founds a poet. That the critic must be aware of the dialectical, "negative" structure of originality is precisely what separates his perspective from the poet's. For the critic the fiction of originality can never be a final term, but this situation does not render the power of the founding fiction any the less efficacious.

The Imaginations usurpation issues for Wordsworth in triumphant self-recognition and self-vindication: "to my Soul I say / I recognise thy glory." The lines which follow spill over from this climatic moment, and they are justly celebrated. But they need to be read as a response not only to the remembered disappointment but also to the anxiety of self-effacement associated with the memory of Gondo Gorge, the memory the Imagination rose to occlude. We need to recover the "negativity" of these lines, the presence in them of what is being magnificently denied:

> ... in such strength
> Of usurpation, when the light of sense
> Goes out, but with a flash that has revealed
> The invisible world, doth greatness make abode,
> There harbours; whether we be young or old,
> Our destiny, our being's heart and home,
> Is with infinitude, and only there;
> With hope it is, hope that can never die,
> Effort, and expectation, and desire,
> And something evermore about to be.
> Under such banners militant, the soul
> Seeks for no trophies, struggles for no spoils
> That may attest her prowess, blest in thoughts
> That are their own perfection and reward,
> Strong in herself and in beatitude
> That hides her, like the mighty flood of Nile
> Poured from his fount of Abyssinian clouds
> To fertilise the whole Egyptian plain.
> [6.599–616]

Where the usurpation is strong, there "greatness" lies; not in the "invisible world" itself, but this side of the supersensible threshold, in a domain properly human. Yet the movement here, from the "light of sense" through the blinding usurpation of Imagination to infinitude, somehow evades or leaps over the mediating signs or characters which abide at the threshold. This is the unmediated path of imagination, from sight to the invisible without the necessity of a signifier. Phenomena can drop away without first becoming signs: Eternity without types and symbols, apocalypse without the characters. Following this path the soul has no anxiety of originality, it "Seeks for no trophies, struggles for no spoils / That may attest her prowess," because it is "Strong in herself" and because the affective exaltation of the self, its beatitude" or "access of joy" (1805) "hides" the soul. "Hides" hints ever so slightly at the necessity of a fiction sustained by joy, without which the soul would lie like a barren plain.[29]

But we cannot expect a poet to subvert his own most fortunate and saving illusion, and the passage is overwhelmingly positive in its claims and its tone. Hence it is that Wordsworth's amnesia is dispelled, and he could go on to Gondo Gorge. The terror of that defile has been answered; with such assurance behind him he could confront and momentarily disappear before the awful characters. In a way the "types and symbols" passage returns to answer and deny the great claims born of Imagination, as it had itself been answered by the Imagination. No moment of consciousness unites the two passages, or the two kinds of greatness they imply. They remain dialectically confronted, side by side in the center of Wordsworth's greatest poem, the positive and negative poles of the Romantic sublime.

NOTES

1. MS. V, *The Prelude*, p. 39.

2. The Prelude, p. 445, app. crit.

3. "Screen Memories," *The Standard Edition of the Complete Psychological Works of Sigmund Freud*, ed. James Strachey et al., 23 vols. (London, 1953–66), III, 322.

4. The Fall of Hyperion, 1.13–15.

5. Geoffrey Hartman, *Wordsworth's Poetry, 1787–1814* (New Haven, 1964), p. 65.

6. *The Prelude*, p. 163.

7. MS. V, *The Prelude*, p. 447.

8. See M. H. Abrams, "The Correspondent Breeze: A Romantic Metaphor," in *English Romantic Poets: Modern Essays in Criticism*, ed. M. H. Abrams (New York, 1960), pp. 37–54 esp. 40–42.

9. *Hamlet*, 1.4.43–44.

10. See Mary Moorman, *William Wordsworth, a Biography: The Early Years, 1770–1803* (Oxford, 1957), pp. 67–70, esp. 68 n.

11. *PWW*, I, 270–83.

12. *The Prelude*, p. 452.

13. "Repression," *Standard Edition*, XIV, 146–58.

14. See Dorothy's journal entry for Tuesday, February 2, 1802, in *Journals of Dorothy Wordsworth*, ed. Mary Moorman (Oxford, 1972). p. 84: "After tea I read aloud the 11th Book of Paradise Lost. We were much impressed and also melted into tears. The papers came in soon after I had laid aside the Book—a good thing for my William." The theme is finely explored by Neil Hertz, "Wordsworth and the Tears of Adam," *Studies in Romanticism*, 7 (1967), 15–33; reprinted in *Wordsworth: A Collection of Critical Essays*, ed. M. H. Abrams (Englewood Cliffs, N.J., 1972), pp. 107–22.

15. *The Letters of John Keats, 1814–1821*, ed. Hyder Edward Rollins, 2 vols. (Cambridge, Mass., 1958), I, 281.

16. Quotations from *The Fall of Hyperion* 1.78, 287–88.

17. See *PL* 7.163 ff.

18. *PWW*, 1, 270.

19. The Simplon sequence is an inevitable occasion in the many discussions of the Wordsworthian imagination and the sublime. The preeminence of Hartman's reading (in *Wordsworth's Poetry*, pp. 39–69) has not in my view been seriously touched by the attempts of subsequent commentators to elide the significance of the Imagination's usurpation at 6.592 ff. My reading is intended to complement Hartman's definition of the Imagination as "consciousness of self raised to apocalyptic pitch" (p. 17) by uncovering the dialectical

status of that consciousness not only with respect to Nature but also with respect to the symbolic order of Eternity. In one sense this makes Imagination a middle term—for the critic, not for the poet. In another sense the Imagination is the final term of this dialectic, for it follows and responds to an intuition—strangely "traumatic" in Wordsworth—of the Word. At all events, the Imagination must certainly be considered in its dialectical "negativity" if we would attend to what Wordsworth does and what happens to him as well as what he says. Hartman brilliantly and persuasively redefines apocalyptic "to characterize any strong desire to cast out nature and to achieve an unmediated contact with the principle of things" (p. x). In the following reading I emphasize the mediating Characters of the great Apocalypse (6.638), which appear to threaten or signify the extinction of self-consciousness as the cost of its identification with the synchronic "principle of things." I therefore neglect the relation of the Imagination to Nature, as I have no fresh light to shed on the problem and no basic objection to Hartman's formulation of it.

20. Max Wildi, "Wordsworth and the Simplon Pass," *English Studies*, 40 (1959) 224–32; see also Wildi's interpretative sequel under the same title, *English Studies*, 43 (1962) 359–77.

21. "Preface to *Poems* (1815);" in *Literary Criticism of William Wordsworth*, ed. Paul M. Zall (Lincoln, Nebr., 1966), p. 149.

22. *The Letters of William and Dorothy Wordsworth*, ed. Ernest De Selincourt, 2d ed., *The Early Years, 1787–1805*, rev. Chester L. Shaver (Oxford, 1967), pp. 33–34.

23. *Macbeth* 2.2.34–36.

24. *Journals of Dorothy Wordsworth*, ed. Ernest De Selincourt, 2 vols. (New York, 1941), II, 258.

25. Wildi, "Wordsworth and the Simplon Pass," p. 232.

26. *PWW*, II, 212. De Selincourt prints "(?1804)" next to the earlier date.

27. Mark L. Reed, *Wordsworth: The Chronology of the Early Years, 1770–1799* (Cambridge, Mass., 1967), pp. 31, 261; see also a reading of the sequence by the same author, "The Speaker of *The Prelude*," in *Bicentenary Wordsworth Studies in Memory of John Alban Finch*, ed. Jonathan Wordsworth (Ithaca, N.Y., 1970), pp. 281–87, esp. p. 286 n. 13.

28. It should be remembered that Wordsworth determined to expand his autobiographical poem and treat of the Alpine tour only in March, 1804, i.e., about a month before the sequence was written.

29. For Coleridge's tentative and interesting objection to the line (616), see *The Prelude*, p. 559.

GEOFFREY HARTMAN

"Was it for this ...?": Wordsworth and the Birth of the Gods

> Was it for this
> That one, the fairest of all rivers, loved
> To blend his murmurs with my nurse's song,
> And from his alder shades and rocky falls,
> And from his fords and shallows, sent a voice
> That flowed along my dreams?
> —THE TWO-PART *PRELUDE* OF 1799, ll. 1–6

Wordsworth's contemporary American reception has been remarkable. For, in general, he is a poet who does not travel well. The Continent still does not recognize his poetry: only his early revolutionary sympathies and illegitimate daughter stir flurries of interest. In America, however, he is taken seriously, more seriously even than in England. Wordsworth seems finally to be creating the taste by which he may be enjoyed. The growth of the poetic mind, or of the sympathetic imagination—his greatest theme—is no longer mistaken as a retreat from otherness into Englishness.

And, as the concrete jungle looks for its ecological saint, Wordsworth's reputation should soar. A *New Yorker* cartoon shows two sixties-style hippies browsing through the outdoor shelves of a bookshop. A bearded youth holds up a slim volume and declaims to his companion: "'I wandered lonely as a cloud'—Hey, wild!" Yet how many of us respond to Wordsworth's kind of

From *Romantic Revolutions: Criticism and Theory*, edited by Kenneth R. Johnston, Gilbert Chaitin, Karen Hanson, and Herbert Marks, pp. 8–25. © 1990 by Indiana University Press.

wildness rather than to Blake's or Whitman's? Our appreciation has increased, yet it is hard to pretend that his age or any age needed the story of Peter Bell the Potter or of Benjamin the Waggoner or other tales of mild idiocy, already ridiculed by Francis Jeffrey.[1] Something less than trumpets, moreover, announces Wordsworth's intended epic: can we really compare his uncertain "Was it for this" to Hölderlin's heroic-hopeful "What are poets for in a time of crisis?" Yet Hölderlin's question too betrays a doubt: it is a modified self-accusation, implying that the age demands Caesars, Napoleons, Nelsons—statesmen and prophets—not poets, and certainly not a Colin Clout "burring" verses in the Cumberland countryside.

Lewis Carroll's Wonderland parodies, placing Wordsworth into the only English tropics around, have not lost their point. They undercut his sentimental and simplistic reception, yet they confirm our sense that conformity has worsted nonconformity, until what's left are droll imaginative doodles. Even those who do not put extreme expectations on poetry have been troubled by Wordsworth's idiosyncrasy. David Ferry saw the precarious quality of his "love of man"; F. W. Bateson caught an unresolved tension between public and private, "Augustan" and "Romantic." Indeed, the charge of solipsism or egotism has never been totally laid to rest, and Jeffrey's comment remains telling. The school of Wordsworth, he said, in distinction from that of Crabbe, does not truly observe nature; its poets excite an interest for their subjects "more by an eloquent and refined analysis of their own capricious feelings, than by any obvious or intelligible ground of sympathy in their situation." All we hear of the Boy of Winander, he complained, is his pastoral game with the owls, "and for the sake of this one accomplishment, we are told that the author has frequently stood mute and gazed on his grave for half an hour altogether!"

Others too, including Coleridge, could not always discern the "intelligible ground of sympathy" that motivated Wordsworth. It may have been this disparity between object and feeling—the lack of a conventional fit between the b(l)eatings of his heart and the ordinary sight or thought, that kept his mind restless, unable to fix its "wavering balance," and obliged him to ask, anticipating Jeffrey, "Was it for this?"

* * *

Let me turn directly to that half line on which so many have commented. The absence of a clear antecedent endows the phrase with a certain independence and pathos. In MS JJ and the Two-Part *Prelude* it gets the narrative started (it is aptly called a launching pad by Kenneth Johnston), but its range of reference remains unclear. The famous verses in JJ on the "mild creative breeze" that becomes a "tempest," disturbing created things by a "redundant energy," indicate that inspiration itself, its duality, may be at issue. This early fragment, as Jonathan Wordsworth has argued, need not connect directly with "Was it for this," yet it is clear from all the versions that Wordsworth was puzzled by the twofold character—mild and wild—of nature's inspiring effect. It is also clear that he believed both types of inspiration had contributed to his growing up as a poet: he was "fostered alike by beauty and by fear" (1805 *Prelude* 1.306), and he finds it strange that so many "discordant elements" have harmonized and formed his "calm existence," one that is obviously not stable but continues to be buffetted by tempestlike motions:

> trances of thought
> And mountings of the mind compared to which
> The wind that drives along the autumnal [?leaf]
> Is meekness.
>   (JJ, 9–12)[2]

I am not confident that we can sort out, better than Wordsworth himself, who is an instinctive phenomenologist, the elements of his character that cohere so strangely. He was, like the Wanderer, a "being made of many beings." But the unsettled question of identity does merge in *The Prelude* with a question about the sources of inspiration: from what depth of otherness do they come, and what do they imply about the relation of mind to nature, even of human existence to other-than-human modes of being? These modes of the other are apostrophized rather than named, and generally they are not developed as pictures or personifications. If the early MSS use traces of the *genius loci* myth, it is because that kind of personification is ancient, allows the vocative, and does not merge beings into being. The later, more complete transformation of such genii into an entirely humanized perception is one of Wordsworth's achievements. But it would not be an achievement if it did not retain a sense that the person speaking is not the only or even major locus of being and that, conversely, the poet's mind is but a "haunt" analogous to the external world: a theater for actions and purposes of larger scope.

"Was it for this" points to this larger scope: sublime, obscure, frightening. The question responds to a demand, an incumbency. The nature of those other modes of being, of Powers and Presences, needs to be defined, together with the poet's own presence among them. He has to represent, even justify, himself. "Was it for this I came into the world?" Without falling back into a romance mode of representation, he inhabits a realm popularized by romance. These genii or Powers are ranged against the human being, who as an alien or interloper is to be admonished, conquered, seduced. "How is the 'I' to enter this scene which has no need for it and in which it has no place?"[3]

The first memory-image of the Two-Part *Prelude* counters that sense of human intrusion:

> Was it for this
> That one, the fairest of all rivers, loved
> To blend his murmurs with my Nurse's song,
> And from his alder shades, and rocky falls,
> And from his fords and shallows, sent a voice
> That flowed along my dreams?

To convey intimacy, there is a deft recomposition of the stream as a flowing voice and of the mind as penetrable. More remarkable still is a hint that we are witnessing the birth of a hero. The child who hears Derwent may be of mixed human and divine origin: his native stream, "fairest of all rivers," is like a nymph or tutelary presence or even genetrix. (Compare the heavier allegory of Romney's "Birth of Shakespeare".) The infant is surrounded from the beginning by other than purely human sounds and sights.

The doubt in "Was it for this" does not diminish, and even motivates, this depiction of a nativity, extended by *The Prelude*. Wordsworth multiplies the gifts of a magian countryside. If "sweetest Shakespeare," in Milton's phrase, was "fancy's child," Wordsworth is nature's child. And he is at pains to emphasize the softer aspects of this prolonged, generous, natural incubation. The euphemistic strain so marked and unsettling in the mature poetry is already in evidence. His native stream is "fairest" and "beauteous"; a "sweet birth-place" is evoked; the child's thoughts are "composed" "To more than infant softness"; the doublets "fords and shallows," "night and day," "fields and groves" evoke complementarity not contraries; and's and or's spring up in profusion; there is a subtle, expansive movement from "one" to "thou," from "Stream" (l. 8) to "streams" (l. 20);[4] and in "the frost and breath of frosty wind" (l. 29) something faintly adversative is at once energized and mellowed by a redundance which doubles the locus of what is later (and more philosophically) named an "active principle." The surplus rhetoric of

> Yes, I remember when the changeful earth
> And twice five seasons on my mind had stamped
> The faces of the changeful year
>   (JJ, 144–46)

is grounded in a natural surplus.

Redundance, classical periphrasis and euphemism combine to convey a multisourced principle of generosity. Sometimes even the locus of perception expands, as when Wordsworth stations the boy within a natural scenery that animatedly and eagerly offers itself. He sees, and is seen:

> The sands of Westmorland the creeks & bays
> Of Cumbria's rocky limits they can tell
> How when the sea threw off his evening shade
> And to the shepherds but beneath the craggs
> Did send sweet notice of the rising moon
> How I have stood....
>   (JJ, 152–57)

This is not the language of mystery, even if the poet does not know why he felt what he felt in moments that seemed primordial:

> How I have stood to images like this
> A stranger linking with the spectacle
> No body of associated forms
> And bearing with [me] no peculiar sense
> Of quietness or peace yet I have stood
> Even while my eye has moved oer three long leagues
> Of shining water, gathering as it seemd
> New pleasure like a bee among the flowers—
>   (JJ, 157–65)[5]

Such experiences allowed Wordsworth to record the phenomena themselves rather than what they meant. An intense outline remains; the rest, affect or meaning, has "Wearied itself out of the memory." This unintelligibility does not seem to be a burden. It is unlike "the heavy and the weary weight / Of all this unintelligible world" characterizing later experience.

Among archetypal moments more permanent than their meanings are the terrifying (wild) and calming (mild) incidents we have mentioned. Wordsworth refuses to see them as irreconcilable. He simply weathers them, and they continue to "work" on him as if he too were water, heath, or mountain. They did not resolve into, or become resolved by, thought. In that formative time the supplement of thought (an interest "unborrowed from the eye") was not there or was not needed. But at present they *are* mediated by thought, and the perplexity he expresses arises from a twofold source: (1) in the past, the fearful incidents outnumbered the calm; (2) at present, the fearful incidents have become an essential part of his "calm existence." He glimpses what the complete *Prelude* calls a "dark inscrutable workmanship" that coheres contrary experiences like music's concordant discord. Given the dominant emphasis on dissonance-resolution, the "this" could be metalinguistic and refer to a recurrent turbulence which has now taken the form of an incessant questioning. "Was it for this kind of questioning, this 'Was it for this.'"

Yet Wordsworth, as he writes on, so enhances the early moments of calm, and so euphemizes the moments of dread, that the opening question, with its hint of continuing turbulence—fretful interludes that threaten a desired equanimity—acts as if it referred to a threatening calm that borders on entropy or the grave. Already by the end of the first paragraph of the Two-Part *Prelude* we have traveled from birth to a composure that has a "rest-in-peace" quality about it. The boy's thoughts were "composed / To more than infant softness" and given "a dim earnest of the calm / Which Nature breathes among the fields and groves."

When Wordsworth later uses the formulaic title "Composed upon Westminster Bridge ...," "Composed by the side of Grasmere Lake ...," does "composed" carry an echo of "made calm" and refer to poet as well as poem? The scenes before him "compose" his thoughts by touching back to those early, calming moments. Yet the calm is not savored for its own sake alone, or because it soothes a fretful mind, but chiefly because in its remembered form it has power—or should I say, powers—in it. To summarize, then, several referents enrich the "this" of Wordsworth's question: fear, or terrible beauty, as a factor in a tempestuous poetic inspiration; the calm that alternates with fear and composes it, but may end by overcoming life itself; the turbulence created by this opposition between poetry's feeding-sources, splitting or unsettling the poet's identity; and the brooding on this, which becomes a "rigorous self-inquisition" in the longer, complete versions of *The Prelude*.

Despite such overdetermination, "Was it for this" potentially simplifies into an "it was for this" and even "it was". The question wants to be a statement about an "it" (nature) that "was" (acted in the past) "for this" (a poetry it calls to birth). Ranged against this affirmation are not only doubts about the tendency of the past but also about the poetry it fosters. While Wordsworth must claim his identity and emerge into major song (*majora canamus*), the very experience that moves him toward self-presentation (the "egotistical sublime") also magnifies a nature that makes the human appear as only one locus of being in an active universe. His privilege is less to say "I" than to identify with nature's purposive and impersonal mode, an "It was" that resembles the ballad's "It is," "There is," "There was"—a "sentiment of being" singled out by Lionel Trilling as the key to Wordsworth's poetic temperament. By the very act of writing *The Prelude*, "Was it for this" turns into "It was for me." The impersonal seems to address and justify Wordsworth's not inconsiderable poetic ego. But his claim to be "a Power like one of Nature's" only revives an ancient question, found in the most lyrical epic of them all. "What is man, that thou dost make so much of him, and set thy mind upon him... ?" (Job 7.17). *The Prelude*'s account of the birth of a poet as "the subject in question" is also a phenomenology of elemental feelings connecting that account with another story: the birth of the gods.

To think of the early versions of *The Prelude as* an embryonic theogony might seem just the wrong context. Such a context fits other Romantics better, especially Blake, Shelley, and Keats. Their revisionary mythic poems are linked to the French Revolution and a change fatal to old ideas about religion. Yet we underestimate Romanticism's connection with the Enlightenment (which it revises not abrogates) if we do not see that Wordsworth too, more radically perhaps, confronts the gods. He does so as part of the history of his development and he brings about a change—even revolution—in the language of representation. Indeed, he naturalizes natural religion so effectively that we barely think of Blake's outraged polemics against it or the psychological aspects of a methodism which Richard Brantley has shown is closest to Wordsworth.

The gorgeous mythopoeia of the other Romantics poses a question of appropriateness. What is special about Wordsworth is that he fashions a language for poetry that does not differ essentially from prose yet allows us to understand myth and religion. He describes their sources in the imaginative life from childhood on and their representational career—the way concepts arising from elemental feelings form and deform mental growth.

The beauty that has terror in it is predominant among those feelings. An old dictum runs that fear founded the gods. The eighteenth century produced a number of sophisticated genealogies expounding the idea. "It was fear," Vico remarks, "which created gods in the world, not fear awakened in men by other men, but fear awakened in men by themselves." That fear, interpreted as self-astonishment, is then connected with figurative language, or with the idiom of our ancestors the giants. Blake also linked fear to figuration, though of a distorted kind. His visionary poems show a continual theogony whose "big bang" is the self-astonishment of an imagination that shrinks from its own power and then abdicates it to the priests. By this recession it also produces the void described in the first lines of Genesis, and a God who has to create something from that nothing. Our present religiously reduced imagination continues to exnihilate creation, that is, to understand created nature as the product of a creator who has raised it from nothing (ex nihilo). The result is a flawed image of power that has inscribed itself in domestic, political, and religious institutions—it has become a second nature, and frozen the hierarchy of human and divine.

The separated gods, then, are forms of fear that terrify, check, and (in the hands of a priestly religion) exploit us. We astonish ourselves with our own conceptions and continue to alienate the modes of mental production by at once abstracting and realizing (reifying) these gods or genii: we forget that "All deities reside in the human breast" (*Marriage of Heaven and Hell*, plate 11). The English Reformation, for both Blake and Wordsworth, began to free the imagination from fears about itself, or "Mystery" in the shrouding and restrictive sense.

Yet the difference between the two poets is striking. Blake's attack on mystery, his redemptive theogony, is a lurid affair, with logos indistinguishable from pathos and with words and emotional states providing the weapons. We are inside some traumatic mental process, or a mock-up of it devised by an ingenious advertising company pushing a mind-altering drug. These decomposing and recomposing gods, these expanding and contracting metamorphs, display recognizable human emotions on a sublime stage that leaves nothing to the imagination because it is the imagination. Instead of mystery, there is too much illumination from Blake's will, burning up and leaving no trace of mystery-religion in any domain. What is missing, even after Yeats, Frye, and Bloom, are the coordinates that would allow reader or spectator to stand on firm ground and not suffer interpretive vertigo. Interpretation, ironically, is the only mysterious thing here, as all that light creates the very darkness Blake wanted to dispel.

In the natural theology that Blake combats, the light of nature goes out when revelation supervenes "dark with excessive bright." But in Wordsworth the light of nature is never totally extinguished by any shade thrown up from the soul. Sense and soul are primordially linked so that fear, whether attributed to nature or mind, is an "impressive agency," an elemental and numinous emotion, not a social construct resulting from age-long imaginative error. Yet no one depicted more sensitively, before Wordsworth, the color of fear and how it might stimulate a demonic religion. In Wordsworth too, fear reflects imagination awakening to a sense of power, though nature's power as well as its own.[6] The child, however, remains ignorant of its own part in this drama till time becomes an interpretant. Blake is all theogony and genealogy; he has nothing to teach about development in time or the growth of the poet's mind. Eternity, not time, is his milieu, even if "Eternity is in love with the productions of Time." But Wordsworth records how the impressive event, being temporalized, opens to interpretation without losing its sensuous hold. The basic shift that time brings about is referential: from nature to imagination, with nature remaining a heavenly agency.

> O heavens, how awful is the might of Souls
> And what they do within themselves while yet
> The yoke of, earth is new to them, the world
> Nothing but a wild field where they were sown.
>   (1850 *Prelude* 3.178–81)

The colloquial oath ironically displaces the heavens it evokes and recalls instead the wars of the imagination on earth. Yet Wordsworth can be nervous about his own discovery, so that a new fear, of interpretation itself, occasionally enters and tempts him to foreclose his insights through euphemism and didactic overlay.

To make these observations more concrete, let me comment briefly on the episode in which the youngster steals a boat and imagines a huge cliff striding after him. Demons are born of that moment of visionary dread, border-images of something alive yet not human. Nature is emptied of the comforts which its shapes and colors normally provide:

>   after I had seen
> That spectacle, for many days my brain
> Worked with a dim and undetermined sense
> Of unknown modes of being: in my thoughts
> There was a darkness, call it solitude
> Or blank desertion: no familiar shapes
> Of hourly objects, images of trees,
> Of sea or sky, no colours of green fields:
> But huge and mighty forms, that do not live
> Like living men, moved slowly through my mind
> By day, and were the trouble of my dreams.
>   (Two-Part *Prelude*, First Part, 120–29)

The light of sense goes out "with a flash that has revealed / The invisible world." Such moments turn nature into theater, a place of heightened action and demand. The poet describes that vividly enough, yet his impressions might have induced romance themes, and even a dramatic form of representation. We want to hear those beings speak "as if a voice were in them" and hear the response of the pursued boy. Can human voice answer to such pressure and remain human, rather than alienating itself and adopting a sublime rhetoric? Can one have a "conversation" in or about such circumstances? Wordsworth talks past the experience, shifting from narrative to apostrophe, from description to an interpretation that assumes a "fellowship" between nature and the developing poet:

> Ah! not in vain ye Beings of the hills!
> And ye that walk the woods and open heaths
> By moon or star-light, thus from my first dawn
> Of childhood did ye love to intertwine
> The passions that build up our human soul...
>   (Two-Part *Prelude*, First Part, 130–34)

This shift, it seems to me, still does not recognize the awful power of imagination. The enumeration and pluralizing (he goes from the one huge cliff to "Beings of the hills" and associates them with "spirits" of the milder sort) take the edge off a singular event. The apostrophe functions as a sublime punctuation mark, a reflective breathing-out that fills the gap between incidents. That gap disturbs me, not so much because Wordsworth's narrative remains episodic but because the episodes that constitute it run off into apostrophe and didactic speech. "Was it for this?" also has no direct addressee: it is uttered, one might say, to the genii of the air. The mind is conversing with itself in the presence of an afterimage that still "works" on the poet, who is never free of the impression it recalls. Solitary recall and reflection may be the best outcome, given the isolating force of imagination, yet Wordsworth continues to represent imagination as destined to become sociable and sympathetic.

The drama on both psychological and expressive levels is not all that different from what Coleridge records in a mountain experience of his own. First described in November 1799, it was reentered in Coleridge's notebooks shortly after his ascent of Scafell, at the time of composing the "Hymn Before Sunrise in the Valley of Chamouny" (September 1802). "Ghost of a Mountain—the forms seizing my Body as I passed and became realities—I, a Ghost, till I had reconquered my substance." Coleridge adopts a sublime or supernatural mode of representation for this kind of experience. The different poetries that emerge from the "dialogue" between the two poets are so absorbing precisely because they question the possibility of a purely human speech, of that conversational style which Coleridge enacts in his famous Conversation poems but then yields to Wordsworth's genius. In this light *The Prelude* is Coleridge's greatest Conversation poem, with "the giant Wordsworth, God bless him!" as the mountain that has "stolen" his substance. Reeve Parker has said a similar thing about the mock-sublime of the Chamouny hymn, and both Kenneth Johnston and Paul Magnuson have rightly called the Two-Part *Prelude* an extended conversation with Coleridge.[7] My main point would be, though I cannot develop it here, that the Romantic poets show us how problematic it is to reduce imagination to conversation, or to a dialogic mode, even as the political ideals they share move in that direction, that is, in the direction of a dismantling of hierarchy and a recovery of vernacular or conversational relationships.

As if inevitably, I have arrived at the political theme haunting contemporary reflections on literature. From the time of Vergil, when the relation of poetry and politics is explicitly raised and the theme of empire and the destiny of nations enters Western literature, poets have never lost sight of the exceptional character of their occupation in the greater world. I cannot say the same about recent commentators, who insist that the political content of literature has been neglected or must be our first if not exclusive concern. No pronouncement of this kind will change the fact that our own occupation as literary scholars working within a university context is as exceptional as poetry itself. The privilege that causes our concern will not be cancelled by mimic wars against the "aesthetic" element in art or art theory. Such attacks deny what is strong and peculiar about both art and art education, and so may be self-scuttling and politically the worst thing to do.

I want to return, therefore, to Wordsworth's self-scrutiny during an era in which, as Napoleon remarked, politics was fate. Poetry, sidelined by the Enlightenment and the beginnings of industry, as well as by the war, was passing again through an identity crisis. An early poem of Hölderlin's sees Napoleon as too transcendent a subject for poetry. "He cannot live or dwell in the poem: he lives and dwells in the world."

Wordsworth's turn to nature meant that an answer to his question had to come from that source. Experientially but also conceptually it was a necessary move. No heavenly voice was expected or even desired. Nature here is not simply the field of the poet's early hauntings; it is the birthplace of genius—"genius" understood as a force of nature, a force of destiny real as any other, including Napoleon's. We are not dealing with daily politics but with visions that ravaged Europe, of empire, revolutionary liberty, and national destiny. A poet gains his legitimacy from the fact that he too has a vision, or counter-vision, inspired by the genius of the place he embodies. "Was it for this?" embraces a doubt— that has to be resolved—about Wordsworth's "leading genius": is he destined to be a poet, and if so, what will be his poetical character? A temperament allied to terror and tempest is indicative of the heroic and suggests not simply an older type of sublimity but also a vocation that is military rather than museal.

What happens when Wordsworth turns to nature? In the "field of light" passage already quoted, he tries, unsuccessfully, to move from sight to insight. He remembers how he used to scan *visibilia*, or the Book of Nature, without understanding the pleasure received and without seeking to go beyond it. He emphasizes the very fact of not-knowing—which does not augur well for his initial question. In the midst of all this light there is opaqueness: why did such scenes hold him? He specifically rules out a psychological interest derived from the mechanism of association: the charm was more elemental than that. Yet his appeal to Cumbria and Westmorland, "they can tell ... how I have stood," suggests an extreme, animistic development of the sympathetic imagination that places the young poet among other consciousnesses and evokes a sense of possible sublimity— enough, perhaps, to feed the feeling that he was Nature's child, and even perhaps the glorious imp whom Vergil celebrated in the *Fourth Eclogue*, his prophetic pastoral. Yet the transition from prelusive trials of strength to a "work of glory" eluded Wordsworth. His self-questioning and apologetic strain impeded what the coda to Vergil's *Fourth Eclogue* called for: "Incipe, parve puer," "Begin, little child...."

Wordsworth refused to step fully into the light with a mythical beginning of this kind. (Even the Great Ode hesitates on the threshold of myth.) Despite teleological breathings he did not claim a manifest destiny but deferred the vision of First and Last, painting nature and his relations to it by a negative knowledge that was his honesty. A higher strain, Miltonic or Vergilian, cuts across the pastoral narrative without transforming it. The deepest feeling of calm, at the same time, though it may purify the quest for meaning, cannot dispel an apologetic or higher consciousness:

> Nor unsubservient even to noblest ends
> Are these primordial feeling[s] how serene
> How calm those seem amid the swell
> Of human passion even yet I feel
> Their tranquilizing power
> (JJ, 166–70)

The question of "ends" always intrudes. Yet here too we find a significant link to Vergil and the rival vocations of poet and leader.

At the conclusion of the *Georgics*, Vergil contrasts the poet's activity with that of Octavius Caesar:

These verses about the culture of the fields, cattle and trees, are what I sang, while great Caesar was unleashing the thunder of war against deep Euphrates and, victorious, imposed his laws on its consenting people, on his way to commanding a place on Olympus. At that very moment sweet Sicily nourished me, Vergil, prospering in the arts of ignoble leisure (*ignobilis oti*)....

This not entirely modest modesty-topos became a literary commonplace. "Inglorious" or "ignoble" in Wordsworth, whether applied to poetry or poetry's description of ordinary childhood, contrasts with the idea of a productive calling, with mature work or "honorable toil." It is not surprising, then, that "Was it for this" is prompted in the 1805 *Prelude* by the New Testament parable of the unprofitable steward. The intensely experienced *otium* must be defended in terms of *negotium*. Wordsworth calls himself "not uselessly employed" in describing childhood activities, his shadowy moods are "not profitless," the pines murmur "not idly." The poet assures himself of the dignity of talking about his youth and its after-images by hinting that there is a noble end. His strong metaphorical use of "work" and "working" derives from the same apologetic vein. The unproductive life is not worth living: *The Prelude* reflects the oldest of bourgeois scruples.

Yet this Wordsworth, "prince of poetical idlers," as Hazlitt dubbed him, had his own way of breaking through to an astute visionariness and representing subliminal modes of action: "The influence of power gently used." Nature's agency in "There was a Boy" quietly counterpoints the exaltation of revolution in the greater world and Vergil's Roman promotion of Caesar to Olympus. A lyrical ballad in which nothing much seems to happen depicts instead the apotheosis of an ordinary child, cousin to Vergil's glorious *puer*. A life is summed up in a few traits that mainly show life taking place elsewhere—a displacement of "heroic argument" more striking than Milton's (compare *Paradise Lost* 9.25–29).

Speech itself, in fact, is almost displaced, so strong is the pressure of a concept of natural development on a concept of formal education. The boy is not given a name, and the opening words are interrupted by an apostrophe to Winander, "ye knew him well" (compare the "you can tell" addressed to Cumbria and Westmorland), which is a first pause in a deepening series. The apostrophe transfers permanent consciousness from man to landscape—subordinating even the poet who utters those words. The narrative almost ends in that first pause, as if "There was a Boy" were story enough, or keenest epitaph.

If Nature intended the youngster to mature into a poet by fostering intuitive rather than tutored speech, her plan is curiously aborted. For

Wordsworth's elegiac "There was" refracts into strong and weak emphases that require an internal echoing or doubling, and so contrasts ironically with the boy's own "speech" that raises echoes yet remains primitive mimicry. "There was," as a narrative opening, is the weak form, though gesturing toward the more dramatic temporality of the traditional ballad. The strong form, "*There* was a Boy," locates him not only in place (time) but also in existence: the essence of childhood is adumbrated as a bond between place and mode of being. Thus the episode as a whole projects an archetype of natural being: the near-silent and inglorious *puer* merges with his birthplace rather than being enskied. He dies into the spot where he was born, becoming a Miltonic *genius loci* who haunts Winander's shore and halts the passer-by.

To juxtapose Milton's *Lycidas*, Vergil's *Eclogue*, and this episode reveals more than the apprenticeship of genre or the influence of the majors. Wordsworth aborts, as it were, the mentality of myth while still allowing access to myth's mode. A complex symmetry builds between the pathos-haunted death of a boy at the threshold of self-awareness and the myth-haunted liminality of Wordsworth's style. Can the force of nature—or vision—be carried over into the next developmental stage? The poet who stands mute, remembering the boy he had been, must save vision not only from the twilight of myth (that is, the Enlightenment), but also from myth itself. The episode poses a double question: Was it for this mythless, muted voice that intimations of immortality dowered childhood? Or, is there a more original form of imagination than myth?

It is far from adequate, then, to define Wordsworth's peculiar strength in terms of a displacement of myth, by internalization or secularization. It is true that he depicts a heroic action removed from its usual martial or worldly locus. Heart and mind, starting with childhood—and almost ending there—are the haunt and the main region of his song. But there is a further displacement, away from visibility, or phenomenality in general, and toward the semiotic.[8] After an eloquent assertion in the third book of *The Prelude*:

> Of Genius, Power
> Creation, and Divinity itself,
> I have been speaking
> (1805 *Prelude*, 3.171–73)

the poet goes on to declare:

> Not of outward things

Done visibly for other minds—words, signs,
Symbols or actions—but of my own heart
Have I been speaking
     (1805 *Prelude*, 3.174–77)

Words and signs are compared to actions, because of their visible, outer-directed nature. It is as if Wordsworth wished to displace even words (the formal subject of *Prelude* 5 is Books) as too external. His argument is supported by the theme of inward (Christian as against Pagan) heroism; what is remarkable, however, is not his extension of the Protestant commonplace but a radical, antiphenomenal attitude that does not spare the spoken word. All the more understandable, then, that the Boy dies before speech makes him known to others. Wordsworth's "ye knew him well" is addressed to native cliffs and islands, not to human companions.

Through this rhetorical turn, however, the displacement that shifts heroic or mythic action inward aligns with a figural displacement that operates independently of the Protestant theme and even preempts it. By the speech act "ye knew him well" a knowledge without speech is evoked: the animating metaphor displaces knowledge, transfers it to a mute observer. Metaphor does "naturally" (that is, conventionally) what on the level of theme is tendentious or exceptional. The quiet(ed) boy and a quiet style go together. We are closer, in this episode, to the birth of words than to the birth of the gods, to verbal figures rather than to myth. It is as if phenomenality had been restored as a property of words rather than "outward things."

The entire episode can now be seen as metaphor writ large rather than myth writ small. Poetry does not compete with Nature as a counterspirit, or with the phenomenal world by a glittering sort of mimesis: it displays a phenomenality of its own that conspires with Nature's milder aspect of "power gently used" (1850 *Prelude* 12.15). We realize that Wordsworth's radical inwardness—so much more, I have suggested, than an extension of Christian or other kinds of internalization—does not disparage language. A poet's words too are "visibly for other minds." A magnification or landscape-enlargement of metaphor creates the subtlest sublimity on record. The point (which Jeffrey missed) is to catch, in poetry, a hint of that apostrophaic and transmuting power[9] Wordsworth ascribes to imaginative action. "Inward light alas," we read in Milton's Samson, "Puts forth no visual beam." Poetic words, ideally, overcome that defect: they endow a silent light with shape, sound, and being. If Derwent, Winander, and all the influences of Nature had raised Wordsworth only for this, it would have been enough.

NOTES

1. Don H. Bialostosky has made a case even for these. See *The Poetics of Wordsworth's Narrative Experiments* (Chicago, 1984).

2. My text is *The Prelude: 1798–1799*, edited by Stephen Parrish (Ithaca, 1977).

3. Thomas Weiskel on the third stanza of "Resolution and Independence," *The Romantic Sublime: Studies in the Structure and Psychology of Transcendence* (Baltimore, 1976), p. 61.

4. All references, unless otherwise indicated, are to the First Part of the Two-Part *Prelude* in Parrish's edition.

5. In the 1805 *Prelude*, 1.607, the leagues of shining water suggest the marvelous, near-Vergilian phrase, "field of light."

6. The role of fear or terror in moving the mind beyond "unregenerate perceiving," is the center of Weiskel's important analyses of Burke and Kant, as well as the Romantic poets.

7. Reeve Parker, *Coleridge's Meditative Art* (Ithaca, 1975); Kenneth R. Johnston, *Wordsworth and the Recluse* (New Haven, 1984); Paul Magnuson, *Coleridge and Wordsworth: A Lyrical Dialogue* (Princeton, 1988). Weiskel makes the interesting claim that when Wordsworth naturalized the archaic and demonic (or divine) sources of power, he discovered "a mode of conversation, now most easily recognized outside of poetry in the domains of the authentic psychoanalyst or a certain kind of expert teacher too tentative to know or say for sure what he 'really' means." Yet he admits, at once, "to describe *The Prelude as* any kind of conversation seems perverse. Its apparent form is closer to monolithic monologue...... (*Romantic Sublime*, p. 169).

8. For Wordsworth's understanding of the radical inwardness (non-phenomenality) of words, see Geoffrey Hartman, *The Unmediated Vision* (New Haven, 1954), the chapter "Pure Representation"; *Wordsworth's Poetry* (reprint, Cambridge, Mass., 1987), pp. 33–69 (these writings of 1954 and 1964 describe not a semiotic process but phenomenality turning against itself); Paul de Man, "Intentional Structure of the Romantic Image" and "Autobiography as De-Facement" (now in *The Rhetoric of Romanticism*, [1984]); Thomas Weiskel, *The Romantic Sublime* [1976], esp. "Wordsworth and the Defile of the Word"; and Hartman, "Words, Wish, Worth," (now in *The Unremarkable Wordsworth* [Minneapolis, 1987]).

9. See 1805 *Prelude* 13.94: [higher minds] "Like transformations, for themselves create"; and 1850 *Prelude* 13.94: "Kindred mutations; for themselves create," "Mutation" suggests, as a word, a turning around of what was *mute*. To "silent light," on Snowdon, voices issue by a reversal or breakthrough that is said to be the express resemblance of imaginative action, human or divine.

DAVID BROMWICH

From Wordsworth to Emerson

M y title says a little more than it means. I will not really be telling how
to get from Wordsworth to Emerson, or describing the forces that
intervened to create some sort of continuity between them. Instead, I want
to point to something in Wordsworth and something in Emerson, and to
show by description why they belong together. I have in mind a thought
which impresses both writers with its difficulty—a thought which resists the
intelligence but which both choose to treat as a communicable truth. It has
to do with the soul and the complex ideas by which the soul may be
defended. Words like *hope* and *trust* sometimes give a name to such ideas, and
I will be alluding to other names presently. Let me now suggest only the
general grounds of argument. Emerson was as happy to declare, as
Wordsworth was reluctant to admit, the thought they shared about self-trust,
or our ability to "keep / Heights which the soul is competent to gain." In
elaborating this contrast between them, I mean to offer an illustrative
anecdote concerning the growth, in the nineteenth century, of an
individualism which was noncontractual and nonpossessive.

There has been a debate about the Immortality Ode among modern
critics of Wordsworth in which most readers feel they have to take a side. In
the terms given by that debate, the poem is about growing old, or about
growing up. Either way, it has a motive related to the poet's sense that he

From *Romantic Revolutions: Criticism and Theory*, edited by Kenneth R. Johnston, Gilbert
Chaitin, Karen Hanson, and Herbert Marks, pp. 202–218. © 1990 by Indiana University Press.

stands at a transition between two kinds of activity. These belong, first, to the imagination, which alone suffices for the creation of poems; and, second, to the "philosophic mind" by which a poet may be accommodated to the proper sympathies of human life. Wordsworth's position on the good of such sympathies is ambiguous. Because they come from unchosen attachments, they can seem to compel us like the force of custom, "Heavy as frost, and deep almost as life." On the other hand, the acts (including acts of love) that we perform from sympathy are just such as we might have performed freely had our minds been unconstrained by an habitual self-regard. In this way the philosophic mind appears to be allied with the poet's imagination after all.

The puzzle remains why Wordsworth should have been so equivocal—compared to other writers of his time—about the sympathies he might expect to share with his readers. He says in the Preface to *Lyrical Ballads* that the poet must give pleasure and that, "Except this one restriction, there is no object standing between the Poet and the image of things."[1] It is odd to think of pleasure, in a sense that allies it with communication, as *limiting* the poet's own sight of the image of things. Maybe the suggestion that the reader's pleasure can hold back the poet's seeing goes some way to explain Wordsworth's uncertainty about how far common sympathies may hinder imagination.

Of course in the debate I mentioned, questions like these are referred to the antithesis between childhood (which is linked with poetic powers) and the philosophic mind (which is linked with "the soothing thoughts that spring / Out of human suffering"). But I do not want to guess at Wordsworth's supposed feelings about his own fate as a poet because I do not think the motive of the poem can be found anywhere in this area. The motive is not Wordsworth's failure or success in cheering himself up but rather a feeling close to guilt. It is a guilt, however, respecting what might as well have been a source of pride: namely, the poet's knowledge that there are certain thoughts all his own, which he, having lived his life and felt the sentiments associated with it, can understand and cherish as no one else can do. What Wordsworth would like to say in this poem is something Emerson does say in "Self Reliance": "Absolve you to yourself, and you shall have the suffrage of the world."[2] But the ideas of obligation in which Wordsworth believed made him reject that as an impossible gesture. What the ode ends up saying is something more like, "Absolve you to the world, and you shall have the suffrage of yourself." The world, however, believes in the suffrage of no power but itself, and it cannot ever wholly absolve him.

From Burke and other moralists, Wordsworth inherited an idea of morality as formed by common interests and tending to subordinate the individual to the community. On this view personal liberty and social order stand in an uneasy tension with each other. The choices of conscience are not beyond challenge, and they are hard to generalize from, being themselves only the internalization of worldly reason and prejudice. It is by coming to know the passions, affections, and sentiments we share with others that we recognize our relationship of mutual attachment to others in a society; by such attachment, in turn, that we are able to see the good of the duties we impose on ourselves as obligations; and by this whole picturing of our selves within the scene of other people's thoughts, feelings, and condition of life that we start to be moral beings and so are humanized. From the beginning of his career, Wordsworth talked in this way about morality; and against this background in another ode, he defined a personal imperative of duty. But in one respect the morality I have described—anti-rationalist, and noncontractual, though it was—spoke in a language that was not his. It seemed to allow no reckoning with the thoughts that made his imagination unlike anyone else's.

For the thoughts that define one's personal character always have to come, says Wordsworth, from an aspect of oneself (a faculty, perhaps) that relates to another aspect of oneself (an instinct, perhaps). These thoughts come to light through the imagination's action upon a deposit so elusive that to catch the sense of it Wordsworth mixes metaphors and calls it a *spot* of *time*. The thoughts in question, that is to say, are discovered by a thinking and writing later self, in a search across moments from an earlier life that can now be looked on as a scene of indefinite striving or possibility. It is for this reason that throughout *The Prelude* Wordsworth describes childhood, in the personal sphere, with the same figures of speech he reserves for the French Revolution in the political sphere. I think Hazlitt was right therefore when he assumed that the phrase, "What though the radiance which was once so bright / Be now for ever taken from my sight," referred at once to youth itself and to the youth of the revolution. But, if that is so, one may conclude that the observance of homecoming in this poem has likewise a double reference. Wordsworth is turning back from the French Enlightenment morality of nature to the still-abiding English morality of sentiments and affections; and, at the same time, from the liberty of an unchartered life to the necessary constraints of a community. Certainly the poem has a good deal of the pathos one associates with an ambivalent return: "We will grieve not, rather find / Strength in what remains behind."

But that only alters the question a little. To whom, or what, does Wordsworth feel answerable for the rightness of his return? Or again (though it is much the same question), to what causes does he lay the unhappiness of his departure? These difficulties the ode does not solve; nor can it, given the nature of the man who wrote it. For Wordsworth's former self-betrayal, like his present self-expiation, is twofold. By wandering to a site of radical enlightenment and reformation, he had turned against England, the place that nursed him, the home (in the largest sense) of all the childhood rovings that first gave him an idea of freedom. And yet by giving up France and its radiance now, and taking on himself the bonds of a native life, he surrenders the very freedom that has been for him a condition of self-knowledge, and that has made him conscious of his separable membership in a community. The last lines of the ode emerge in so unbroken a cadence that one can fail to notice how strangely they recur to the note of ambivalence.

> Thanks to the human heart by which we live,
> Thanks to its tenderness, its joys, and fears,
> To me the meanest flower that blows can give
> Thoughts that do often lie too deep for tears.

We live by the human heart; but the thoughts come to *me*. The shared joys and fears of this conclusion recall the wedding, the funeral, and other ceremonial occasions that have appeared rather grimly in the more conventional part of the poem. Amid all this grand evocation of public observances is one who stands alone aware of thoughts the meanest flower can give; just as, earlier in the poem, with children culling flowers on every side, only the child Wordsworth could feel "The Pansy at my feet / Doth the same tale repeat."

Plainly something in the poem, including one part of Wordsworth, wants us to be able to say that these solitary thoughts are the same as those "soothing thoughts that spring / Out of human suffering." In that case they would truly belong to Wordsworth's new and comparatively selfless existence. But the poem only half conceals an allusion to the fact that his thoughts are of a different kind. They can often be, it says, "too deep for tears," which means that they come with no affections of the usual sort. So a principle of self, and even of self-reliance, has tacitly been declared at the end of a poem that aimed from the first at an other-regarding dedication of the poet's imaginings. The result must appear difficult, almost opaque, if placed beside the poem's moral directives elsewhere. A person gazing earnestly at the meanest flower will look anomalous compared to someone contemplating a picturesque landscape of fountains, meadows, hills, and groves. But for Wordsworth it is enough to know that his choice is intelligible to him. I take the end of the ode to suggest that any venture of Wordsworth's life, however it affects the community he lives in, will be justified only in the light of a personal principle from which finally there is no appeal—not even to responses like tears, which others can be imagined to share. Leigh Hunt thought that tears were "the tributes, more or less worthy, of self-pity to self-love. Whenever we shed tears, we take pity on ourselves; and we feel ... that we deserve to have the pity taken."[3] I think this helps in reading the last line of the ode. Wordsworth's conviction about his own thoughts has deepened beyond the want even of an appeal to *self*-sympathy. He no longer expects others to pass in sad review the events of his life (as if those events added up to a tale worthy of their pity). And he tells us that he himself is unable to see his life in this way.

I have concentrated thus far on the end of the ode both because it is decisive and because it is memorable. But, in looking back on the poem, one may come to feel that its frequent turnings, the very traits that make it an ode, were the result of an effort to control and render outstanding what is always inward in the poet's thoughts. I can give two examples of this, the first structural and general, the second figural and particular. The poem, we know, was written in two parts, the first four sections at one time and then the last seven; and it does feel as if it had been written that way. The whole first part is imagined by Wordsworth with a persistent intensity of grief for himself: it is "I," writing about me and the things that are mine. "Two years at least," according to the Fenwick Note, elapsed between the last line of the fourth section ("Where is it now, the glory and the dream?") and the first line of the fifth ("Our birth is but a sleep and a forgetting"), and if we ask what has come into the poem in that time, the answer is the "we" that steals upon us quietly and that dominates the rest of the ode.

This is, if I may put it so, the first Arnoldian consolation in English poetry. It works its way by various ruses in the next several sections: first Wordsworth tries out the myth of preexistence, then he supposes the child a foster-child nursed by mother earth (so he has already lost something; there never was a time when he had not lost it); then, in a curious and unassimilable satirical bit, he dandles and pokes the child some more, and pushes him back among his proper companions, regarding him now as a conscious, imitative being ("A six years' Darling of pigmy size!"). In this perspective the address to the child as "Mighty Prophet! Seer blest!" which strikes many readers as hyperbolic, may have seemed to Wordsworth a compensation for the liberty he took with the child in the preceding sections.

So much for the structural effort of control—the movement from I to We, from an inward and incommunicable subject to an outward and common one—and Wordsworth's feeling that this is both a necessary passage and a focus of new anxieties. For the figural representation of that effort, I turn to the ninth section, in which, as I read it, nothing at last is controlled. The hope that nature, being the source of a shared sentiment, will therefore be translatable to other people, seems here as precarious as ever. Wordsworth has spoken of "Delight and liberty, the simple creed / Of Childhood," but now he adds:

> Not for these I raise
> The song of thanks and praise;
> But for those obstinate questionings
> Of sense and outward things,
> Fallings from us, vanishings;
> Blank misgivings of a Creature
> Moving about in worlds not realised,
> High instincts before which our mortal Nature
> Did tremble like a guilty Thing surprised:
> But for those first affections,
> Those shadowy recollections,
> Which, be they what they may,
> Are yet the fountain light of all our day,
> Are yet a master light of all our seeing;
> Uphold us, cherish, and have power to make
> Our noisy years seem moments in the being
> Of the eternal Silence....

Note that, in this analysis of thought, Wordsworth gives three distinct moments, with corresponding kinds of moral agency, which seem to stand for three different phases of consciousness. In the creed of childhood liberty, the child possesses himself without knowing that he does. Grown up and joined to our mortal nature, he will be unable to imagine such freedom except in grown-up terms, as a prompter of fear and guilt. But Wordsworth is interested in neither of these moments, neither of the extremes. He chooses rather to celebrate the child-consciousness at the moment of farewell, when the boy is just starting to know the "blank misgivings" (blank, because why should he feel them?) that signify his passage into the moral life of society. His instincts even at this moment are high, for he is sure, without having to be conscious, of his difference from other people and the rightness of that difference.

Yet the common moral life deals not so much with high instincts as with middling hopes and fears and prudential arrangements, and, once committed to these, the child will participate in our mortal nature. He is, however, thereby diminished only with respect to his own instincts, which he has disappointed. What is cryptic about the whole passage is that it speaks as if the loss related mostly to perception; the "fallings from us, vanishings" are fallings and vanishings from sight; and we know (among other sources, again, from the Fenwick Note) that perception formed a large part of Wordsworth's thinking about the idealisms of childhood. However, on the interpretation I have sketched, the great lines of the ninth section were not written by a man reflecting on the character of his perceptions. In all of these metaphors, the tenor belongs to morality and not metaphysics—but morality in the reverse of Wordsworth's usual self-distrustful sense. The child himself was a principle all his own before he could ever reflect on the fact, but his individual character, his soul, becomes definite to him only as he begins to see it passing; and he sees that happen vividly whenever he is imposed on by other people's claims.

Such, then, is the moment Wordsworth selects for thanks and praise: the moment when, having fallen part way from our selves, we discover that we exist, and look for certain traces of past seeing to uphold and cherish. But that is not quite right either. By resorting to normal ideas of cause, effect, and agency to explain Wordsworth's conception, I have distorted it. According to the grammar of the lines, we do not uphold and cherish anything; rather, it is those recollections, instincts, misgivings, in their very falling from us, that uphold and cherish us: they compose whatever we are, and we are nothing else, even if the consequent sense of ourselves has come from nothing but impressions caught in flight. Wordsworth's practice of self-recovery does not reach beyond this fact which resists all further discussion. The knowledge we have of our own identity is the representation, by a conscious self, of something fugitive in the life of a creature not yet individuated, with whom we share some memories and a name.

Emerson read the ode early and pondered it often, and was, in fact, among the first to have called it an Ode on Immortality. I want to begin this inquiry into his relationship to the poem by asking what he meant by a difficult sentence in the first paragraph of "Self Reliance": "In every work of genius we recognize our own rejected thoughts; they come back to us with a certain alienated majesty." What kind of thoughts did Emerson mean? One feels that he was trying to describe, and trying not to illustrate, a scene of the uncanny return of something repressed in ourselves—just the kind of scene Wordsworth did commonly illustrate, as in the boat-stealing episode of *The Prelude*. I do not tell myself (Emerson would thus be saying), till I discover it unbidden in some external thing, how thoroughly a principle of self-trust governed even the things I could care for. That principle has made the world over, in keeping with my character and moods; so that I suppose for me to respond to them, they must always have been mine.

In the light of this clue I think it is worth recalling the history of the composition of "Self-Reliance." Emerson occasionally mentions Wordsworth in his lectures of the 1830s, though some of his praise is rather equivocal.[4] Then in January 1839 at the Masonic Temple in Boston, he delivers a lecture on genius, with a draft of some remarks he will work in to "Self-Reliance":

> To believe your own thought,—that is genius.... In every work of genius, you recognize your own rejected thoughts. Here as in science the true chemist collects what every body else throws away. Our own thoughts come back to us in unexpected majesty. We are admonished to hold fast our trust in instincts another time. What self-reliance is shown in every poetic description! Trifles so simple and fugitive that no man remembers the poet seizes and by force of them hurls you instantly into the presence of his joys.[5]

Fugitive and *instincts* have come back to him from the ode. And a little further on, he generalizes: "The reason of this trust is indeed very deep for the soul is sight, and all facts are hers; facts are her words with which she speaketh her sense and well she knoweth what facts speak to the imagination and the soul."[6] However, between the two passages above Emerson needed to quote some poetry; he chose the lines about skating that later went into *The Prelude*, beginning "So through the darkness and the cold we flew," and ending "Till all was tranquil as a summer sea." It is one of the earliest quotations I know by any critic of materials from Wordsworth's autobiographical poem; though the passage was available to others where Emerson found it, in the four-volume edition published in Boston in 1824.

He quoted well from a new source, but he was thinking about the ode, of which "Self-Reliance" gives an original reading. If for us now, his individualism is generally accounted more radical than Wordsworth's, that is because he made himself be the sort of reader Wordsworth could not afford to be. Across the divide of those vanishings, and writing wholly from the side of our mortal nature, Wordsworth had come to have too many misgivings. The particular use of Emerson therefore, for someone interested in English Romanticism, is that he recovers a revolutionary idea of Wordsworth's aims. But, as in Wordsworth after 1797 or so, it is a revolution without a social medium in which to operate. The beautiful sublimation that Wordsworth had performed, by speaking of the French Revolution in a parable about childhood, Emerson continues by speaking of American democracy in a parable about the self. And on a single point of terminology, the two authors do converge. The individual power which they aim to preserve they call neither the child nor the self but the soul.

Yet in the sentence of "Self-Reliance" that I began with, much of Emerson's thought turns on his use of a rarer word, "alienated." It can have a religious sense of course, and maybe that is the primary one here: having alienated myself from the god who is my self, I find that my face is turned toward him again in every meaningful look I give or receive. But there is also a social sense of the word (the alienation of property) which stays near the surface with almost the force of a pun. I have alienated myself from my own estate; but wherever I cast my eye I find it still before me. That would be sufficiently Wordsworthian; and it fits in with the following sentence from "Self Reliance," about the power we can call upon if we have once been strong in the past: "That is it which throws thunder into Chatham's voice, and dignity into Washington's port, and America into Adam's eye." So the two metaphors that alienation can imply—the religious one about sight and the social one about property—are suggested together in Adam's gaze at his lands. It is important that the lands be inherited as naturally as an instinct, and not earned as the reward of labor or service. For Emerson will also want to say: "Prayer that craves a particular commodity, anything less than all good, is vicious."

I shall return later to Wordsworth's and Emerson's ideas of property. Besides, there is a connection between the immortality Ode and "Self-Reliance" which ought to concern us more. I mean the path by which Wordsworth moves from his intimations to the glimpse of the "immortal sea which brought us hither"; by which Emerson is able to pass from the accusing philanthropists who muddle his thoughts to the conception of an aboriginal Self. Both proceed by means of an inverted genealogy. Wordsworth says, "The Child is Father of the Man." Emerson says, "Is the acorn better than the oak which is its fulness and completion? Is the parent better than the child into whom he has cast his ripened being? Whence this worship of the past?" Which is very strange, until one realizes it is playing against the Wordsworth, and even then it is not much less strange. Wordsworth's little allegory itself is grotesque if one tries to picture it rather than reason about it. But once we scale it down from allegory to mere exaggeration, it seems to say that the child is both wiser, in his closeness to the source of things, and at the same time more capable than the father, in having not yet had to acquiesce in the ways of custom and habit. Because he establishes the character the man will have to obey, the child is father to him. On the other hand—what *could* Emerson have meant? One expects the acorn will be compared to the oak as the child to the parent, but he works it the other way around, and says the oak is the child "into whom [the parent] has cast his ripened being." So the child there stands above the parent by being the realized thing that is livelier to the imagination than the potential thing. The child, in his characteristic independence, outranks the parent in his thoughtless conformity, as the fully developed entity does the inchoate or elementary.

One cannot help being struck as well by a difference in the function of the metaphors. The child, as Wordsworth sees him, can actually come before, precede, influence the man *in the continuity of a single life*, and in that sense be his own father. But there is no sense in which the child Emerson imagines (with the integral strength Emerson imputes to such a creature) will admit that the parent came before, preceded, or influenced him in any but the trivial manner in which an acorn comes before an oak. The reason Emerson can do without this admission is that he is not in fact talking about the continuity of a single life. Why look to virtuous actions, he asks, when you have before you the man who is himself the embodied virtue? Start thinking about acts and you scatter your forces. On this view the composition of a life by particular choices of conduct toward others looks like a chimerical aspiration. Even the possibility of knowing days "bound each to each by natural piety" may come to seem an invention of institutional morality which one could very well do without. I am alluding here to Wordsworth's use of the phrase *natural piety* in the epigraph to the ode: as far as I know, *The Prelude* is the first work of moral reflection in which virtue is made to depend on a conscious attempt to compose a life of such naturally linked actions.

Emerson would have found this way of thinking antipathetic, for to judge particular acts somehow implies judging them from outside; which is done by rules, or at least by conventions of judgment; which, in turn, bring to mind the kind of scrutiny that can make society "a conspiracy against the manhood" of each of its members. But there may be another clue to his reaction in the word piety. It shares a root with *expiation*, about which Emerson has this to say: "I do not wish to expiate, but to live. My life is for itself and not for a spectacle." To the extent that Wordsworth does regard his life as a spectacle, his thinking seems to be in line with ordinary republican sentiments about how one has to live with respect to others. One acts, that is, under a consciousness of fortune and men's eyes. By contrast, Emerson has already so far sacrificed consistency, and with it even the aim of being the hero of his own life, that he is hardly susceptible to much anxiety about the story others may make of it. Indeed the very idea of story is non-Emersonian. He says, still in "Self-Reliance," that "all history resolves itself very easily into the biography of a few stout and earnest persons," and he might as fairly have added that biography itself is only the insight of believing persons into "a great responsible Thinker and Actor working wherever a man works." We sympathize with such a man and want to imagine his life in just the degree that we find our own thoughts come back in his with a certain alienated majesty.[7]

I said earlier that Emerson, like Wordsworth, appeals from an idea of the self to an idea of the soul. Here is the passage from "Self-Reliance" in which he declares his faith:

> The magnetism which all original action exerts is explained when we inquire the reason of self-trust. Who is the Trustee? What is the aboriginal Self, on which a universal reliance may be grounded? What is the nature and power of that science-baffling star, without parallax, without calculable elements, which shoots a ray of beauty even into trivial and impure actions, if the least mark of independence appear? The inquiry leads us to that source, at once the essence of genius, of virtue, and of life, which we call Spontaneity or Instinct. We denote this primary wisdom as Intuition, whilst all later teachings are tuitions. In that deep force, the last fact behind which analysis cannot go, all things find their common origin. For the sense of being which in calm hours rises, we know not how, in the soul, is not diverse from things, from space, from light, from time, from man, but one with them and proceeds obviously from the same source whence their life and being also proceed. We first share the life by which things exist and afterwards see them as appearances in nature and forget that we have shared their cause. Here is the fountain of action and of thought. Here are the lungs of that inspiration which giveth man wisdom and which cannot be denied without impiety and atheism. We lie in the lap of immense intelligence, which makes us receivers of its truth and organs of its activity. When we discern justice, when we discern truth, we do nothing of ourselves, but allow a passage to its beams. If we ask whence this comes, if we seek to pry into the soul that causes, all philosophy is at fault. Its presence or its absence is all we can affirm. Every man discriminates between the voluntary acts of his mind and his involuntary perceptions, and knows that to his involuntary perceptions a perfect faith is due. He may err in the expression of them, but he knows that these things are so, like day and night, not to be disputed. My wilful actions and acquisitions are but roving; the idlest reverie, the faintest native emotion, command my curiosity and respect. Thoughtless

people contradict as readily the statement of perceptions as of
opinions, or rather much more readily; for they do not
distinguish between perception and notion. They fancy that I
choose to see this or that thing. But perception is not whimsical,
but fatal. If I see a trait, my children will see it after me, and in
course of time all mankind,—although it may chance that no one
has seen it before me. For my perception is as much a fact as the
sun.

When Emerson writes "We lie in the lap of immense intelligence," I think
he means that our nurse or foster-mother (the same one who "fills her lap
with pleasures all her own") is *not* the earth. We do not belong to someone
who can speak for nature and human nature, and by doing so wean us from
ourselves, and make us forget the glory from which we came. Rather that
intelligence is simply ourselves. So that the receding of its power from us is
a tendency of life to which we need not submit. Emerson, of course, can
make his claim the more plausibly because he conceives of the soul as
somehow beyond the reach of our experiential self: it is "that science-baffling
star, without parallax, without calculable elements ... the last fact behind
which analysis cannot go."

Seeking a clue to his intentions here, let us recall that in the paragraph
quoted above, as in some other celebrated passages, Emerson speaks of the
soul's force in a metaphor borrowed from electromagnetism. The soul makes
a current of being, and can do so merely by having brought two things into
relation, like a coil of wire with a magnet. This explains his confidence about
the fatality of perception once a given character and the physical universe
have been brought into contact with each other. For the power that is
generated as a result may appear to be both timeless and oddly
undifferentiated. True, one of Emerson's aims is to concentrate all energy in
the present: it seems to be part of his larger project of disencumbering the
self, and America, of a grave and incapacitating reverence for the past. But
though the entire figure concerning magnetism has this form, it is intended
above all as a metaphor about process, and the power in question can hardly
be constant or static. We come to know it, indeed, only in moments of
passage from one state to another—that is to say, in fallings from us which
are also fallings toward something deeper in ourselves. As Emerson remarks
a little further on, in a striking revision of the ninth section of the ode: "Life
only avails, not the having lived. Power ceases in the instant of repose; it
resides in the moment of transition from a past to a new state, in the shooting
of the gulf, in the darting to an aim. This one fact the world hates; that the
soul *becomes....*"

Wordsworth had placed the moment of repose in the past, though it is a question whether he really thought it belonged there: he seems to have wanted to defend himself from the knowledge that it might still lie in the future. When, in the "Ode to Duty," he writes "I long for a repose that ever is the same," it is a longing against both imagination and freedom.

Emerson for his part believed that individual power tends to harden soon enough into just such a repose; but he wants us to believe that the opposite is always possible; and his departure from Wordsworth is connected with his own violent hatred of memory. To the conspicuous faith of the ode, that our memories leave the deposit from which our profoundest thoughts derive, Emerson replies in "Self-Reliance": "Why should you keep your head over your shoulder? Why drag about this corpse of your memory, lest you contradict somewhat you have stated in this or that public place? Suppose you should contradict yourself; what then?" We are once again at the point where natural piety, consistency of opinion, and a respect for duties laid upon oneself as actor in the spectacle of social morality, come to seem names for the same thing. Wordsworth, however reluctantly, is responsive to their call, and Emerson is not.

Every other divergence I have noticed between Wordsworth's and Emerson's reading of the self plainly follows from their opposite prejudices about memory. But I want to close by remarking a slightly different, almost physical, correlative of the self which both writers treat allusively and which may bring out a permanent difference in the social backgrounds from which English and American Romanticism took shape. The self-trust of an individual in the writing of both Wordsworth and Emerson has something to do with the secure possession of property. Wordsworth uses a complex word for the motive by which property and the self are linked: the word is *hope*. Thus we are told of the hero of "Michael" that the news of his forfeit of lands

> for a moment took
> More hope out of his life than he supposed
> That any old man ever could have lost.

Hope, in this Wordsworthian grammar, has to be represented as a partitive substance, like land or earnings. But hope for Michael is the imaginative measure of that practical thing, property. To put it another way, a strong self like Michael finds in property the sanction of his individual way of life. The model both for the poet, who dwells in effort and expectation and desire, and the citizen who lives an exemplary life of natural piety, is the return to a given spot of earth by a Cumbrian freeholder. It was of such people that

Wordsworth observed in his letter of 1801 to Charles James Fox: "Their little tract of land serves as a kind of permanent rallying point for their domestic feelings.[8]

On the face of things Emerson, notwithstanding his popular reputation, has a much more disdainful view of property, and in "Self-Reliance" preeminently. He says near the end of the essay that "the reliance on Property, including the reliance on governments which protect it, is the want of self-reliance." (It is pertinent that he also says, "Fear and hope are beneath [the soul]. There is somewhat low even in hope.") And yet, Emerson is always close to a figurative language that keeps in view associations of property; as, for example, in the long passage above, with its rhetorical question, "Who is the Trustee?" He seems, in short, to have been interested in property as a material instance of a principle which the soul prefers to keep ideal. Though not, therefore, connected as cause and effect, secure property and self-reliance know each other as versions of autonomy, and are perhaps justly suspicious of each other's claims. But Emerson writes of a society in which this kind of sanction could be taken more for granted than in England. Little of the available land in America had yet been either claimed or enclosed. It is in fact the apparent detachment of the self from property that makes Emerson so elusive a guide to readers who expect a writer like him to be involved in the work of social criticism, whereas Wordsworth, though his politics at any time of his life are difficult to characterize, has been steadily serviceable to radical as well as reactionary communitarians.

Maybe Emerson's unsatisfactoriness here, his intention not to satisfy interests like these, marks a more general refusal of the spectacle of expiation. It may also seem to mark the point at which we have to start reading him against no writer earlier than himself. I have been arguing only that the peculiar quality of his detachment was a possible development from Wordsworth. He said of Wordsworth in *English Traits* that "alone in his time, he treated the human mind well, and with an absolute trust. The Ode on Immortality is the high-water mark which the human intellect has reached in this age. New means were employed, and new realms added to the empire of the muse, by his courage." This is conventional language but for Emerson its meaning was not conventional. The high-water mark had to be very high indeed to reach us, as far inland as we were in conformity and habitual practices. And, for Wordsworth, whose deference to the bonds of custom was great in exact proportion to his self-doubt, to show the thoughts of the soul must have seemed an even stranger undertaking than it has been for his successors, who have had his own example to invigorate them. All I have tried to explain in this essay is what Emerson rightly called Wordsworth's *courage*.

NOTES

1. "Preface to *Lyrical Ballads*," in *Selected Poems and Prefaces*, ed. Jack Stillinger (Boston, 1965), p. 454. All quotations of Wordsworth's poems are from this edition.

2. "Self-Reliance," in *Selections from Ralph Waldo Emerson*, ed. Stephen E. Whicher (Boston, 1957), p. 149. All quotations of "Self-Reliance" are from this edition.

3. Leigh Hunt, *Imagination and Fancy* (London, 1883), p. 302.

4. He more than once refers to Wordsworth's poetic talents as "feeble." I take it he meant by this to deny Wordsworth the power of a rich inventiveness while granting him a power much stranger and less parochially literary.

5. *The Early Lectures of Ralph Waldo Emerson*, ed. Robert E. Spiller and Wallace E. Williams (Cambridge, Mass., 1972), 3:77. The overt echoes of the ode in "Self-Reliance," of which I have little to say here, may be useful to list for the reader who hoped for a different kind of commentary. They seem to me these: "[A boy] cumbers himself never about consequences, about interests.... But the man is as it were clapped into jail by his consciousness." "[Man] dares not say 'I think', 'I am', but quotes some saint or sage. He is ashamed before the blade of grass or the blowing rose."

6. Ibid., 3:78.

7. Carlyle wanted the majesty to return, unalienated, in the life of a hero, who would make a great figure for a race, and not merely for individual readers. The choice has broad consequences for his thinking about history. It cannot be for him (what Emerson says it is) "an impertinence and an injury if it be any thing more than a cheerful apologue or parable of my being and becoming." The Carlyle parable is gloomy because it always belongs to a whole people, over the heads of the individuals who recall it.

8. *Early Letters of William and Dorothy Wordsworth* (1787–1805), ed. Ernest De Selincourt (Oxford, 1935), p. 262.

KENNETH R. JOHNSTON

"While We Were Schoolboys":
Hawkshead Education and Reading

> a scanty record is deduced
> Of what I owed to books in early life;
> *Their later influence yet remains untold....*
> (V.630–32; italics added)

In Wordsworth's Hawkshead, the boys always seem to be running, never reading; it's hard to find the school in the midst of all this activity. The first two books of *The Prelude* both have "School-Time" in their titles, but there is not a line in them describing school activity: no masters, no subjects, no punishments, no tedium, nothing. As far as they tell it, Wordsworth's Hawkshead curriculum was entirely extracurricular. He was at an excellent school at the top of its form, but in *The Prelude* he had an interest in minimizing his debt to culture and society, relative to nature. But *The Prelude* is not literally his biography, and we have to hold ourselves at a distance from his romantic nature myth to recognize that most of his time in Hawkshead was in fact spent in school and that he was an excellent, very bookish student.

Scholars charmed by the energy of Books I and II of *The Prelude* have speculated that Hawkshead grammar school's educational philosophy was influenced by the theories of Rousseau, stressing children's natural innocence.[1] This we may very much doubt. Wordsworth's *description* of it was indeed influenced by his admiration for the more optimistic parts of

From *The Hidden Wordsworth: Poet, Lover, Rebel, Spy*, pp. 69–92. © 1998 by Kenneth Richard Johnston.

Rousseau's pedagogical theory. But the academic discipline at Hawkshead grammar school was hard old-fashioned classicism, combined with hard new-fashioned mathematics, and the value of the boys' freedom out of class was more accidental than philosophically inspired. Much of the time the school had the appearance of a library: one hundred boys and four or five masters working in a building not much larger than a comfortable two-story house, with two large rooms on each floor. Reading and study took place in the library on the upper floor; lessons and recitations were done on the ground floor. Founded in 1585 by Edwin Sandys, archbishop of York, who was born at Esthwaite Hall, the school was one of about four hundred grammar schools in Great Britain to which the gentry and well-to-do merchants could send their sons; sons of the very rich were still tutored at home.[2] It was also one of the best, both in its traditional, classical curriculum and in its modern, scientific one. The school's proximity to Scotland helped it participate in the "Northern Enlightenment," evident in its strong emphasis on mathematics. Then as now, schools that specialized in preparing students for admission to the most prestigious universities often provided a more rigorous education than the universities themselves. Hawkshead's success was prodigious, in placing students at Cambridge and helping them to succeed there. Sandys had gone to St. John's College, Cambridge, and so did many of the Hawkshead schoolboys, where they did very well indeed: four of the six senior wranglers at Cambridge between 1788 and 1793 came from Sandys's school.

There were great expectations behind John Wordsworth's expedient decision to send the Wordsworth boys to Hawkshead. Although founded as a charity school for local boys, it had by Wordsworth's time become a thriving establishment for the preparation of sons of the rising middle class. Only about 10 percent of its hundred students were still charity boys, and they were usually on one- or two-year rotating scholarships. The grammar school should not to be confused with the local village schools, which were start-and-stop, one-room affairs dealing in basic literacy and catering to children who were either too young (under ten), or not clever enough or rich enough to attend the grammar school.[3] It was a point of pride in the villagers' lives (such as Hugh Tyson's) to have been fortunate enough to spend a term or two in the privileged precincts of the grammar school. The school's endowment kept tuition down to a "cockpenny" per year, about a guinea and a half, derived from the ancient custom of awarding prize money to the student with the best fighting cock.[4] Room and board cost thirty to forty pounds per year on a national average, but charges for each of the Wordsworth boys' "Sabine fare" ran less, in the twenty-pound range.[5] Lawyers and estate agents like John Wordsworth, local squires, wool merchants from Kendal and slate traders from Coniston, and other gentry from as far away as Carlisle and even Edinburgh were happy to pay these charges for a school that could virtually assure their sons a place at Cambridge.[6]

This was the route Wordsworth was supposed to follow, and he had every intention of doing so. John Wordsworth's career plans for his sons continued to mold them even after his death: he succeeded with three of them, but William spoiled the family plan. Richard became a lawyer like his father, leaving school early to clerk with his Whitehaven uncles and cousins. John was slated for the sea, and dutifully left school at age fifteen for the East India Company, starting out in the Wordsworth "family bottom" sailing from Whitehaven. Christopher, the youngest, was the most successful of all, in a career that can be viewed as filial overcompensation along the path his older brother William was supposed to tread: B.A. Trinity in 1796 (tenth wrangler); fellow in 1798 until his marriage in 1804; then successive rectorships in Norfolk, Surrey, and Kent, with prestigious intervals as chaplain to the archbishop of Canterbury and the House of Commons; then back to Trinity as master in 1820 until his retirement in 1841, serving two elected terms as vice-chancellor of the university.[7] The social history of the Wordsworth family in the nineteenth century is a chapter in the story of the formation of England's intellectual aristocracy out of its educated middle class, and in this history it is Christopher and his sons and grandsons who are the success stories, not his rebellious older brother.

At Hawkshead, Wordsworth was supposed to begin his conventional success, and by all accounts he did so very well, in both the classical and the modern parts of the curriculum. One of his masters once left him alone in his office for a moment, looking at Newton's Opticks; he found him still poring over it an hour later, when he returned after a delay, and was astonished to hear the boy ask if he could take the book with him to read more.[8]

The literary curriculum was of course in Greek and Latin, included the standard authors (Anacreon, Homer, Ovid, Virgil), and moved smartly along from linguistic to literary training, as translating led to "imitating" the classics in both English and the original language, a popular genre throughout the eighteenth century. Wordsworth was quickly awakened from his dame-school slumbers by Mr. Shaw, one of the ushers, "who taught me more of Latin in a fortnight than I had learnt during two preceding years at the school of Cockermouth."[9] Translation was still a dominant literary genre; the mighty achievements of Dryden's Virgil (1697) and Pope's Homer (1715–25) remained unsurpassed for at least another century. The curriculum was arranged to take the boys up the ladder of genres from epigrams to lyrics to epistles and narratives, and finally to epics. Wordsworth expressed an early independence by preferring Ovid over Virgil. "Before I read Virgil I was so strongly attached to Ovid, whose Metamorphoses I read at school, that I was quite in a passion whenever I found him, in books of criticism, placed below Virgil [i.e., almost always]. As to Homer, I was never weary of travelling over the scenes through which he led me."[10] This was a mildly naughty predilection, for Ovid is the classical "nature poet" whose Just-So stories reveal natural forms as the result of men or women's attempt to escape from—or the consequences of their not escaping from—the lascivious embraces of the gods.

But he soon graduated to Virgil, and later in life began a project to translate the *Aeneid* which, had he completed it, might well have supplanted Dryden's.[11] Virgil marked the acme of the Latin curriculum, but his *Georgics* were more important than the *Aeneid* in eighteenth-century pedagogy and general culture.[12] These four long poems celebrating rural labor in the unsettled period following the Roman civil wars had an explicit ideological role in Neoclassical, Augustan England. They represented the classical ideal of rural republican virtue checking urban imperial excess, which Whig philosophers and pedagogues skillfully used to distance the country from the trauma of its own civil wars of 1642–60.

Thanks largely to his Hawkshead training, Wordsworth was a lifelong student and master of languages, in fact a formidable linguist. His knowledge of—and debts to—a variety of literary traditions is usually not appreciated, because it often suited his purposes to minimize such debts in the interest of promoting his views about "natural" imaginative creativity.

Wordsworth was not simply the beneficiary of large sociocultural educational trends, however. They had a human face in Hawkshead, and its name was William Taylor (1754–1786), schoolmaster from 1782 till his death, during Wordsworth's critically important twelfth through sixteenth year. There were three other masters during Wordsworth's years at the school, but none of them had anything like Taylor's impact on him. James Peake was master when he arrived, but had little responsibility for the younger boys. Edward Christian, though a family friend and legal defender, was master for less than a year (1781–82), and not much in residence. Thomas Bowman took over from Taylor in Wordsworth's final year. Bowman modestly admitted he taught Wordsworth more by the books he suggested to him than through lessons: "Tours and Travels ... Histories and Biographies," George Sandys's *Travels in the East*, Ovid's *Metamorphoses*, Foxe's *Book of Martyrs*, Evelyn's *Forest Trees*, and many contemporary poets, such as Cowper and Burns "when they first came out" (1785 and 1786, respectively).[13]

The measure of Wordsworth's high esteem for Taylor is paradoxically indicated by his not saying a word about him in *The Prelude* until Book X, "Residence in France and the French Revolution." This chronological displacement juxtaposes his gentle, beloved schoolteacher to, of all people, the archfiend of revolutionary demonology, Maximilien Robespierre. Wordsworth first learned of Robespierre's death (July 28, 1794) in early August of 1794, when crossing Leven Sands during a summer visit to relatives on Morecambe Bay. A passing traveler told him the news, and Wordsworth in a flash associated the news with the fact that he had just come from visiting Taylor's grave at Cartmel Priory, directly behind him on the east side of the bay, with its inscription from Gray's "Elegy Written in a Country Church Yard." He also connected it with Hawkshead, which "lay, as I knew," slightly to the north, beneath some very impressively represented clouds:

> ... clouds, and intermingled mountain-tops,
> In one inseparable glory clad—
> Creatures of one ethereal substance, met
> In consistory, like a diadem
> Or crown of burning seraphs, as they sit
> In the empyrean.
>   (X.478–83)

In this elaborate Miltonic diction, the clouds are made to gather over Hawkshead like the crown of heaven over—in a word—God.[14] Wordsworth never backed away from representing his poetic calling in the highest rhetorical terms available to him: he means to suggest that his becoming a poet, thanks to Taylor, made his career a creative challenge to, and ultimately an imaginative victory over, the misplaced redemptive energies of Robespierre's Jacobins, who are duly represented as a consistory of fallen angels from Milton's Hell. The angels and devils come from *Paradise Lost*, the landscape is Wordsworth's boyhood paradise, Taylor was his favorite teacher, and Gray was Taylor's favorite poet. By connecting Taylor to Robespierre, and Gray to Milton, and placing himself at the nexus of them all, Wordsworth suggests that Taylor helped him to be the next English Milton.

Taylor's influence on the young Wordsworth was underscored with the psychological authority of a deathbed commission. Before he died, in June 1786, Taylor called in some of the older boys to say a last good-bye: "He ... said to me, 'My head will soon he low'" Wordsworth never forgot the encouragement Taylor gave him: "[hc] Would have loved me, as one not destitute / Of promise, nor belying the kind hope / Which he had formed when I at his command / Began to spin, at first, my toilsome songs" (X.510–14). Taylor had chosen four modest lines from Gray's "Elegy" for his tombstone, praying for repose in "the bosom of his Father and his God." Wordsworth does not mention which lines of Gray *he* had in mind, but we can easily find them by cross-referencing the allusions in his *homage* to Taylor, for they are the heart of the lesson Gray teaches from "the short and simple annals of the poor": "Some mute inglorious Milton here may rest, / Some Cromwell guiltless of his country's blood."[14a]

William Taylor was a Cambridge graduate, and like many eighteenth-century schoolmaster-vicars combined his duties with a cultured love of literature, construing his profession as essentially "literary," though he was also well trained in mathematics. He had excellent ideas about literary instruction. He set his young charges to imitate not only the best classical models but also a wide range of contemporary literary ones: not just Homer, Ovid, and Virgil but also Gray, Collins, Goldsmith, and other mid-century poets of "Sensibility," who reacted sentimentally against the urbane, satiric verse of Dryden, Pope, and Swift. These poets, many of whom lived unhappy, reclusive lives and wrote poems to match, raised a self-consciously minor poetry to the status of a major genre, or at least a very popular one, in the half century between the deaths of Pope and Swift in 1744 and 1745 and the publication of *Lyrical Ballads* by Wordsworth and Coleridge in 1800. They were the poets of an age of prose. To be sure, the Hawkshead boys read Shakespeare, Spenser, Milton, Dryden, and Pope as well. But Taylor gave his best boys extraordinary opportunities to read poetry by living writers. He and other masters or ushers lent the boys their own books and encouraged them to join book clubs and lending libraries in Kendal and Penrith, where the boys read Gray, Goldsmith, Thomson, Collins, Cowper, Burns, Akenside, Williams, Shenstone, the Warton brothers (Joseph and Thomas), Percy, Smith, Beattie, Chatterton, Crabbe, Langhorne, Carter, and Aikin. Few twentieth-century readers who are not literary specialists will get very far in that list before starting to inquire, "Who?" It was as if students born in 1970 were, as they finished high school in the late 1980s, reading not only Eliot, Yeats, Pound, Stevens, and Frost but also Larkin, MacNeice, Hughes, Harrison, Muldoon, and Heaney—or, in the United States, Lowell, Sexton, Wright, Rich, Nemerov, and Levine.

These long roll calls give the lie to Wordsworth's disingenuous claim in 1791 to William Mathews, one of his best college friends, who had asked him for some contemporary reading suggestions: "God knows my incursions into the fields of modern literature, excepting in our own language three volumes of *Tristram Shandy*, and two or three papers of the

Spectator, half subdued—are absolutely nothing."[15] The facts are far different.[16]

The range and energy of Wordsworth's early reading, both in and out of school, is revealed in two quite different accounts of it. In the *Memoirs*, his nephew reported that "the Poet's father set him very early to learn portions of the works of the best English poets by heart, so that at an early age he could repeat large portions of Shakespeare, Milton, and Spenser."[17] This sounds right; it fits with what we see elsewhere of Wordsworth's linguistic precocity. But in his "Autobiographical Memoranda," the poet himself says this: "Of my earliest days at school I have little to say, but that they were very happy ones, chiefly because I was left at liberty, then and in the vacations, to read whatever I liked. For example, I read all Fielding's works, Don Quixote, Gil Blas, and any part of Swift that I liked, Gulliver's Travels and the Tale of a Tub, being both much to my taste."[18] This also sounds true, but very different from the other statement.

The first comment shows Wordsworth's literary precociousness, how he was trained by his father from a very early age to succeed in a certain professional line—not that of meagerly self-supporting poet, but the general arena of "literary" accomplishments associated with university fellowships, lucrative positions in great men's houses (tutor, chaplain, or secretary), comfortable church livings, or, at the bottom of this professional line, school-mastering. This is the kind of training William Taylor had had, that Christopher Wordsworth would have, and that many of the poets of Sensibility used as the basis for their amateur standing in the arts. A clear performance ethic was at work in the boy's being "set" to "learn portions" of the "best," and to "repeat large portions" from memory. This is not all bad, as we know from the nearly contemporaneous example of Mozart's father's severe regimen for his son.

But, set against this rigorous standard for high achievement, the feeling of release and enthusiasm in the second quotation is notable: "happy ... at liberty ... to read whatever books I liked." It sounds like the book-reading equivalent of his breakneck horseback rides. This description confirms the educational romanticism which Wordsworth celebrated in Book V ("Books") of *The Prelude* and exemplified with apparently innocuous fairy tales, *The Arabian Nights*, Jack the Giant Killer, Robin Hood, and "Sabra in the forest with St. George." But his enthusiasm for the raffish, amoral picaresque novels in his second list was based on his personal inclination toward their very similar heroes and plots. Like their fairy-tale counterparts, they are all underdogs who become rescuing heroes: precisely the deep-structure plot of *The Prelude*. They are all stories of young men at large, on the road, alone, seeking their fortune. They are orphans,

foundlings, or other family castoffs—Tom Jones, Joseph Andrews, and Gil
Blas—or inspired, half-crazed wanderers moving through worlds of
imagined wonderment: Don Quixote, Lemuel Gulliver, and Sterne's
"Yorick." They are all "road novels" in the way that much of Wordsworth's
life from 1790 to 1800 will be a "road" experience, and like his poems of the
same period. Some of them are tours that unravel, trailing off into quests for
life directions. Their young hero is seeking his fortune but also seeking to
"find himself," and trying to understand the people he meets along the
way—who, by virtue of their also being out on the road, are frequently poor
and lost themselves.

The story of Tom Jones the foundling, who is revealed to be a
gentleman's son and thus eligible to claim the hand of the beautiful heiress,
Sophia Western, played as lively in Wordsworth's youthful imagination as it
did for many other hopeful, up-and-coming young Englishmen, making it
one of the first best-sellers in the dawning age of the novel. But the influence
of Alain-René Lesage's *Gil Blas of Santillane* has been entirely neglected by
Wordsworth scholars. Lesage's rambling novel, beautifully translated by
Smollett in 1749, delighted Wordsworth when his father purchased its four-
volume edition on December 27, 1781.[19] It was an interesting gift to set
before an eleven-year-old son. Gil Blas is sent off by his poor father to be
educated by his clerical uncle, who turns out to be a fake, who turns Gil over
to an increasingly dubious set of tutors, until he sets out to complete his
education at Salamanca. He reaches it only after hundreds of pages of
adventures, captures, escapes, and seductions, by the end of which he has
become a practiced gigolo, go-between, and double agent. Like the works of
Cervantes, Fielding, and Swift, *Gil Blas* has a much larger element of sexual
adventure and misadventure than we are used to associating with
Wordsworthian delight. (It also uses the word "madcap" in contexts
suggesting homosexuality, reminding us of Wordsworth's fond reference to
Robert Greenwood as a "male mad-cap").[20]

All of these heroes are more seduced than seducing, but none is
excessively moral. They all skirt deliciously close to total ruin, but they
triumph by gaining the goal—financial independence—which made them so
popular with their rapidly expanding audience of middle-class readers. As
cautionary tales, they were the radical alternative, or therapeutic detour, to
the route from respectable family to proper school to best university to
quasi-independent profession which was so assiduously mapped out by
Wordsworth's elders. They were precisely about what promising young men
should *not* do, which is why they were so popular. Young Wordsworth's life
until he was well past thirty must often have looked to his guardians like the
self-indulgent acting out of a picaresque novel.

But Wordsworth's future course of development is best charted through his Hawkshead reading in contemporary poetry. Even if he did not read the complete works of all the poets listed above, it is still a remarkable range, and anticipates much of his later achievement. Hour for hour, book reading took up as much of his time as ice-skating, bird nesting, horseback riding, and boat racing. Just as he knew Philip Braithwaite, John Gibson, and the Castlehow boys, so too he knew and "conversed" with Helen Maria Williams, Joseph Warton, James Thomson, and many others, and the traces of *these* boyish acquaintances can be followed in the textures of his work with as much confidence as his references to boyhood games and sports in Hawkshead. Even when Wordsworth wandered at night, or when he and his friends played at minstrelsy, they were not "just being boys"; they were trying on ready-to-wear cultural fashions.

A common understanding of the influence of contemporary eighteenth-century poets on Wordsworth's youthful development simply takes him at his word in the preface to *Lyrical Ballads* and grants him high cultural status as a wholly original Romantic poet. A somewhat more sophisticated approach allows that he was indeed influenced in his youth by the "poetic diction" of his Sensibility predecessors, but asserts that he recognized the error of his ways and created the new poetry of ordinary language for which he is deservedly famous, "a man speaking to men." A still more comprehensive view recognizes not only that these poets influenced his immature juvenile verse but that their signatures can be traced even in the revolutionary work of Wordsworth's first maturity, *whose novelty is presented by Wordsworth as if it rejected the habits of thought, diction, and imagery characteristic of the poetry of Sensibility*. This "later influence" has indeed, for the most part, "yet remain[ed] untold," as Wordsworth plainly admitted in his discussion of his early reading. In his notes to his poems he was not forthcoming about these influences, usually associating the poems with their time and place of composition but saying little or nothing about their literary debts. There is nothing unusual or reprehensible about this: Wordsworth is not required to be the scholar of his own work. But when time and place and local inspiration are wholly substituted for other literary influences, we have not learned all we should about the process of Wordsworth's self-creation.

The poetry of Sensibility permeates the great work of Wordsworth's first maturity: that of the Poet of *Lyrical Ballads*. Just a few salient examples will show strong influences in the themes and subjects of his poetry, as well as in settings, imagery, and other aspects of his style. Equally noteworthy in the Poet's self-creation, and even more frequently overlooked, are the ways in which the careers and "lifestyles" of these men and women provided models for Wordsworth to follow—and ultimately to reject. Not only what they wrote and how they wrote it, but also the career conditions these poets established in order to give themselves time to write, were matters of keen estimation for the young Wordsworth, especially the degrees to which these writers depended on the old system of patronage or on the emerging new one of marketplace capitalism. For both options the mighty figure of Samuel Johnson (d. 1784) was highly symbolic, from his famous rejection of Lord Chesterfield's patronage to his heroic endeavors in producing the first great English *Dictionary* virtually single-handed.

In varying degrees, the two dozen or so poets that Wordsworth read and imitated at Hawkshead all wrote elaborate descriptions of rural scenes of natural beauty, with intermittent scenes of Sublime terror and apostrophes to mytho-religious "Powers!" that were vaguely orthodox or Deistic. Their descriptions were marked by a new realism, or attention to detail, and an interest in describing common rural sights and objects (such as sunsets and peasants' cottages) that had not appeared much in English poetry before. They often expressed a desire for simplicity in life and expression, in language that was anything but. These elements were frequently cast into the theme of returning, sadder but wiser, to one's "native vales," sometimes motivated by loss of youth, love, and success in the larger world, and sometimes in revolted reaction against the high degree of corruption in urban centers, particularly London. In this outline of elements, we can already see the main outlines of Wordsworth's poetical career image.

The desire to go back to simple places with simple manners and sincere language was often extended historically into a broad program for recovering older, more genuine ways of living and speaking. Sometimes this focused on the era just before the national trauma of the civil war, the reign of Elizabeth I, but more often it tried to go "all the way" back, not only to the antique Greek and Roman patterns of England's Neoclassical myth, but to ancient or fictitious traditions of Welsh, Scottish, and generally Celtic bards and minstrels, as in Percy's *Reliques of Ancient English Poetry* (1765) and Beattie's *The Minstrel* (1770). The semifictions of James Macpherson's *Fragments of Ancient Poetry Collected in the Highlands of Scotland* (1760), "translated" from fragments of oral tradition about third-century Gaelic warrior-bards named Fingal and Ossian, and the brilliant if fraudulent imitations of Thomas Chatterton's "Rowley Poems" (1770), which he claimed to have recovered from fifteenth-century manuscripts in Bristol, were another part of this enthusiasm for native origins. So too were the recurring fads for more or less authentic "primitives" like Stephen Duck, called the Thresher Poet, Mary Collier, the Poetical Washerwoman, Ann Yearsley, the Bristol Milkmaid (a.k.a. Lactilla), and other farmer or plowboy poets from Robert Burns to

John Clare.[21] It is not hard to associate much of Wordsworth's oeuvre with this broad program.

Sophisticated theorists of the simple life diffused it into fashionable intellectual life. Hugh Blair's *Critical Dissertation on the Poems of Ossian* (1763) and *Lectures on Rhetoric and Belles Lettres* (1783) are one source for the literary impact of these ideas on Wordsworth, as are the various literary essays and dissertations of Blair's fellow Scot James Beattie.[22] Thomas Warton's history of English literature (1774–81) is generally acknowledged to be the first systematic attempt to establish a *history* of English cultural artifacts—that is, poems—that had heretofore been taken for granted. By the time Wordsworth arrived at Hawkshead, despite ferocious rearguard actions by Johnson and his London circle against what they regarded as "the dangerous prevalence of imagination," such views were nearly official culture: Thomas Warton was named poet laureate in 1775.

The philosophical basis for the liberating value of emotion, against the rigidifying claims of reason, had long been reasserted, most notably by Anthony Ashley Cooper, the third earl of Shaftesbury (1671–1713). But a poet was wanting to make them good. Calls for original new bards went out regularly, but in poems whose melancholy tone undercut their effectiveness. They simply re-expressed the problem, and faded away from the challenge of a solution. Manifestos of imaginative freedom were written in the most regretful ways imaginable, enlivened with merely histrionic exclamation marks. Joseph Warton—for the movement was most often called "the school of Warton"—said forthrightly in the "Advertisement" to his *Odes on Various Subjects* (1746) that "the fashion of moralizing in verse has been carried too far" and that his poems were "an attempt to bring Poetry back into its right channel": more imaginative and descriptive, and less didactic. His first ode, "To Fancy," calls for "some chosen swain" who sounds very like Wordsworth's later estimation of himself as "a chosen Son": "Like light'ning, let his mighty verse / The bosom's inmost foldings pierce; / With native beauties win applause, / Beyond cold critic's studied laws." But Warton could not do it himself: he kept up his spirits with some odes on Liberty, on Health, and against Superstition, but gradually he turned away from his intellectual message toward his melancholy medium, with odes on Despair, Evening, Solitude, and "To a Lady Who Hates the Country." Similarly, William Collin's "Ode on the Poetical Character" (1746) starts strong but ends weak: England's poets were once inspired by godlike power, but "Heav'n, and *Fancy*, kindred Pow'rs, / Have now o'erturned th'inspiring Bow'rs."

Since Wordsworth is the poet of origins and originality par excellence, he has stimulated, from the beginning, a search for the Ur-point of his imagination, despite his sensible disclaimer:

> Who knows the individual hour in which
> His habits were first sown even as a seed,
> Who ... shall point as with a wand, and say
> "This portion of the river of my mind
> Came from yon fountain"?
>   (II.210–15)

But readers have never wearied of seeking that fountain, either in a place (Hawkshead?), a person (Ann Wordsworth?), or a poem—many poems. The search is appropriate, given the subject, but it is also endless, or rather beginning-less. As Wordsworth went on to say, in his self-protective advice to himself it is a "Hard task to analyse a soul, in which ... each most obvious and particular thought— ... in the words of reason deeply weighed— / Hath no beginning" (II.232–37).

Hence it is fitting that "the first poem from which he remembered to have received great pleasure," an "Ode to Spring" attributed to Elizabeth Carter, should turn out not to be by her but by Lucy Aikin, known to contemporaries as Mrs. Anna Barbauld (1743–1825), a consistently successful author of poems for children who also enjoyed a wide adult readership.[23] Elizabeth Carter (1717–1806) owed her literary reputation to Samuel Johnson, based primarily on her translations of Epictetus. But her *Poems on Several Occasions* (4th ed., 1789) contained many elegies and odes in the new Sentimental style, including several that anticipate its Romantic revival, such as her "Ode to Melancholy."

Carter and Barbauld were not typical of the poets who influenced Wordsworth at Hawkshead. Their combination of emotion with natural metaphors was still strongly framed by didactic abstractions, just the sort of thing Joseph Warton wanted to get away from. They were entirely appropriate for William Taylor to introduce into the Hawkshead schoolroom, but different from what he offered his older, more intelligent boys outside of class.

Yet Carter and Barbauld were typical of Wordsworth's earliest influences in another way: they were women. Wordsworth's share in the sector of the literary market sometimes called "women's writing" is notable, because his first productions were so conversant in this mode and because his poetic revolution depended in part on distinguishing what he was doing from its characteristic and highly successful productions: novels and poems of sentiment and romance. Though Wordsworth is, as Coleridge said, one of the most "masculine" of poets (referring to his ability to distance himself emotionally from his subjects), he like the other major Romantic writers sought to retain a "feminine" valuation of emotion that was supposed to be part of women writers' natural stock-in-trade.[24]

Much stronger feminine influences on the young Wordsworth's reading and writing were Charlotte Smith and Helen Maria Williams. Wordsworth's first published poem was addressed to Williams, and he went to France in 1791 with a letter of introduction to her from Smith, to whom he was distantly related by marriage: she was John Robinson's sister-in-law. From Helen Williams, Wordsworth got emotion and lots of it. "She wept" is the opening phrase of his "Sonnet on Seeing Miss Helen Maria Williams Weep at a Tale of Distress." Tears are shed on virtually every page of her *Poems* of 1786; one of her special effects was to represent tears as if falling on the very page we are reading. But Williams's locales and situations were of more lasting interest to Wordsworth than her language. Her "Edwin and Eltruda: A Legendary Tale" opens "where the pure Derwent's waters glide ... [and] A castle rear'd its head"—that is, Cockermouth Castle, a neighborly setting for a fantastic love story of immediate adolescent interest to Wordsworth.

Extensive borrowings from Helen Williams's friend Charlotte Smith (1749–1806) have been found in many of Wordsworth's poems, especially from her *Elegiac Sonnets*, first published in 1784.[25] Wordsworth's own copy is inscribed, "St. John's Cambridge '89."[26] In 1833 he backhandedly acknowledged his debt to her in a note to his "Stanzas Suggested in a Steamboat off St. Bees' Head": "The form of the stanza in this poem, and something in the style of versification, are adopted from the 'St. Monica,' a poem of much beauty upon a monastic subject, by Charlotte Smith: a lady to whom English verse is under greater obligations than are likely to be either acknowledged or remembered. She wrote little, and that little unambitiously, but with true feeling for rural nature, at a time when nature was not much regarded by English poets; for in point of time her earlier writings preceded, I believe, those of Cowper and Burns."[27] This is really quite disingenuous, especially the vague "I believe," from the poet who had, by 1833, established in perpetuity the priority of *his* claims on true feelings for rural nature. For Smith's "earlier writings" also "preceded" those of Wordsworth, whose verse is therefore also "under greater obligation" to hers than he has "either acknowledged or remembered."

The dominant theme of her poems is the loss of youth and happiness, in contrast to the constant beauty of her beloved home district. She celebrates the river Aurun in much the same way that Wordsworth does the river Derwent, and the difference in quality between her expressions of this theme and his is moot. Smith: "Ah! hills beloved!—where once, a happy child, / Your beechen shades, your turf, your flowers among. / I wove your blue-bells into garlands wild, / And woke your echoes with my artless song" ("To the South Downs," ll. 1–4). Wordsworth: "Fair scenes! with other eyes, than once, I gaze, / The ever-varying charm your round displays, / Than when, erewhile, I taught, 'a happy child,' / The echoes of your rocks my carols wild" (*An Evening Walk*, ll. 17–20). Smith identifies her internal quotation (from Gray) in a note; but Wordsworth's quotation—of Smith (he removed the quotation marks in his final, 1849 edition)—was not attributed until 1982, with the deadpan scholarly comment "It seems clear that the ... passage contains Wordsworth's first acknowledgment of his obligations to Charlotte Smith's poetry."[28] If this be acknowledgment, what constitutes neglect?

The male poets of Sensibility were stronger influences on Wordsworth, not because they were better poets, but because they enjoyed by right of cultural tradition precisely what the women poets lacked: careers whose patterns could be studied and imitated by young admirers.

James Thomson's "Winter" (1726) and *The Seasons* (1730) anticipated Joseph Warton's call to return poetry "into its right [descriptive] channel" by nearly a generation, and became one of the most popular poems in Europe. Thomson described the appearances of the seasons elaborately but not naturally. Or rather—since the question of what constitutes a "natural" description of natural phenomena is logically undecidable—he used very ornate diction to describe many ordinary natural occurrences. Samuel Johnson was still admiring *The Seasons* in the 1770s, though he criticized its "lack of method." But Wordsworth as a fourteen- to seventeen-year-old boy was more interested in images and actions than abstract ideas, and his debt to *The Seasons* was first incurred by adapting Thomson's descriptions directly to his Hawkshead activities.[29] For example, ice-skating: "they sweep / On sounding skates a thousand different ways / In circling poise swift as the wind along ... / Their vigorous youth in bold contention wheel / The long resounding course" ("Winter," ll. 768–70, 774–75). "I wheeled about / Proud and exulting, like an untired horse / That cares not for its home. All shod with steel / We hissed along the polished ice in games / Confederate, imitative of the chace" (*Prelude* ll. 458–62). Or nutting, where Wordsworth picked up Thomson's romantic, idyllic swains and virgins—

> Ye swains, now hasten to the hazel bank ...
>   In close array
> Fit for the thickets and the tangling shrub,
> Ye virgins, come ...
>   ... the clustering nuts for you
> The lover finds amid the secret shade;

And, where they burnish on the topmost bough,
With active vigour crashes down the tree ....
　("Autumn," ll. 611ff.)

—and transferred their emotions to his own sexual intercourse with the
natural scene:

　　　　... the hazels rose
Tall and erect, with tempting clusters hung,
A virgin scene!—A little while I stood,
Breathing with such suppression of the heart
As joy delights in; and, with wise restraint
Voluptuous, fearless of a rival, eyed
The banquet ....
　　　　　　　Then up I rose,
And dragged to earth both branch and bough, with crash
And merciless ravage ....
　("Nutting," 19–25, 43–45)

Where Thomson's "shepherd stalks gigantic" through the fog ("Autumn,"
727), Wordsworth's follows him, "In size a giant, stalking through the fog"
(VIII.401).[30] When Thomson's "western sun withdraws the darkened day"
("Autumn," 1082), Wordsworth's "western clouds a deepening gloom
display."[31]

At this point we may simply feel we have reached the limits of what
sixty years of stylized descriptive language can do with sunsets. But
Thomson's introduction to "Autumn" is so like Wordsworth's in "The
Ruined Cottage" that it's clear his early reading of Thomson went far beyond
sharing common literary conventions. "'Tis raging noon; and, vertical, the
Sun / Darts on the head direct his forceful rays. / O'er heaven and earth, far
as the ranging eye / Can sweep, a dazzling deluge reigns; and all / From pole
to pole is undistinguished blaze" ("Autumn," 432–36). Here is Wordsworth's
similar scene: "'Twas was Summer, and the sun was mounted high, / Along
the south the uplands feebly glared / Through a pale steam, and all the
northern downs / In clearer air ascending shewed far off / Their surfaces on
which the shadows lay / Of many clouds far as the sight could reach" ("The
Ruined Cottage," 1–6). These close verbal parallels continue for nearly fifty
lines. The story that Wordsworth proceeds to tell in this setting shows great
advances upon Thomson, but the close similarity of the two passages
indicates that Wordsworth's advance depends upon Thomson's text as much
as—if not more than—the observations of landscapes and poverty in Dorset

to which Wordsworth attributed his descriptions: "All that relates to Margaret and the ruined cottage, etc., was taken from observations made in the South West of England."[32]

Thomson was a precursor of the new school, and, as a Scotsman who succeeded in London (thanks to Pope's patronage), he also anticipated the frequency with which practitioners of the new descriptive poetry hailed from the north. Thomas Percy, James Beattie, and Robert Burns were other authors in this northern constellation whom Wordsworth read toward the end of his Hawkshead years. Each in his own way called for a national cultural revival to rise from approximately the region where Wordsworth lived, and each located the source of a new imaginative power in a romantically historicized "north countrie" setting, peopled by simple folk following rural pursuits far from urban corruption, and speaking a native dialect.

Thomas Percy (1729–1811) changed his name from Piercy when he took up his first parish, in Northampton, after his M.A. from Oxford. Although born a grocer's son in Shropshire, he associated himself with the Percys of the north for both cultural and practical reasons; he eventually became chaplain and secretary to the duke of Northumberland.[33] He dedicated his famous *Reliques of Ancient English Poetry* (1765) to the countess of Northumberland, a well-known "romantic" diarist, who lived near his parish. His career as a literary priest, like many of these authors' lives, was another influence on Wordsworth, who was intended for the same profession and who knew these writers' lives well from the biographical notices and memoirs which prefaced their works.

Percy's essay "The Ancient English Minstrels" stimulated young Wordsworth's developing sense of himself as a poet. It stresses the northern associations of minstrelsy—signifying Scotland and all of England north of the Humber. "There is hardly an ancient Ballad or Romance, wherein a Minstrel or Harper appears, but he is characterized by way of eminence to have been 'of the North Countrie': and indeed the prevalence of the Northern dialect in such kind of poems, shews that this representation is real."[34] Whatever the Welsh or the Irish may have thought of this, such a nearby geographical identification enthused the self-conscious "Minstrels of Winandermere," Charles and John Farish, Robert Greenwood, and William Wordsworth. Many of the ballads have local settings, like "The Nut-Brown Maid," a popular favorite, who is sorely tested by her lover, "a squyer of low degre," but finally taken home in triumph "to Westmarlande, / Which is myne herytage."

As in *Lyrical Ballads*, there is a series of Mad Songs in the *Reliques*, though Percy notes this was more of a southern specialty: "the English have more songs and ballads on the subject than any of their neighbors." One of these, "The Frantic Lady," has very close parallels to Wordsworth's "The Mad Mother."[35] Wordsworth's poem is also indebted to Percy's "Lady Bothwell's Lament" for its question-and-answer dialogue between mother and her baby. Percy's Frantic Lady was mad for love, but not evidently a mother, whereas his Lady Bothwell is not mad but has a baby, her husband having divorced her to marry Mary, Queen of Scots: "Balow, my babe, ly stil and sleipe! / It grieves me fair to see thee weipe: / If thou be silent, Ise be glad, / Thy maining maks my heart ful sad." Wordsworth: "Sweet babe! they say that I am mad, / But nay, my heart is far too glad; / And I am happy when I sing / Full many a sad and doleful thing." Wordsworth brilliantly combined the two themes of motherhood and madness, creating a dangerous instability in his speaker that his two models individually lack. But his only note to the poem shifts the debt for its inspiration from literature to life: "Alfoxden, 1798. The subject was reported to me by a Lady of Bristol who had seen the poor creature." Percy's two Ladies, Frantic and Bothwell, must share in the credit given to this Bristol Lady, if indeed she existed.

Within five years Percy's call for a modern revival of old minstrelsy was taken up by his countryman James Beattie. The first version of *The Minstrel* (1770) was so successful that a second installment was called for; Books I and II were published together in 1774. Like Percy, Langhorne, Crabbe, and others in this group—including Wordsworth—Beattie came of poor but respectable professional gentry background. But without benefit of a university education and contacts, he achieved his independence by stitching together schoolmastering jobs and low-level church appointments. He had made a stout defense of Scotland's honor against Charles Churchill's hilarious attack, in *The Progress of Famine* (1763), which ut its finger exactly on the way these "rude" bards were condescendingly adopted by London:

> *Thence* simple bards, by simple prudence taught,
> To this *wise* town by simple patrons brought,
> In simple manner utter simple lays,
> And take, with simple pensions, simple praise.

Beattie's *Minstrel* was well received by the conservative old literary lions in London, as well as by the young literary cubs in Hawkshead. Wordsworth and his friends adopted the style and manners of this ersatz chivalric minstrelsy, in Charles Farish's *The Minstrels of Winandermere* and in the boys' picturesque placing of Greenwood, "the minstrel of our group," on the Windermere "holmes" for relaxing, pseudo-sophisticated sunset concerts. The Hawkshead boys aped the mannerisms of Beattie's poem with a devotion akin to that of late twentieth-century teenagers adopting the dress, style, speech, and mannerisms of contemporary rock stars, and their youthful minstrelsy on the lakes echoes in the sound of amateur rock-and-roll groups practicing in garages and basements around the world.

Remarkable similarities of tone, theme, and attitude between Beattie's minstrel persona, Edwin, and Wordsworth's developing poetical role have been noted.[36] The minstrel was a prototype of Wordsworth's juvenile poet figure, and Beattie's subtitle, "The Progress of Genius," parallels Wordsworth's working title for *The Prelude,* "the poem on the growth of my own mind," but on a national rather than an individual level. Such was Beattie's plan for Edwin: educated by a wise old hermit, "He meditates new arts on Nature's plan,"and is tutored in the history of poetry to a new level of achievement. Exactly how he does this, Beattie "fain would sing: but ah! I strive in vain," and so he too dwindles into the characteristic melancholy of Sensibility.

The earliest commentator to recognize Beattie's influence on Wordsworth was his sister, Dorothy. In her charming letters of 1787 to her friend Jane Pollard, recording her rediscovery and exploration of her long-lost brothers, she presents "my dear William" as a version of Beattie's model: "'In truth he was a strange and wayward wight fond of each gentle &c. &c.' That verse of Beattie's Minstrel always reminds me of him, and indeed the whole character of Edwin resembles much what William was when I first knew him after my leaving Halifax—'and oft he traced the uplands &c, &c, &c.'"[37] Doubtless she was prompted in this identification by the favorite parts of Beattie that William read or recited to her, which are reflected in various ways throughout his works. When he represented himself as "singled out ... from a swarm of rosy boys ... For my grave looks, too thoughtful for my years" (*The Excursion,* I.56–59), he was adapting Beattie's words for Edwin: "no vulgar boy, / Deep thought oft seem'd to fix his infant eye" (I.16).

Robert Burns (1759–1796) took the innovations of Thomson and Beattie a big step further by writing many of his poems in the regional dialect of southern Scotland, and on contemporary topics. Wordsworth purchased Burns's most important volume, *Poems, Chiefly in the Scottish Dialect* (1786), from the Penrith book club as a present for Dorothy before he went to Cambridge in 1787, having read it enthusiastically during his last year at Hawkshead.[38] Burns's use of Scottish (though a third of the poems are in standard English) marks a shift in theme and focus not present in the tamer innovations of Beattie and Thomson. Like all the writers of Sensibility, they were mild rebels, proffering their works from the margins of contemporary literature as self-consciously minor productions hopeful of acceptance by mainline culture, symbolized by the "Great Chain," Samuel Johnson.

But Robert Burns was not such a co-optable rebel. He interwove poems about the proper language and subjects for poetry with poems about country manners and problems. On the first manuscript page of "The Ruined Cottage," Wordsworth penned an epigraph from Burns, the first two and last two lines of this stanza from "Epistle to J.L. L*****k [John Lapraik], an Old Scots Bard. April 1st, 1785":

> Gie me ae spark o' Nature's fire,
> That's a' the learning I desire;
> Then tho' I drudge thro' dub an' mire
> At pleugh or cart,
> My Muse, tho' hamely in attire,
> May touch the heart.

These are the same sentiments that Burns had prefixed to his own volume, in English:

> The Simple Bard, unbroke by rules of Art,
> He pours the wild effusions of the heart:
> And if inspir'd, 'tis Nature's pow'rs inspire;
> Her's all the melting thrill, and her's the kindling fire.

Burns's volume ends with "A Bard's Epitaph," which uses the same. sequence of challenges delivered to other, supposedly more useful vocations (soldier, priest, merchant) that Wordsworth later adopted in "A Poet's Epitaph" to arrive at a remarkably similar conclusion: "Is there a Bard of rustic song / Who, noteless, steals the crouds among ... / ... Here pause—and thro' the starting tear, / Survey this grave" (7–8, 17–18). Wordsworth: "But who is He, with modest looks, / And clad in homely russet brown? ... / ... Here stretch thy body at full length; / Or build thy house upon his grave" (37–38, 59–60). Both poems are indebted to the pastoral tradition of one shepherd piping a lament at the grave of another. But Burns invoked this tradition mainly to distinguish his poems from it: "The following trifles are not the production of the Poet, who, with all the advantages of learned art, and perhaps amid the elegancies and idlenesses of upper life, looks down for a rural theme, with an eye to Theocritus or Virgil." This, the lead sentence of Burns's preface, helped prepare the way for Wordsworth's great preface of 1800.

The Scottish or Northern Revival was not the only kind of poetry that interested William Taylor and his best students. The contemporary English poets George Crabbe, John Langhorne, and William Shenstone were also high on their lists of extracurricular reading. These were some of the first poets who took it upon themselves to describe the plight of the poor as a fit subject for serious poetry. The literature of Sensibility, with its large funds of pathos, expended much emotion on the poor, but predominantly in sentimental pastoral rhetoric like Thomson's and Beattie's. The one great poem that transcends this level before the 1780s is Gray's "Elegy Written in a Country Church Yard" (1751), which purports to read "the short and simple annals of the poor." But we do not look to Gray to learn what poverty is like, still less what to do about it, unless we are disposed to accept his view that its greatest claim on our attention is to "implore the passing tribute of a sigh."

Crabbe's *The Village* (1783) was written against these fashions of affected pastoral representations of poverty, but it was not a protest poem in the modern radical sense. Crabbe, another of the many literary divines on Wordsworth's extracurricular reading list, was surely "against" poverty, but his best hope was for an enlightened aristocracy to take better paternal care of the peasants in their parishes, following the example of his patron the duke of Rutland. Wordsworth read Crabbe as early as 1783, when the best parts of *The Village* were excerpted in the *Annual Register*, available at Hawkshead.[39] These were Crabbe's set pieces of naturalistic description, the worn-out laborer, the parish poorhouse, the cheating apothecary, the jovial hunting parson, and the pauper's funeral.

Crabbe knew the world of parish politics that Wordsworth also knew from Cockermouth, where many social issues were resolved by "the yearly dinner, the septennial bribe" (I.114). His exhausted old laborer anticipates Wordsworth's Simon Lee, the Old Huntsman: "He once was chief in all the rustic trade; / His steady hand the straitest furrow made; / Full many a prize he won, and still is proud / To find the triumphs of his youth allow'd; / A transient pleasure sparkles in his eyes, / He hears and smiles, then thinks again and sighs" ("The Village," 188–93).

The situation of Crabbe's laborer is the same as that of Wordsworth's "Old Cumberland Beggar." Both authors describe the same social phenomena: "roundsmen," paupers sent around the parish from house to house by the overseer of the poor to get work (for about sixpence a day) and food.[40] But what Crabbe simply reports with pity, Wordsworth finds a way to celebrate as the occasion for virtuous philanthropy: "the villagers in him / Behold a record which together binds / Past deeds and offices of charity." Whether his view or Crabbe's description of villagers' "ruthless taunts of lazy poor" is more accurate depends a lot on the parish in question. Both men deplored the alternative, the poorhouse, which was in many parishes purposely left in a terrible state to discourage applicants. But though Crabbe represented the condition of the poor more realistically than the fashionable conventions of picturesque description, he did not have a theory of language and its relations to culture and politics such as Wordsworth proposed in 1800.

In 1837, when he was nearly seventy, Wordsworth compared Crabbe to John Langhorne (1735–1779), "our Westmorland Poet," on the question of poverty as a subject for poetry, with a side glance at Shenstone:

> ["The Country justice"] is the first Poem, unless perhaps Shenstone's Schoolmistress be excepted, that fairly brought the Muse into the Company of common life, to which it comes nearer than Goldsmith, and upon which it looks with a tender and enlightened humanity—and with a charitable, (and being so) philosophical and poetical construction that is too rarely found in the works of Crabbe. It is not without many faults in style from which Crabbe's more austere judgment preserved him—but these to me are trifles in a work so original and touching.[41]

Wordsworth made this subtle discrimination for an admirer who accepted the new opinion that the great poet of the poor was now Wordsworth. He apportions value to Langhorne for content and to Crabbe for style, and modestly leaves unspoken the name of the poet who might be said to have united the two. He unfairly links Crabbe's "austere" style to his ostensibly less charitable views of common life, for Crabbe was nothing if not a social critic. Today Crabbe remains an important minor poet, but Langhorne is almost completely forgotten, except for his associations with Wordsworth, which are worth remembering because Langhorne also combined Lake District origins with poetical attentions to social suffering.

Possibly Wordsworth did not actually read Langhorne until he was at Cambridge,[42] but Langhorne's influence on him is close to Crabbe's, as his proprietary phrase "our Westmorland Poet" indicates. For their differences, we have only to imagine Wordsworth's reaction if he were called "our Cumberland Poet"! Langhorne, born in Kirkby Stephen and schooled in Appleby, offers another instance of a local boy struggling through difficulties to make good. He did not have Wordsworth's social advantages, for his formal education, like Beattie's, ended with grammar school. But by dint of tutoring and schoolmastering he was able to register for an extramural B.D. degree from Cambridge at age twenty-five, the same age at which Beattie achieved the same shaky start, and the age at which Wordsworth would depart for London to throw himself into political journalism. Langhorne's path also led him toward London, "the metropolis, that mart for genius and learning"[43] (Wordsworth would call it "that mighty gulph ... of talents" when he made the same move),[44] where he became a reviewer and writer for the *Monthly Review* from 1764 until his death in 1779.

His "Ode to the Genius of Westmorland" was one of many contemporary stimuli to Wordsworth to praise the Muse in the Lakes. It runs over all the usual picturesque keys—"wild groves," "mountains grey," "dark woods," the poet claiming that he has caught from them "the sacred fire, / That glow'd within my youthful breast," and that he will eventually return to repay his debt to them. But Langhorne's "Ode to the River Eden" (1759), on the Lake District river that flows just east of Penrith into Solway Firth, points to even more specific similarities between these two poets' recognition of their muse in the features of their childhood landscape.

> Delightful Eden! parent stream,
>   Yet shall the maids of Memory say,
> (When, led by Fancy's fairy dream,
>   My young steps trac'd thy winding way)
> How oft along thy mazy shore,
> That many a gloomy alder bore,
>   In pensive thought their Poet stray'd;
> Or, careless thrown thy banks beside,
> Beheld thy dimply waters glide,
> Bright thro' the trembling shade.

These opening lines prepare the way for perhaps the most famous of all Wordsworth's beginnings:

> Was it for this
> That one, the fairest of all rivers, loved
> To blend his murmurs with my nurse's song,
> And from his alder shades and shallows, sent a voice
> That flowed along my dreams? For this didst thou,
> O Derwent, travelling over the green plains
> Near my "sweet birthplace," didst thou, beauteous stream,
> Make ceaseless music through the night and day ....
>   (1799 1.1–9)

Wordsworth's lines read almost like a translation of Langhorne into another language. But Wordsworth's memory—which must include his memory of Langhorne—shares many elements of setting and attitude with Langhorne: the river as parent/nurse, the shady alders (Langhorne has "the poplar tall"), the flowers, the boyish play, the passage's movement toward sunset, and the question if imagination can respond adequately to childhood memories. Wordsworth's lines are of course remarkable for their clear, modern simplicity, though written only forty years later. But perhaps most telling, as his response to a remembered text, is the subtle symbolism by which he transmutes Langhorne's allegorical and abstract personifications into organic metaphors. Langhorne pleasantly imagines old Father Time skipping like a boy, but Wordsworth much more impressively, yet without sacrificing the charm of the situation, manages to suggest that Skiddaw is something like a "bronzed" primitive deity and he a little "naked savage" worshiping before it.

The stylized, artificial quality of nature in these and other contemporary poems owes more to William Shenstone (1714–1763), who was criticized during his lifetime for the excessive prettiness of his poetry. Shenstone's favorite topics are a veritable roll call of Sensibility, featuring elegies on retirement, simplicity, death, friendship, domesticity, disinterestedness, humility, solitude, and benevolence. Shenstone's "Schoolmistress" is another prototype for Wordsworth's idyllic portrait of Ann Tyson (above), in parallels of tone rather than diction.

> Here oft the dame, on Sabbath's decent eve,
> Hymned such psalms as Sternhold forth did mete;
> If winter 'twere, she to her hearth did cleave,
> But in her garden found a summer-seat:
> Sweet melody!
>   (118–22)

Wordsworth's idyllic descriptions of his Hawkshead "School-Time" also owe a debt to the idealized school in Shenstone's popular poem. The single longest section of Shenstone's poem describes the punishment of a wild, wayward boy, but ends with a caution against too severe punishments that might cramp future great spirits:

> E'en now sagacious foresight points to show
> A little bench of heedless bishops here,
> And here a chancellor in embryo,
> Or bard sublime, if bard may e'er be so,
> As Milton, Shakespeare, names that ne'er shall die!
>   (245–49)

The immediate source of such sentiments is Gray's "mute inglorious Miltons," but the theme of a hoped-for new poetic savior echoed through the works of almost all these poets, and it resonated loudly with Wordsworth at Hawkshead, stimulating thoughts about the creation of the Poet that became his master theme.

Wordsworth's sense of the power of his imagination is often expressed in the contrary terms of how great his loss would be if imagination should fail him. Hence it is not surprising that one of Shenstone's clearest influences on him should be in the Lucy poems, those privately coded meditations on the imagined death of his sister, Dorothy, or, what amounted to the nearly same thing, a loss of his confidence in his developing genius. Many of Lucy's characteristics are borrowed from Shenstone's "Nancy of the Vale." The rivers Dove and Avona are far apart, but the maids the poets place on their banks are virtually twin sisters—one generation removed: "'Twas from Avona's banks the maid / Diffus'd her lovely beams, / And ev'ry shining glance display'd / The Naiad of the streams" (Shenstone, 18–21). "She dwelt among the untrodden ways / Besides the banks of Dove ... Fair as a star, when only one / Is shining in the sky" ("She dwelt among the untrodden ways," 1–2). Wordsworth's terse late note, "1799. Composed in the Hartz Forest," again identifies only the physical time and space of his poems' composition: their roots in creative memory very evidently go to "hiding places" at least ten years further back, in Hawkshead.

William Cowper's *Poems* (1782) and *The Task* (1785) were both critical and popular successes when they appeared in the middle of Wordsworth's Hawkshead years, but Cowper's influence on Wordsworth, though long felt, has only recently begun to get its due.[45] Lines like "I gaz'd, myself creating what I saw" (*Task*, IV.290) touch very closely on "Tintern Abbey's" "mighty world / Of eye and ear, both what they half create, / And what perceive." This influence was first set in motion when Wordsworth, like all the other Hawkshead schoolboys, was set to write celebratory verses on the Bishop Sandys's school's bicentenary in 1785. They had immediately before them Cowper's new poem "Tirocinium; or, A Review of the Schools" (1785), which they were expected to refute, since it argued against public school education like theirs in favor of the older aristocratic idea of private education at home by tutors.

But Cowper's influence is as broadly cultural as it is specifically literary. The cool, sensible blank verse of *The Task* is only a step or two from the limpid clarity of *The Prelude* at its best, but those two steps are the stride from talent to genius. Cowper's unassuming voice of personal meditation encouraged Wordsworth's self-examination, though Cowper stopped far short of Wordsworth's claims for his imagination: "no prophetic fires to me belong; / I play with syllables, and sport in song" ("Table Talk," 504–5). The similar motives but different outcomes of these two long poems make all the difference between a major Romantic poem and an amusing, intelligent, but finally unchallenging poem like *The Task*. Many of its episodes start out like those in *The Prelude*, but they never develop into visionary "spots of time." Cowper presciently imagined the fall of the Bastille: "There's not an English heart that would not leap / To hear that ye were fall'n at last" (V.389–90). But his lines "leap" nowhere near the height Wordsworth's heart did when the event actually occurred: "Bliss was it in that dawn to be alive, / But to be young was very heaven!"

These moments of poetic influence are very close, but worlds apart. Cowper's best-loved, most poignant poem, "The Castaway," was written in 1799, the same year that Wordsworth began *The Prelude*. Both *The Task* and *The Prelude* are preparatory, therapeutic poems. But one was written from the last stages of mental debility, while the other took its first steps toward recovery by imagining the creation of a new kind of mind. Cowper's "warfare [was] within" (VI.935), as was Wordsworth's, but Wordsworth raised the stakes of mental struggle much higher. Yet there is no point using Wordsworth as a stick to beat Cowper. The point, rather, is to see how close Cowper, like all these poets of Sensibility, came to Wordsworth, and how far Wordsworth went beyond them.

The time, the place, the occasion, and the mastership of William Taylor combined to make Wordsworth's response to Cowper, his first extended verse production, an unexceptionally positive celebration of his school. What might not have been expected was that the assignment led Wordsworth into a course from which he never thereafter was fundamentally diverted: "This exercise ... put it into my head to compose verses from the impulse of my own mind."[46]

NOTES

1. *EL*, 31, 55–57.

2. John Burnett, A *History of the Cost of Living* (Harmondsworth: Penguin, 1969), 147.

3. TWT, 151.

4. MM1, 25n.

5. Burnett, *Cost of Living*, 158; TWT, 115, 104.

6. MM1, 26.

7. TWT, 85.

8. Eileen Jay, *Wordsworth at Colthouse* (Kendal: Westmorland Gazette, 1981), 28. Some scholars have found mathematical principles deeply functional in Wordsworth's oeuvre: Geoffrey H. Durrant, *Wordsworth and the Great System: A Study of Wordsworth's Poetic Universe* (Cambridge: Cambridge Univ. Press, 1970); Lee M. Johnson, *Wordsworth's Metaphysical Verse: Geometry, Nature, and Form* (Toronto: Univ. of Toronto Press, 1982).

9. *Prose*, 3:372.

10. IF, *PW*, 4:422. Ovid was a general Hawkshead favorite, not just Wordsworth's special taste, since his *Metamorphoses* had been famously translated by George Sandys (1579–1644), son of the school's founder (I am grateful to John West, present curator of the school, for this and other information).

11. Bruce Graver, "Wordsworth's Translations from Latin Poetry" (Ph.D. diss., Univ. of North Carolina, 1983), ii, 65–68.

12. Annabel Patterson, *Pastoral and Ideology: Virgil to Valéry* (Berkeley: Univ. of California Press, 1987), 193–262.

13. Jay, *Wordsworth*, 28–29; TWT, 344–45.

14. WAG, 384, n. 3, citing Paradise Lost, Paradise Regained, and At a Solemn Music.

14a. Curiously, Gray's "Elegy" was also the favorite poem of Wordsworth's nemesis James Lowther, who could quote from it at length and who appreciated it in terms not unlike Wordsworth's coming revolution in English poetics: "I love elevated thoughts, but I'd like 'em as well when plainly expressed" (Hugh Owen, *The Lowther Family* [Chichester: Phillimore, 1990], 300).

15. *LEY*, 56.

16. Scholarly research on Wordsworth's *reading*, as distinct from the literary influences that can be traced in his writing, has in a sense only just begun. Duncan Wu, *Wordsworth's Reading, 1770–1799* (Cambridge: Cambridge Univ. Press, 1993); idem, *Wordsworth's Reading, 1800–1915* (Cambridge: Cambridge Univ. Press, 1995); Robert Paul Kelley, "The Literary Sources of William Wordsworth's Works, 10 July 1793 to 10 June 1797" (Ph.D. diss., Univ. of Hull, 1987).

17. *Memoirs*, 34.

18. *Memoirs*, 10.

19. *CEY*, 54, n. 5.

20. *Gil Blas*, vol. 1, bk. 1, chap. 2.

21. Marilyn Gaull, *English Romanticism: The Human Context* (New York: Norton, 1988), 259.

22. E. H. King, "James Beattie's Literary Essay: 1776, 1783," *Aberdeen University Review* 45 (1974):389–401.

23. MM1, 54.

24. The full story of male Romantic writers' debt to their female contemporaries is just now being written. It frequently presents the unsavory spectacle not only of unacknowledged debts but also of nonpayments accompanied (or disguised) by critical denunciations of precisely the qualities that the male poet loved most. Among many others that might be cited are Marlon Ross, *The Contours of Masculine Desire: Romanticism and the Rise of Women's Poetry* (New York: Oxford Univ. Press, 1989); Stuart Curran, ed., *The Cambridge Companion to British Romanticism* (Cambridge: Cambridge Univ. Press, 1993); Anne K. Mellor, ed., *Romanticism and Feminism* (Bloomington: Indiana Univ. Press, 1988); and Anne K. Mellor, *Romanticism and Gender* (New York: Routledge, 1993).

25. Bishop Hunt, "Wordsworth's Marginalia on Paradise Lost," *Bulletin of the New York Public Library* 73 (1969): 85–103; Kelley, "Literary Sources," 220; Mary Jacobus, *Tradition and Experience in Wordsworth's "Lyrical Ballads" (1798)* (Oxford: Oxford Univ. Press, 1976), 244n, 258n.

26. In WL, DC.

27. *PW*, 4:403.

28. Kelley, "Literary Sources," 220.

29. Jacobus, *Tradition*, 39–44, 105–9, gives excellent accounts of Thomson's philosophical influence on Wordsworth's verse, and of such compositional devices as the

"topographical episode" (which anticipates the "spots of time") and the placement of another figure, or companion, in the scene to give plausible human scale to the rhapsodic praises of nature.

30. WAG, 286, n. 6.

31. "How sweet the walk along the woody steep" (Isle of Wight, 1793), Hayden, 116.

32. *PW*, 5:410.

33. Edward Walford, "Life of Bishop Percy," in his edition of the *Reliques*.

34. *Reliques* (1765), 1:xxi.

35. Hayden, 945–46.

36. See Everard King, *James Beattie* (New York: Twayne, 1977). King may overstate Beattie's influence at times, but most early influences on Wordsworth have been so understated that one can hardly blame him. See Abrams, "Wordsworth and Coleridge on Diction and Figures," *English Institute Essays* (New York: Columbia Univ. Press, 1954), 171–201, and Oliver Elton, *A Survey of English Literature, 1730–1780* (London: Arnold, 1928), viii, which notes that in The Minstrel "'the growth of a poet's soul' [is] mildly anticipated."

37. *LEY*, 100–101.

38. MM1, 73–74.

39. SG, 29, n. 73.

40. George Crabbe, *The Complete Poetical Works*, ed. Norma Dalryrmle-Champneys and Pollard, 3 vols. (Oxford: Clarendon Press, 1988), 1:668.

41. *LLY*, 3:348.

42. MM1, 101–2.

43. *The Poetical Works of John Langhorne, D.D.*, ed. J. T Langhorne [his son] (London: Mawman, 1804), 13. All quotations of Langhorne's work are from this edition.

44. To William Mathews, Nov. 7, 1794, *LEY*, 135.

45. Jacobus, *Tradition*, 44–51 and passim; also Jonathan Wordsworth, *William Wordsworth: The Borders of Vision* (Oxford: Clarendon Press, 1982), 231–32, 248–49, 295–98, 333–59.

46. *Memoirs*, 11–12.

JONATHAN WORDSWORTH

William Wordsworth, The Prelude

*T**he Prelude* was written in four major stages, or versions, over a seven-year period, 1798–1805, but not published till after Wordsworth's death in 1850. It is the great epic of human consciousness, measuring Wordsworth's own position against the aspirations of Milton and the thinking of Coleridge. Milton saw his Christian epic, *Paradise Lost*, as replacing Homer and Virgil. Wordsworth noted the progression and, in an extraordinary passage of 1805, Book III, confidently added himself to the list. It is not that he regards his work as post-Christian, but that he has taken for his theme the human mind, a subject truly modern, without earlier parallel:

> Of genius, power,
> Creation and divinity itself
> I have been speaking, for my theme has been
> What passed within me! Not of outward things
> Done visibly for other minds—words, signs,
> Symbols, or actions—but of my own heart
> Have I been speaking, and my youthful mind.
>   (1805: III. 171–6)[1]

From *A Companion to Romanticism*, edited by Duncan Wu, pp. 179–190. © 1998 by Blackwell Publishers Ltd.

Coleridge, in whose terms Wordsworth was 'at least a semi-atheist', must have found these lines disquieting. They have a bravura which exceeds his most outspoken Unitarian assertions, and hardly square with the Trinitarian orthodoxy he was by now trying to accept. Yet they are clearly related to his own claims for the grandeur of the human imagination. Wordsworth's tones are almost contemptuous as he speaks of his predecessors, who have written the old-fashioned epic of action, battle, 'outward things / Done visibly for other minds'. He himself has looked inward, and found 'genius, power, / Creation and divinity itself'. There could hardly be a grander assertion, but it is not the egotism that it might seem. Wordsworth is strongly aware of his own individuality—'Points have we all of us within our souls / Where all stand single' (ibid., ll. 186–7)—yet rests his claim for the new epic on a godlike capacity that we are assumed to have in common: 'there's not a man / That lives who hath not had his godlike hours' (ibid., ll. 191–2).

Wordsworth is writing in January 1804, a week or two before completing *Ode, Intimation of Immortality from Recollections of Early Childhood*. *The Prelude* has been in abeyance for two years; he takes it up now, aware that it is going to be a longer poem—than he had predicted, and announces as his theme 'the might of souls, / And what they do within themselves while yet / The yoke of earth is new to them' (ibid., ll. 178–80). 'This', he tells us, 'is in truth heroic argument / And genuine prowess' (ibid., ll. 182–3). Both halves of the sentence come as a surprise. The words are an allusion, however, and we are expected to notice the source. Faced with describing the Fall of Man in *Paradise Lost* Book IX, Milton had compared his task to those of Homer and Virgil:

> sad task, yet argument
> Not less but more heroic than the wrath
> Of stern Achilles on his foe, pursued
> Thrice fugitive about Troy wall; or rage
> Of Turnus for Lavinia, disespoused ...
>   (13–17)

Prowess, shown in turn, by the *Iliad*, singing the deeds of Grecian heroes; by its sophisticated Latin counterpart, the *Aeneid*, telling of the founding of Rome and Roman values; and by Milton's seventeenth-century English adaptation of pagan form to Christian purposes, will be shown by Wordsworth himself in a revelation of the godlike nature of man—the 'majestic sway we have / As beings in the strength of nature' (1805: III. 193–4). Though quietly introduced, this is one of *The Prelude*'s major rethinkings of the Coleridgean higher imagination. For both poets, imagination is the godlike faculty unique in man's nature. Coleridge would not dissent from the view that it gives to man 'majestic sway' over the natural world. But the thought that it does so 'in the strength of nature' is essentially Wordsworthian. In exercising his 'sway' over nature, man demonstrates a power belonging to nature herself, of which he, man, is part.

Wordsworth's confidence in what he is doing is all the more astonishing if one looks back to the origins of *The Prelude*. The first brief version of October 1798, *Was It For This* (*WIFT*), begins fluently but tentatively. Wordsworth is thinking his way through a problem:

> Was it for this
> That one, the fairest of all rivers, loved
> To blend his murmurs with my nurse's song,
> And from his alder shades and rocky falls,
> And from his fords and shallows, sent a voice
> To intertwine my dreams? For this didst thou,
> O Derwent, travelling over the green plains
> Near my sweet birth-place, didst thou, beauteous stream,
> Give ceaseless music to the night and day,
> Which with its steady cadence tempering
> Our human waywardness, composed my thoughts
> To more than infant softness, giving me
> Amid the fretful tenements of man
> A knowledge, a dim earnest, of the calm
> That nature breathes among her woodland haunts?
> Was it for this ...
>   (*WIFT*, 1–16)

In the manuscript the poem starts not only in mid-line, but with a small 'w'. It is a very unobtrusive beginning—almost, it seems, accidental. Wordsworth doesn't know that he has embarked on a major poem. Yet his thoughts fall instinctively into blank verse. Coleridge and Milton are present already, looking over his shoulder: Coleridge in the quotation from *Frost at Midnight*, 'my sweet birth-place', at line eight; Milton in the urgent, rhetorical questioning—'Was it for this ... For this didst thou / O Derwent ... Was it for this ... ?' The pattern had been used by others, Pope and Thomson among them, but it takes us more importantly to *Samson Agonistes*. 'For this', Manoah asks his blinded and imprisoned son,

> did the angel twice descend? For this
> Ordained thy nurture holy, as of a plant

> Select and sacred?
> (361–3)

Wordsworth, it seems, as he begins what turns out to be *The Prelude*, thinks of himself as having been singled out, and as failing. The task on which he should have been at work was *The Recluse*, the great philosophical poem that Coleridge had six months earlier persuaded him it was his duty to write. Looking back to his 'nurture' among the Cumbrian mountains, he felt reproached. With such a childhood to prepare him, surely he should have been able to get on? But as the reproaches prompt his memory, new and more productive questions are raised. What is the nature of these early experiences? How do they contribute to adult strength, consciousness, creativity? Moving on to ask, and answer, these questions, Wordsworth comes upon what is the great theme of *The Prelude* in all its stages and versions: education.

Was It For This is immensely important, showing us how quickly, and how inevitably, the theme of education is established. In 150 lines—just six paragraphs—Wordsworth creates a new idiom. In place of the public poetry and grand affirmations of *Tintern Abbey* (written only three months before), we hear the voice of *The Prelude*. *Tintern Abbey* is the seminal poem of the Romantic age, quoted, touched upon, imitated, again and again; yet it is a sequel to Coleridge's *Frost at Midnight*, and offers in its affirmations a version of Coleridge's early Unitarian faith. *Was It For This* is Wordsworth with no sources but the memory, imagination and speculative power of his own mind. At once we are offered 'spots of time' (isolated memories, made vivid by the imagination that is itself, in part, the subject of the poetry):

> Oh, when I have hung
> Above the raven's nest, have hung alone
> By half-inch fissures in the slippery rock
> But ill sustained, and almost (as it seemed)
> Suspended by the wind which blew amain ...
> (*WIFT*, 37–11)

and at once we are offered the ruminative voice, that takes a larger, longer view, thinking things through as we listen. The forces that govern human education

> love to interweave
> The passions that build up our human soul
> Not with the mean and vulgar works of man,

But with high objects, with eternal things,
With life and nature, purifying thus
The elements of feeling and of thought,
And sanctifying by such discipline
Both pain and fear, until we recognize
A grandeur in the beatings of the heart.
    (*WIFT*, 50–8)

The final line might almost stand as a definition of imagination. As Keats put it, 'I am certain of nothing but of the holiness of the Heart's affections and the truth of Imagination' (to Bailey, 22 November 1817).[2] Wordsworth would have agreed, but as an instinctive follower of Burke on the sublime he tended to associate 'the beatings of the heart' with fear, pain, guilt. *Was It For This* contains not merely the birds-nesting episode, by the woodcock-snaring; within a matter of days, Wordsworth would go on to write the boat-stealing, thus completing the first three 'spots of time' of the 1799 two-part *Prelude*, all of them showing the power of the sublime.

Not that he discounts the beautiful. At this stage (perhaps at all stages) he associates it with 'those first-born affinities which fit / Our new existence to existing things' (*WIFT*, 120–1), the bonding of the child and nature that precedes education through the sublime. The cadence of the River Derwent, blending its murmurs with his nurse's song, is our introduction to this way of thinking, but *Was It For This* includes, too, a unique passage ascribing the 'first-born affinities' to the work of a Platonic eternal spirit, the 'soul of things':

        he who painting what he is in all
    The visible imagery of all the worlds
    Is yet apparent chiefly as the soul
    Of our first sympathies
        (*WIFT*, 106–9)

It is the child's partaking of this world-soul that enables him, in this original *Prelude* version, to hold

                        unconscious intercourse
    With the eternal beauty, drinking in
    A pure organic pleasure from the lines
    Of curling mist, or from the smooth expanse
    Of waters coloured by the cloudless moon.
        (*WIFT*, 127–31)

Was It For This did not simply grow into the 1799 *Prelude*. Wordsworth rethought his poem. Soon after Christmas 1798 he defined for himself a link between childhood imaginative experience and adult creativity:

> There are in our existence spots of time
> That with distinct preeminence retain
> A fructifying virtue, whence, depressed
> By trivial occupations and the round
> Of ordinary intercourse, our minds—
> Especially the imaginative power—
> Are nourished and invisibly repaired
>   (1799: I.288–94)

The key to this, and to the three 'spots' that cluster round Wordsworth's definition, appears in a link-passage that is, for no obvious reason, left out of the 1805 and 1850 versions of *The Prelude*. 'I might advert', Wordsworth writes, 'To numerous accidents in flood or field':

>   tragic facts
> Of rural history that impressed my mind
> With images to which in following years
> Far other feelings were attached—with forms
> That yet exist with independent life,
> And, like their archetypes, know no decay.
>   (Ibid., 279–87)

What is being described is an associative process within the mind that relies on Hartley's *Observations on Man* (reissued 1791), and ultimately on Locke, but which is peculiarly Wordsworthian in its application. Response to tragic occurrences in the region, traditional or recent, has the effect of 'impressing' (imprinting, stamping) images upon the mind—images of places where the occurrences took place, or where the poet heard of them. Over the years these images are visited, and revisited, within the mind, becoming the focus of new imaginative feelings, such as the child could not have had.

It is the process that is described in *The Pedlar* of spring 1798:

> In such communion, not from terror free...
> He had perceived the presence and the power
> Of greatness, and deep feelings had impressed
> Great objects on his mind with portraiture
> And colour so distinct that on his mind

They lay like substances, and almost seemed
To haunt the bodily sense.
   (30–4)

It is the process that leads on Wordsworth's first visit to Tintern Abbey to his storing-up of the 'forms of beauty' that later have such influence on his mind. And it is the process that underlies the imagery of association in *Was It For This*. More especially, it explains Wordsworth's reference to the 'characters' (handwriting) of 'danger and desire', which, 'impressed' through 'the agency of boyish sports' onto the Cumbrian landscape, have power to make

The surface of the universal earth
With meanings of delight, of hope and fear,
Work like a sea.
   (*WIFT*, 69–75)

The new emphasis present in Wordsworth's *1799* link-passage is upon continuity and permanence: the 'forms' (images) stamped upon the mind *yet* (still, at the time of writing) exist, with their independent life, achieving within the mind a permanence comparable to that of their 'archetypes' (the landscapes, natural forms, from which they derive). With this as our introduction to the 'spots of time' definition, it is clear that we should expect the 'spots' to be not just memories where time stands still, but images, pictures in the mind, imprinted as the result of more than usually important emotional experience.

The final 'spot' of 1799 Part I shows the process at work. First we see the child, 'feverish, and tired, and restless', waiting on the hill above his school at Hawkshead for horses that will take him and his brothers home for the Christmas holidays. Then we cut to his father's sudden death:

             Ere I to school returned
That dreary time, ere I had been ten days
A dweller in my father's house, he died,
And I and my two brothers (orphans then)
Followed his body to the grave. The event,
With all the sorrow which it brought, appeared
A chastisement; and when I called to mind
That day so lately passed, when from the crag
I looked in such anxiety of hope,
With trite reflections of morality,
Yet with the deepest passion, I bowed low

To God who thus corrected my desires.
    (1799: I.349–60)

Revisiting the Hawkshead landscape in his remorseful mind, the child attaches to it 'far other feelings' than the hope with which it had so recently been associated. But Wordsworth is not merely writing about an episode in his past, he is telling us of its importance for the present. The details of the landscape become 'spectacles and sounds' to which he consciously returns to 'drink as at a fountain'. 'And I do not doubt', he concludes impressively,

> That in this later time, when storm and rain
> Beat on my roof at midnight, or by day
> When I am in the woods, unknown to me
> The workings of my spirit thence are brought.
>   (Ibid., 368–74)

The Hawkshead landscape—associated first with 'anxiety of hope', next with guilty thoughts that the child is responsible for his fathers death—changes, over the 15-year period before the poetry is written, into a source of strength, support for the workings of the adult poet's spirit. This time Wordsworth is no more able than we are to say what has taken place. These are experiences of the mind,

>   Which, be they what they may,
> Are yet the fountain-light of all our day,
> Are yet the master light of all our seeing.
>   (*Intimations*, 153–5)

1799 Part I has it in common with *Was It For This* that it deals primarily in terms of an education through the sublime. At a secondary stage, however, Wordsworth inserts the skating episode (lines 150–98) and the 'home amusements' section (lines 198–233), designed to show that his boyhood was not always lonely and subject to fear and guilt. And in Part II he takes his account of childhood through into adolescence, consciously offering beauty as a sequel to the sublime:

>   But ere the fall
> Of night, when in our pinnace we returned
> Over the dusky lake, and to the beach
> Of some small island steered our course, with one,
> The minstrel of our troop, and left him there,
> And rowed off gently while he blew his flute

Alone upon the rock, oh, then the calm
And dead still water lay upon my mind
Even with a weight of pleasure, and the sky,
Never before so beautiful, sank down
Into my heart and held me like a dream.
     (1799: II.204–14)

In Part II, as in Part I, we are offered vivid personal memories, intensified within the mind because they are associated with particular landscapes. Halfway through the part, however, Wordsworth becomes aware that he has unfinished business. Having dropped from his text the *Was It For This* sequence on the eternal spirit, he has left himself with no answer to the question, what does enable us to 'fit our new existence / To existing things?' What are the origins of the imaginative power seen so vividly in his remembered early experience? The 'spots of time' told of memories by which the mind, 'especially the imaginative power', is nourished and made fruitful by its own self-generated power; but where did the power come from? Wordsworth's thoughts took him once again to Coleridge and to Milton—to Coleridge, to whom 'The unity of all [had] been revealed' (1799: II.256), and to Milton, who had in *Paradise Lost* offered the Christian myth of origins that no longer seemed sufficient.

     No less than Milton, Wordsworth felt it to be his task to 'trace / The progress of our being' (1799: II.268–9), but he did so, not from the Garden of Eden, but from an infant at the breast:

                 blest the babe
     Nursed in his mother's arms, the babe who sleeps
     Upon his mother's breast, who when his soul
     Claims manifest kindred with an earthly soul
     Does gather passion from his mother's eye.

'Such feelings', Wordsworth continues,

                 pass into his torpid life
     Like an awakening breeze, and hence his mind,
     Even in the first trial of its powers,
     Is prompt and watchful ...
          (1799: II.269–77)

Clearly, he has *Was It For This* in his thoughts. 'Oh bounteous power', he had written, addressing the eternal spirit,

> In childhood, in rememberable days,
> How often did thy love renew for me
> Those naked feelings which when thou wouldst form
> A living thing thou sendest like a breeze
> Into its infant being.
>   (*WIFT*, 109–14)

In each case the 'awakening breeze' of life is associated with love, but the Platonic eternal spirit gives place in the 1799 *Prelude* to the tenderness of a human mother. Along the child's 'infant veins are interfused', not the pantheist 'something far more deeply interfused' of *Tintern Abbey*, but

> The gravitation and the filial bond
> Of nature that connect him to the world.
>   (1799: II.292–4)

As in *Was It For This* Wordsworth is concerned with 'those first-born affinities which fit / Our new existence to existing things', but now it is the gravitational pull of nature (personalized in the mother's love) that makes the infant part of the world in which he lives.

The mother's effect upon her child, it has to be said, is extraordinary. He becomes not merely 'prompt and watchful', capable (as we should expect) of the associative process of storing up images, but also 'powerful in all sentiments of grief, / Of exultation, fear, and joy' (1799: II.300–1). Two things are happening at once within the poetry: we are to see the child both as the credible human infant, and, symbolically, as the poet in embryo—one whose mind,

> Even as an agent of the one great mind,
> Creates, creator and receiver both ...
>   (Ibid., 302–3)

In the terms that Coleridge will later use in *Biographia Literaria*, the child is, from his earliest days, a fully imaginative being. Capable at once of creation and perception, he exercises the full powers of the primary imagination. At the day-to-day level he orders experience, builds the parts of his universe into a whole; as 'an agent of the one great mind', he performs the higher imaginative act that is 'a repetition in the finite mind of the eternal act of creation in the Infinite I AM' (God's eternal creative assertion of self, that brings into existence the other). As he grows, the child will develop— through the beautiful influence of his mother, through the more often sublime influence of nature—but already his imaginative capacity has been established.

That the two-part *Prelude* should end in a farewell to Coleridge is doubly appropriate. In the first place, Coleridge had decided in early December 1799, when Wordsworth was writing, to pursue his career as a journalist in London, leaving William and Dorothy to establish themselves in their new Lake District home at Dove Cottage, Grasmere. In the second, Wordsworth's poem had been from the outset addressed to his friend. The quotation from *Frost at Midnight* in Part I, line eight (originally *WIFT*, 9) had signalled this fact, and now, in rounding off Part II, Wordsworth alludes again to the same poem: 'Thou, my friend, wast reared / In the great city, mid far other scenes' (1799: II.496–7). Throughout Wordsworth's life *The Prelude* was to be known as 'The Poem' to Coleridge; until the later revisions, each successive version is in some new way importantly bound up with him and his thinking. Each, it should be said, is also more strongly Miltonic than the last.

An effort was made in December 1801 to extend the 1799 poem into a third part, taking the study of Wordsworth's education up to his Cambridge days. After 167 lines, however (mostly old material, drawn from *The Pedlar*), the attempt broke down. It took the impetus of Coleridge's imminent departure for the Mediterranean in early 1804 to get Wordsworth restarted. On 4 January Coleridge records in his notebook a reading of 'the second part of (William's) divine self-biography' in 'the highest and outermost of Grasmere' (Easedale, perhaps?). Ten days later he leaves for London. Wordsworth falls to work, and by early March has at least nearly completed a *Prelude* in five books for Coleridge to take with him on his voyage. Then suddenly, around the tenth of the month, he takes it apart, and begins work on a still longer, and radically different, version. All texts of *The Prelude* (even the first edition) have their problems. *Was It For This*, however, is in the poet's hand, the 1799 and 1805 *Preludes* exist in duplicate fair-copies; the five-book poem has to be reconstructed from drafts and imperfect manuscripts. For all this, it is a poem of great importance. Broadly speaking, it consists of the first three books of the 1805 text, followed by a fourth containing the bulk of the material in 1805's Parts IV and V, and a fifth made up of the 'spots of time' sequence (revised and augmented as in 1805 Part XI), plus the Climbing of Snowdon (finally 1805: XIII.1–65). As always, education is Wordsworth's theme. Imagination, built up through childhood and adolescence among the mountains, is impaired by exposure at Cambridge to sophistication and artificiality. Through the workings of the 'spots of time', however, it is restored ('nourished and invisibly repaired'), and the poem shows it at its new adult height in the epiphany on Snowdon. With its Miltonic paradise-lost-

and-regained structure, it is (or was, or would have been) a highly impressive work. Why, then, did Wordsworth dismember it? Not so much, probably, because he was dissatisfied, as because, like Penelope, he dared not finish his task. Coleridge had agreed that *The Prelude* should form part of *The Recluse*, but the central philosophical section still had to be written. An attempt to write it in *Home at Grasmere* (spring 1801) had merely shown how great was the problem. Wordsworth had no system to offer. Only Coleridge could supply such a thing, and he now (March 1804) was leaving for Malta, perhaps in fact dying. Hearing on the 29th that he has been dangerously ill, Wordsworth writes: 'I would gladly have given 3 fourths of my possessions for your letter on *The Recluse* ... I cannot say what a load it would be to me, should I survive you, and you die without this memorial left behind.'

No notes on *The Recluse* were forthcoming (at one point Coleridge claimed that they had been written, and sent off, but unfortunately burnt when his messenger died of the plague). In their absence, Wordsworth reworked his material, sent Coleridge 1805 Books, I–V to take abroad, put Snowdon and the 'spots of time' on one side for future use, and embarked on Book VI. With the subject of his undergraduate travels through France in 1790, he introduced into his poem revolutionary politics. It is fairly certain that after completing Book VI in late March, he went on to write IX and the first half of X, carrying his readers up to the death of Robespierre. In the autumn of 1804 he added VIII (retrospect of childhood) and VII (London as Underworld), before completing X (politics and alienation in post-Revolutionary London). After a pause marking the death of Wordsworth's brother, John, in February 1805, the poem was brought to a conclusion with three brief final books: XI (incorporating the 'spots of time', set aside from the five-book *Prelude*), XII (producing the poet's definition of 'the ennobling interchange / Of action from within and from without', lines 376–7) and XIII, with its climactic ascent of Snowdon.

The Prelude emerges as a poem not merely of different versions, but of essentially different structures. Though it is in a sense autobiography, it nowhere attempts to tell the story of Wordsworth's life. Even the 1799 version, where the division into childhood and adolescence appears straightforward, in fact disregards chronology. Of the major 'spots of time', the first takes place when the child is nine, the second when he is five, the third when he is thirteen. By the same token, in the 1805 version the Climbing of Snowdon should chronologically have been placed between Wordsworth's two visits to France, but is reserved to form a conclusion. Book VII (including London experiences of 1793–5) is placed for overall effect, as a descent into hell after the sublime of the Alps, and followed in VIII by a retrospect of childhood.

Four great similes show Wordsworth's awareness of the complexity of his structures. 'Who that shall point as with a wand', he demands in 1799 Part II, 'and say / "This portion of the river of my mind / Came from yon fountain?"' (lines 247–9). In 1805 Book V we see him 'Incumbent o'er the surface of past time', attempting from his boat to distinguish on the bottom of a lake 'The shadow from the substance' (lines 247–64). 'As oftentimes a river', Wordsworth writes at the opening of Book IX,

> Turns and will measure back his course—far back,
> Towards the very regions which he crossed
> In his first outset—so have we long time
> Made motions retrograde ...
>   (1–9)

And in Book XIII we have, in the last of these water-images of *The Prelude*, a tracing of the stream of imagination which is in effect a synopsis of the poem itself:

> we have traced the stream
> From darkness and the very place of birth
> In its blind cavern, whence is faintly heard
> The sound of waters; followed it to light
> And open day, accompanied its course
> Among the ways of nature, afterwards
> Lost sight of it bewildered and engulfed,
> Then given it greeting as it rose once more
> With strength, reflecting in its solemn breast
> The works of man and face of human life...
>   (172–81)

Wordsworth is structuring his poem, telling us what to see and how to read.

Finally, the unity of *The Prelude* depends upon our sense of the mind that is at its centre, the consciousness of the adult poet looking into the deep that is his own identity, examining the emotions of the child whose mind is, and is not, his own. The Climbing of Snowdon is the ultimate achievement, and revelation, of this mind. Ascending the mountain by night, the poet emerges into the moonlight above the clouds: 'on the shore / I found myself of a huge sea of mist, / Which meek and silent rested at my feet' (1805: XIII.42–4). For the last time in the poem the beautiful gives way to the sublime, as Wordsworth singles out from his moonscape the strange chasm at its centre:

> And from the shore
> At distance not the third part of a mile
> Was a blue chasm, a fracture in the vapour,
> A deep and gloomy breathing-place through which
> Mounted the roar of waters, torrents, streams
> Innumerable, roaring with one voice!
>   (Ibid., 54–9)

In this 'dark deep thoroughfare', we are told, has 'nature lodged / The soul, the imagination, of the whole' (Ibid., 64–5). It is a strange, impressive claim, leading us to wonder at what seems to be Wordsworth's anticipation of modern concepts of the unconscious. The poetry needs no explication, but a year after composing the narrative of the ascent Wordsworth was prompted to add a gloss:

> A meditation rose in me that night
> Upon the lonely mountain when the scene
> Had passed away, and it appeared to me
> The perfect image of a mighty mind,
> Of one that feeds upon infinity,
> That is exalted by an underpresence,
> The sense of God, or whatsoe'er is dim
> Or vast in its own being.
>   (Ibid., 66–73)

The landscape as a whole has become a mind 'that feeds upon infinity', but the infinity upon which it feeds comes from within, welling up through the 'deep and gloomy breathing-place' as 'the roar of waters, torrents, streams / Innumerable'. The streams, we have noticed, roar 'with one voice', achieving unity, wholeness. And Wordsworth has dignified them already in his reference to 'the soul, the imagination' that is 'lodged' in the cloud-rift. But nothing has led us to expect that he would gloss the 'underpresence' in terms of such grandeur, and such clarity. In words that show just how far he is prepared to go beyond Milton, beyond Coleridge, he tells us that it doesn't matter whether the highest achievement of the human imagination is a perception of God. It is equally important if it is a sense of that which is 'dim / Or vast in [our] own being'. Either way, it is the ennobling interchange / Of action from within and from without' that is his theme.

NOTES

1. All quotations from *The Prelude* are from the texts in *The Prelude:, The Four Text)* *(1798, 1799, 1805, 1850)*, ed. Jonathan Wordsworth, Harmondsworth, Penguin, 1995.

2. Rollins, I, 184.

REFERENCES AND FURTHER READING

Gill, Stephen, (ed.) *William Wordsworth*, Oxford, Oxford University Press, 1984.

———. *William Wordsworth: A Life*, Oxford, Oxford University Press, 1989.

Hartman, Geoffrey H., *Wordsworth's Poetry 1787–1814*, New Haven, Yale University Press, 1964.

Manning, Peter J., 'Reading Wordsworth's revision: Othello and the drowned man', in *Reading Romantics: Texts and Contexts*, New York, Oxford University Press, 1990, pp. 87–114.

Wordsworth, Jonathan, *William Wordsworth: The Borders of Vision*, Oxford, Clarendon Press, 1982.

DENNIS TAYLOR

Wordsworth's Abbey Ruins

One of the perennial questions in Wordsworth criticism is: where is the abbey in "Tintern Abbey"? The easiest answer is that it is merely a place in Wordsworth's title, "Lines Composed a Few Miles above Tintern Abbey, on Revisiting the Banks of the Wye during a Tour. July 13, 1798." Though Wordsworth called the poem "Tintern Abbey," the abbey is arguably merely a place used to identify the spot on the river Wye that Wordsworth revisited in 1798. Presumably the poem might have been subtitled "A few miles above Chichester Common" or "Above Birnum Woods" if these had been the nearby places.

One oddity is that Wordsworth's tour at this time included several visits to the abbey itself. Another is that the nature scene described in the poem might well have been inspired by Wordsworth's early experience in the Lake Country, by the river Derwent celebrated in *An Evening Walk*. Another oddity is that Wordsworth referred to the poem as "Tintern Abbey," though this may have been simple shorthand. And still another is simply the fact that Tintern Abbey is the major signifying marker for the poem in the minds of generations of readers.

But there is occasional speculation that the abbey does in fact cast its shadow in the poem, if only by its absence.[1] Indeed an influential new historicist interpretation of recent years argues that Wordsworth forcibly

From *The Fountain Light: Studies in Romanticism and Religion*, edited by J. Robert Barth, S.J., pp. 37–53. © 2002 by Fordham University Press.

keeps out of the poem the beggars and industrial pollution associated with the abbey in 1798 and described by William Gilpin in his *Observations on the River Wye* (1782). Thus the vagrants and smoke in the first verse paragraph indicate a reality that Wordsworth has chosen to suppress in favor of the imaginative subjectivity of the poem.[2]

But I would argue that the real question is not "Where are the beggars?" but rather "Where is the Abbey?" Tintern Abbey is, like Poe's purloined letter, visible throughout but unseen by the untrained eye. We need to look, once more, at the opening lines:

> Five years have past; five summers, with the length
> Of five long winters! and again I hear
> These waters, rolling from their mountain-springs
> With a soft inland murmur.—Once again
> Do I behold these steep and lofty cliffs,
> That on a wild secluded scene impress
> Thoughts of more deep seclusion; and connect
> The landscape with the quiet of the sky.
> The day is come when I again repose
> Here, under this dark sycamore, and view
> These plots of cottage-ground, these orchard-tufts,
> Which at this season, with their unripe fruits,
> Are dad in one green hue, and lose themselves
> 'Mid groves and copses. Once again I see
> These hedge-rows, hardly hedge-rows, little lines
> Of sportive wood run wild: these pastoral farms,
> Green to the very door; and wreaths of smoke
> Sent up, in silence, from among the trees!
> With some uncertain notice, as might seem
> Of vagrant dwellers in the houseless woods,
> Or of some Hermit's cave, where by his fire
> The Hermit sits alone.[3]
>   (1–22)

I would argue that the Abbey is all through these lines, but first we need to look at an unnoticed part of Wordsworth's career, his empathy for the Catholic spirituality especially associated with monasteries and convents. I should caution that this argument is not of the "Shakespeare was an Irish Catholic" school of thought. Wordsworth thought of himself as a good Protestant, nationalistic, loyal (increasingly) to the Church of England, deeply suspicious of papal power and priestly superstition. He is rightly thought of as the poet of imaginative liberty, of natural landscape, even at his best as a poet who secularizes the religious tradition into a celebration of "the very world which is the world / Of all of us, the place in which, in the end, / We find our happiness, or not at all."[4] But this is only half the story.

If we simply numbered the Catholic images, or Catholic words, in Wordsworth, he would seem the most Catholic of poets. His poems abound with images of monasteries, hermitages, hermits, Catholic shrines, Catholic processions, nuns, saints, the Virgin Mary, priests. A few of these are, of course, Anglican, but the vast majority are specifically papist. Many of these images occur in poems that are not much discussed in Wordsworth criticism, and therefore the images and their importance go unnoticed. But they also abound in the canonical poems, so much so that there almost seems a conspiracy of silence about them. For what it is worth, a simple check of the concordance[5] shows how frequently Wordsworth uses Catholic terms and their cognates with positive connotation, like *nun* (17), *convent* (30), *Mass* (11), *cell* (81), *cloister* (19), *anchorite* (4), *abbey* (17), *recluse* (6), *Virgin* (12), *monk* (35) (though *monkish* occasionally carries a negative weight), *hermit* (34) and manifold references to the Virgin Mary and to Catholic saints. *Hermit*, incidentally, carries for Wordsworth a specifically Catholic association, as in "The Excursion" (7.302–305):

> The hermit, lodged
> Amid the untrodden desert, tells his beads,
> With each repeating its allotted prayer
> And thus divides and thus relieves the time....

In addition to these words are a host of terms which often. take on Catholic associations: hallowed, litany, sainted, saint, altar, church, prayer, chapel, priest, holy, shrine, pilgrim, retreat, Madonna, benediction, altar, sacred, grace, sanctity, votary, angels, temple, blessed, rite, prayer, etc. Distinguishing the Catholic, Anglican, and secularized associations of these words is, of course, part of the critical task.

What was the importance of Catholicism for Wordsworth? I would argue that it offered him a major analogy for his most important psychological experience, the experience of "spots of time." The analogy is that of the solitude of contemplation experienced by the monk or hermit. We can illustrate this by glancing at one of Wordsworth's earlier poems, written before his career took a more overtly religious turn after 1805. "Descriptive Sketches," written in 1790–1792, after his first trip to France, begins (I am quoting the revised version of 1836):

Were there, below, a spot of holy ground,
Where from distress a refuge might be found,
And solitude prepare the soul for heaven;
Sure, nature's God that spot to man had given
Where falls the purple *morning* far and wide
In flakes of light upon the mountain-side,
Where with loud voice the power of water shakes
The leafy wood, or sleeps in quiet lakes.
    (1–10)

This is a generic description which could apply to Wordsworth's early experience of the Lake Country, as well as the French and Swiss countryside of his walking tour. Wordsworth is larger than his critics because his poetry defines the sacred moment in a way much richer than any critic has been able to parse. In these opening lines, we can simply point to the idea of a sacred place, a refuge, where a deeply religious solitude is experienced, a sense of "peculiar grace, / A leading from above, a something given" (in the words of "Resolution and Independence") in a setting often surrounded by mountains, as if by walls, creating a valley filled with light, both physical and spiritual.

But these lines are only a beginning. Where they lead is not to Paris, the scene of revolutionary liberty (which Wordsworth then applauded), but to a place not often discussed in Wordsworth criticism: the Cistercian monastery of La Grande Chartreuse in France. To describe the effect of the monastery on Wordsworth at this time, I will use later lines from the 1850 *Prelude*:

                              ... an awful *solitude*:
        Yes, for even then no other than a place
        Of soul-affecting *solitude* appeared
        That far-famed region, though our eyes had seen,
        As toward the sacred mansion we advanced,
        Arms flashing, and a military glare
        Of riotous men commissioned to expel
        The blameless inmates, and belike subvert
        That frame of social being, which so long
        Had bodied forth the ghostliness of things
        In silence visible and perpetual calm.
        —'Stay, stay your sacrilegious hands!'—The voice
        Was Nature's, uttered from her Alpine throne;
        I heard it then and seem to hear it now—
        'Your impious work forbear, perish what may,

Let this one temple last, be this one spot
Of earth devoted to eternity!'
She ceased to speak, but while St. Bruno's pines
Waved their dark tops, not silent as they wave,
And while below, along the several beds,
Murmured the sister streams of Life and Death,
Thus by conflicting passions pressed, my heart
Responded....

>   '... be the house redeemed
With its unworldly votaries, for the sake
Of conquest over sense, hourly achieved
Through faith and meditative reason, resting
Upon the word of heaven-imparted truth,
Calmly triumphant; and for humbler claim
Of that imaginative impulse sent
From these majestic floods, yon shining cliffs,
The untransmuted shapes of many worlds,
Cerulean ether's pure inhabitants,
These forests unapproachable by death,
That shall endure as long as man endures,
To think to hope, to worship, and to feel,
To struggle, to be lost within himself
In trepidation, from the blank abyss
To look with bodily eyes, and be consoled.'
   (VI, 414–436, 451–466)

The 1850 version intensifies and expands the experience given in "Descriptive Sketches" and again in the 1805 *Prelude*. "Solitude" is italicized, as though being discovered clearly for the first time. The monastery, about to be stripped, has "bodied forth the ghostliness of things," an embodiment of those eternal intersections characterizing the more personal spots of time, but a ghostly one, eerily Gothic in some respects. And Nature enforces the parallel with the other spots of time by insisting: "be this one spot / Of earth devoted to eternity!"

There are various complications to the passage, and to Wordsworth's experience of Catholicism generally. On the one hand, these places of monastic solitude are the "real thing," in Henry James' sense, where monks contemplated nature and God, and where their contemplation was authenticated by centuries of religious practice. On the other hand, Chartreuse is also a stern and forbidding place, with its history of harsh penitence, "conquest over sense, hourly achieved." This aspect of monastic discipline threatens Wordsworth's liberty of imagination, and indeed underscores for him the more sinister aspects of Catholicism, its cold power, its tyranny, its Gothic dark. But even in these lines, Wordsworth puts the harsher silence next to a softer mode, for he also credits the Chartreuse with the "humbler claim / Of that imaginative impulse sent / From these majestic floods, yon shining cliffs / ... These forests." So Catholic solitude can go either into the richness of gentle personal contemplation in a natural setting, or into something threatening to Wordsworth's sense of his own individuality, not to speak of his loyalty to his beloved English countryside, dotted with Anglican spires.

There are at least two things that connect the passage with "Tintern Abbey." One is the use of the word *mansion*, used here to describe the "sacred mansion" of Chartreuse, and in "Tintern Abbey" to describe the imaginative mind, in this case Dorothy's:

> ... thy mind
> Shall be a mansion for all lovely forms,
> Thy memory be as a dwelling-place
> For all sweet sounds and harmonies....
>   (139–142)

Another connection is the very shape of the setting, where the "imaginative impulse" is "sent / From these majestic floods, yon shining cliffs / ... These forests." This sense of enclosure connects with lines from "Tintern Abbey":

> these steep and lofty cliffs,
> That on a wild secluded scene impress
> Thoughts of more deep seclusion; and connect
> The landscape with the quiet of the sky.
>   (5–8)

The Chartreuse experience contains another theme of profound importance to Wordsworth, a theme increasingly important in recent "revisionist" discussions of English Reformation history. It is a theme embodied in Eamon Duffy's title, *The Stripping of the Altars*, a book that describes the destruction of English Catholic culture and religion during the Elizabethan years.[6] This theme is not just confined to the English Reformation; it extends itself in other recent works into discussions of the way modern Protestant culture is haunted by its destroyed Catholic past. A preeminent example of this latter discussion is Jenny Franchot's *Roads to Rome*, which discusses how nineteenth-century Protestant culture in America is haunted by its Catholic 'other,' the alien Italianate Christianity that both attracts and repels writers like Longfellow and Hawthorne.[7] In alluding so briefly to an immense body of scholarship, of which Duffy and Franchot are only the tips of the iceberg, I simply want to suggest how the topic of Wordsworth and Catholicism is part of a much larger topic of growing importance: English (and American) Catholic and Protestant relations. Wordsworth, I would argue, is an unnoticed major participant in this discussion, as suggested by this passage from *The Prelude*:[8]

> —'Stay, stay your sacrilegious hands!'—The voice
> Was Nature's, uttered from her Alpine throne;
> I heard it then and seem to hear it now—
> 'Your impious work forbear, perish what may,
> Let this one temple last, be this one spot
> Of earth devoted to eternity!'
>   (*1850* VI, 425–430)

The warning against sacrilege comes not from the Church, but from Nature. The symbiosis between the abbey and the natural setting is so close that to destroy one is to destroy the other. The stripping of the altars becomes a stripping of nature, a destruction of the sacred place where the spot of time occurs.

So we see another connection with "Tintern Abbey." The poem does not refer to a living monastery, like the ones Wordsworth experienced in France, but to a ruin, a set of gutted rooms, an outline only of chapel and dormitory, "bare ruined choirs where late the sweet birds sang," now overgrown with moss and ivy and brush. Wordsworth had experienced such abbeys before he went to France; and one of them, Furness Abbey, was a companion to some of his earliest spots of time. But Wordsworth's trip to the continent taught him an astonishing lesson. What was now happening to the monasteries on the continent had happened to the monasteries in England. The raw ragged ruins of the freshly destroyed buildings in France were the same as those in the English countryside, but these English ruins had been overgrown, had become picturesque, had become the setting of paintings and poems and a whole school of melancholy. Startlingly, so I would argue, Wordsworth realized the parallel between the continent now and England then. Chartreuse now was Tintern Abbey then.

William Gilpin's book, a likely source for Wordsworth and one invoked by the new historicists, can be our guide here:

> A more pleasing retreat could not easily be found. The woods,
> and glades intermixed; the winding of the river; the variety of the

ground; the splendid ruin, contrasted with the objects of nature; and the elegant line formed by the summits of the hills, which include the whole; make all together a very inchanting piece of scenery. Every thing around breathes an air so calm, and tranquil; so sequesterd, a man of warm imagination, in monkish times, might have been allured by such a scene to become an inhabitant of it.... Nature has made it [the abbey] her own. Time has worn off all traces of the rule; it has blunted the sharp edges of the chissel; and broken the regularity of opposing parts.... To these [windows] are superadded the ornaments of time. Ivy, in masses uncommonly large, has taken possession of many parts of the wall.... Mosses of various hues, with lychens, maiden-hair, penny-leaf, and other humble plants, overspread the surface.... The pavement is obliterated: the elevation of the choir is no longer visible: the whole area is reduced to one level ... covered with neat turf, closely shorn.[9]

There follows the description of the homeless inhabitants of the abbey, including one poor woman who had taken over "the remnant of a shattered cloister.... It was her own mansion." Again the word, mansion!

The parallels with the first stanza of "Tintern Abbey" should now be more clearly coming into view:

> These plots of cottage-ground, these orchard-tufts,
> Which at this season, with their unripe fruits,
> Are clad in one green hue, and lose themselves
> 'Mid groves and copses. Once again I see
> These hedge-rows, hardly hedge-rows, little lines
> Of sportive wood run wild: these pastoral farms,
> Green to the very door, and wreaths of smoke
> Sent up, in silence, from among the trees!
> With some uncertain notice, as might seem
> Of vagrant dwellers in the houseless woods,
> Or of some Hermit's cave, where by his fire
> The Hermit sits alone.
>   (11–22)

The scene here is one of effaced outlines, hedgerows overgrown and losing themselves in one green hue, running wild like sportive woods, the boundary between nature and the human habitation blurred; and behind this screen of overgrown outlines, the sense of someone dwelling there, in silence, a hermit telling his beads. Tintern Abbey itself is a palimpsest in the first verse paragraph of "Tintern Abbey."

So half our job is done. But why is the abbey there? What function does it serve? The plot of the poem moves quickly away from the opening setting and into the subject of Wordsworth's imagination. We need to look at those ruins more closely.

What made the ruins? The answer is given in other lines from the Chartreuse passage quoted above:

> Thus by conflicting passions pressed, my heart
> Responded; Honour to the patriot's zeal,
> Glory and hope to new-born Liberty!
> Hail to the mighty projects of the time!
> Discerning sword that Justice wields, do thou
> Go forth and prosper; and, ye purging fires,
> Up to the loftiest towers of Pride ascend,
> Fanned by the breath of angry Providence.
> But oh! if Past and Future be the wings
> On whose support harmoniously conjoined
> Moves the great spirit of human knowledge, spare
> These courts of mystery....
>   (*1850* VI, 435–446)

What made the ruins was the spirit of "new-born Liberty" to which Wordsworth wholeheartedly aspired, but with "conflicting passions." Wordsworth could see how "Liberty" threatened tradition and order. He could see this not just in political terms, but in personal terms. Geoffrey Hartman, in *Wordsworth's Poetry*, has discussed how Wordsworth fears the overweening power of a self-sufficient imagination and needs to bind that imagination into some sense of natural continuity.[10] In his own imagination, Wordsworth could feel the same dazzling power that led to the destruction of the monasteries. When he discusses the "sacrilege" that threatens the monastic silence, he knows he is capable of the same thing in homefelt terms.

The situation is complicated. Spots of time are experienced by the free imagination that finds itself wandering—going on a pilgrimage, in a sense—in a natural setting. In the sacred solitude, the imagination finds its sustenance. But it does so out of a sense of its own freedom, a freedom that contributes to the sense of blessing, of being an imagination finding its home in a sacred place. It experiences the blessing of having a mind able to perceive a beautiful world, fitting and being fitted. But that freedom fears something about the solitude—namely: its potential stasis, its capability of paralyzing the imagination, of imprisoning it like Ariel in a tree. The solitude can turn Gothic, superstitious, soul-destroying. It can become Roman Catholicism.

So what Wordsworth discovered at Chartreuse was a prime analogy, which connected a massive cultural fact with a personal experience: the analogy between the Protestant stripping of Catholic sacred places and the imagination's violation of its sacred sources. To see this analogy more clearly in "Tintern Abbey," we need once again to consider part of its title: "July 13, 1798." Critics have puzzled over the fact that the date is not July 14, the great anniversary of the Bastille (whose celebrations Wordsworth witnessed on his 1790 trip to Chartreuse). However, the date, July 13, does signal the date of Wordsworth's first visit to France, on July 13, 1790, and also the date of the assassination of Marat, July 13, 1793, which some see as the beginning of the Terror.[11] What is puzzling is the way Wordsworth describes his memory of 1793 as he looks back in 1798:

> here I stand, not only with the sense
> Of present pleasure, but with pleasing thoughts
> That in this moment there is life and food
> For future years. And so I dare to hope,
> Though changed, no doubt, from what I was when first
> I came among these hills; when like a roe
> I bounded o'er the mountains, by the sides
> Of the deep rivers, and the lonely streams,
> Wherever nature led: more like a man
> Flying from something that he dreads, than one
> Who sought the thing he loved. For nature then
> (The coarser pleasures of my boyish days,
> And their glad animal movements all gone by)
> To me was all in all.—I cannot paint
> What then I was. The sounding cataract
> Haunted me like a passion: the tall rock,
> The mountain, and the deep and gloomy wood,
> Their colours and their forms, were then to me
> An appetite; a feeling and a love,
> That had no need of a remoter charm,
> By thought supplied, nor any interest
> Unborrowed from the eye.
>   (62–83)

What is curious is that if this refers to five years previous, it refers to a time, 1793, when Wordsworth was twenty-three and a revolutionary sympathizer, not fourteen and bounding about in the Lake Country. In 1793, Wordsworth was a very sophisticated young man, back from his second trip and long stay in France, back from Annette Vallon and Michel Beaupuy (whose influences on his Catholic sympathies were very important), back in London for several months and perhaps revisiting Paris where he may have witnessed an execution of one of the Girondists, the more conservative of the republicans, and also the year when Wordsworth wrote his republican "Letter to the Bishop of Landaff." Sometime between 1793 and 1798 he became profoundly disillusioned with revolutionary politics; a disillusionment recorded in "Tintern Abbey," which attempts to recover the sacred sources of his imagination.

In his memory, Wordsworth points to several stages of his joy, from late childhood (a time of "coarser pleasures") when he bounded over the mountains, through adolescence when he played truant from school and rode to Furness Abbey, to his young adulthood, when he strode across France and felt the winds of freedom. The five-year-old joy, really five- and ten- and twenty-year-old joy, is in modern parlance "overdetermined." But somehow a loss has occurred, a stripping of the imaginative altars; so that all he has left are "beauteous forms" but empty, only "a picture of the mind," an outline, like the abbey outline, needing to be filled in. He needs to recover La Grande Chartreuse. We need to discern yet another palimpsest, that of Chartreuse, in the following lines:

> for such loss, I would believe,
> Abundant recompence. For I have learned
> To look on nature, not as in the hour
> Of thoughtless youth; but hearing oftentimes
> The still, sad music of humanity,
> Nor harsh nor grating, though of ample power
> To chasten and subdue. And I have felt
> A presence that disturbs me with the joy....
>   (87–94)

Wordsworth learned this lesson at Chartreuse. I say this because of a passage in *The Prelude* where Wordsworth identifies the moment when he turned consciously from nature to humanity. In Book VIII of *The Prelude*, Wordsworth praises the figure of the shepherd, and draws upon the memory of his 1790 visit to Chartreuse:

> His form hash flashed upon me glorified
> By the deep radiance of the setting sun;

Or him have I descried in distant sky,
A solitary object and sublime,
Above all height, like an aerial cross,
As it is stationed on some spiry rock
Of the Chartreuse, for worship. Thus was man
Ennobled outwardly before mine eyes,
And thus my heart at first was introduced
To an unconscious love and reverence
Of human nature....
    (*1805* VIII, 404–414)

And at the end of this passage, Wordsworth praises "the mind / That to devotion willingly would be raised, / Into the temple and the temple's heart" (469–471), thus enforcing the parallel of nature's temple, the mind's temple, and the monastic temple. The passage is very important for crediting Chartreuse, and the worshipping shepherd, with the move to "love and reverence / Of human nature."

Now, this connection with Chartreuse is hardly explicit in "Tintern Abbey," where the Tintern Abbey outlines fade in and out like the Cheshire cat's smile. But one thing that is explicit in the poem is the constant uncertainty and tentativeness of several moments of the poem: "If this / Be but a vain belief," "And so I dare to hope," "for such loss, *I would believe*, abundant recompense" (emphasis added), "Nor perchance if I were not thus taught." These hesitancies have been much remarked, and they are indeed odd since Wordsworth has been describing an experience of blessed joy, not merely a hope for it. But what we are seeing is the dialectic of the free imagination—able to doubt and fly away from its moorings—and the original sacred place of holy seclusion experienced in nature and confirmed in the abbey setting. Wordsworth must somehow re-create this joy and this monastic setting in a new subjective way. Though he has the experience, he needs to see if the experience is permanent and embodies an immortal value. This need is what made him so grateful to discover the monastic equivalent to his early spots of time, for the abbey spirituality provided a religious mooring for his private experience. So in the poem, he needs to recontact that support for his early experience. He needs to re-experience the abbey.

He does so by turning to his sister Dorothy. Dorothy in the poem has characteristics that we find in other distinctive characters in Wordsworth:

    Therefore let the moon
Shine on thee in thy solitary walk;
And let the misty mountain-winds be free

To blow against thee: and, in after years,
When these wild ecstasies shall be matured
Into a sober pleasure; when thy mind
Shall be a mansion for all lovely forms,
Thy memory be as a dwelling-place
For all sweet sounds and harmonies; oh! then,
If solitude, or fear, or pain, or grief,
Should be thy portion, with what healing thoughts
Of tender joy wilt thou remember me,
And these my exhortations!
    (134–146)

What Wordsworth here says of Dorothy is similar to what he says of the "Old Cumberland Beggar" in that poem also written in this year:

Be his the natural silence of old age!
Let him be free of mountain solitudes;
And have around him, whether heard or not,
The pleasant melody of woodland birds....
    (182–185)

The old Cumberland beggar has connections with the leech-gatherer in "Resolution and Independence," whose connection with the hermit is discussed by Geoffrey Hartman in *The Unmediated Vision*.[12] Dorothy's "mansion" also connects here with Gilpin's description of one of the inhabitants of the abbey, the old pauper woman whom he describes: "She could scarce crawl; shuffling along her palsied limbs, and meagre, contracted body, by the help of two sticks" (36). So also the leech-gatherer, whose body was "bent double, feet and head / Coming together in life's pilgrimage" (66–67): "Himself he propped, limbs, body, and pale face, / Upon a long grey staff of shaven wood" (71–72). Gilpin's poor woman serves as the tour guide who had taken over "the remnant of a shattered cloister.... It was her own mansion."

    Dorothy is connected with the Cumberland beggar, with the leech-gatherer, with Gilpin's beggar woman, and thus becomes the re-encountered hermit in the poem. She internalizes in herself the monk's mansion, now a mental mansion "for all lovely forms."[13] Just as Wordsworth is supported by nature and by the abbey setting in his spots of time, now he is supported by Dorothy: "with what healing thoughts / Of tender joy wilt thou remember me"—a phrase meant as encouragement to her, but in fact carrying the personal accent of his own appeal. With Dorothy, he will reconstitute a monastic community, as "worshipper[s] of Nature ... Unwearied in that service ... with far deeper zeal / Of holier love." The moment will recover "these steep woods and lofty cliffs," the enclosing setting of the sacred place, for which the abbey is a prime symbol, and where worship, service, holier love is carried out in ancient traditional style.

There is another example that reinforces the parallel of Dorothy to the monastic hermit. Years later, in 1835, Wordsworth was to compose a poem, "Written after the Death of Charles Lamb," in which he speaks not only of Lamb but of his sister Mary, who may be seen as parallel to Dorothy:

> O gift divine of quiet sequestration!
> The hermit, exercised in prayer and praise,
> And feeding daily on the hope of heaven,
> Is happy in his vow, and fondly cleaves
> To life-long singleness; but happier far
> Was to your souls, and, to the thoughts of others,
> A thousand times more beautiful appeared,
> Your *dual* loneliness. The sacred tie
> Is broken; yet why grieve? ...
>   (121–129)

There are many further questions that cannot be adequately considered here: the relation of Wordsworth's Catholic sympathies to his high church Anglicanism; their consistency with his furious anti-papalism at the time of the Catholic Emancipation Act; their relevance to the question of the continuity and discontinuity of his career; their relation to the question of Romantic escapism from social ills (like the Tintern Abbey beggars); their consistency with the secularized Wordsworth of the modern critical tradition. Let me only say a concluding word about this last topic.

M. H. Abrams has argued influentially, in *Natural Supernaturalism*, that Wordsworth secularized the religious—so influentially in fact that it constitutes current orthodoxy:

> The Christian theodicy of the private life, in the long lineage of Augustine's Confessions, transfers the locus of the primary concern with evil from the providential history of mankind to the providential history of the individual self, and justifies the experience of wrongdoing, suffering, and loss as a necessary means toward the greater good of personal redemption. But Wordsworth's is a secular theodicy—a theodicy without an operative *theos*—which retains the form of the ancient reasoning,

but translates controlling Providence into an immanent teleology, makes the process coterminous with our life in this world, and justifies suffering as the necessary means toward the end of a greater good which is nothing other than the stage of achieved maturity.[14]

Such Wordsworthian theodicy, he goes on, "translates the painful process of Christian conversion and redemption into a painful process of self-formation, crisis, and self-recognition, which culminates in a stage of self-coherence, self-awareness, and assured power that is its own reward." About this view, I have written elsewhere: "The distinction is familiar, but because of it, the old religious theodicy seems flat and conventional, the new secular theodicy seems bland and aimless. In any event, New Historicism has hatcheted Wordsworth's 'self-discovery' into a thing of shreds and patches. In fact, might there be a way of reinvigorating both religious and psychological traditions by bringing them into new forms of contact with each other?"[15]

I am quoting myself here because at the time I did not see the way through the disabling alternatives of old orthodoxy and secular blandness. But I would now argue that Wordsworth keeps returning to the religious as a base from which he can spring, again and again. He needs to keep returning to the sources and mainstay of his imaginative life, sources that are associated with natural solitude, and whose prime analogy is with the experience of Catholic monks and hermits. And we are speaking of the religious not in some vague sense, but in the specific historical sense of the Catholicism of pre-Reformation England and pre-Revolutionary France, but continuing in "Roman Catholic" form into Wordsworth's time. The scope of Wordsworth is immense in that he takes on the whole span of English religious history—thus the importance of his long look at the subject in *Ecclesiastical Sonnets*. Because of revisionist Reformation history, we are beginning to see the power of the Catholic past in England, and can now see it here in the most famous English poet of nature and imagination.

NOTES

1. See Peter A. Brier, "Reflections on Tintern Abbey," *The Wordsworth Circle* 5 (1974): 5–6.

2. See Marjorie Levinson, *Wordsworth's Great Period Poems* (Cambridge, 1986) 37–38.

3. Quotations from Wordsworth's poetry, except *The Prelude*, are taken from Wordsworth, *The Poems*, ed. John O. Hayden (New Haven, 1981).

4. Wordsworth, *The Prelude* (1805), X, 725–727. Quotations from *The Prelude* are taken from *The Prelude 1799, 1805, 1850*, ed. Jonathan Wordsworth, M. H. Abrams, and Stephen Gill (New York, 1979).

5. See Lane Cooper, ed., *A Concordance to the Poems of William Wordsworth* (London, 1911). This concordance does not include some poems like "The Tuft of Primroses" which is laden with the relevant words.

6. *The Stripping of the Altars: Traditional Religion in England c. 1400–c. 1850* (New Haven, 1992).

7. *Roads to Rome: The Antebellum Protestant Encounter with Catholicism* (Berkeley, 1994).

8. Wordsworth's *Ecclesiastical Sonnets* are also an important part of this tradition. Although the sonnets defend Protestantism, "yet the negative always seems tinged with some regret that the delicate balance of reforming and preserving had not been maintained"; John L. Mahoney, *William Wordsworth: A Poetic Life* (New York, 1997) 249.

9. *Observations on the River Wye* (1782; Oxford, 1991) 32–34.

10. *Wordsworth's Poetry, 1787–1814* (New Haven, 1964) 41–42, 212.

11. See J.R. Watson, "A Note on the Date in the Title of 'Tintern Abbey,'" *The Wordsworth Circle* 10 (1979): 379–380.

12. *The Unmediated Vision: An Interpretation of Wordsworth*, Hopkins, Rilke, and Valéry (New Haven, 1954) 33–35.

13. A related passage is *The Prelude* (1805) II, 294–296, "The props of my affections were removed, / And yet the building stood, as if sustained / By its own spirit!" This passage is discussed as a symbol of the imagination by J. Robert Barth, SJ., "'The Props of My Affections': A Note on *The Prelude* II, 276–281," *The Wordsworth Circle* 10 (1979): 344–345.

14. *Natural Supernaturalism: Tradition and Revolution in Romantic Literature* (New York, 1971) 95–96.

15. Dennis Taylor, "The Need for a Religious Literary Criticism," *Religion and the Arts* 1 (1996): 142.

WORKS CITED

Abrams, M.H. *Natural Supernaturalism: Tradition and Revolution in Romantic Literature.* New York: Norton, 1971.

Barth, J. Robert, S.J. "'The Props of My Affections': A Note on *The Prelude* II, 276–281." *The Wordsworth Circle* 10 (1979): 344–345.

Brier, Peter A., "Reflections on Tintern Abbey." *The Wordsworth Circle* 5 (1974): 5–6.

Cooper, Lane, ed. *A Concordance to the Poems of William Wordsworth.* London: Smith, Elder, 1911.

Duffy, Eamon. *The Stripping of the Altars: Traditional Religion in England c 1400–c. 1580.* New Haven: Yale University Press, 1992.

Franchot, Jenny. *Roads to Rome: The Antebellum Protestant Encounter with Catholicism.* Berkeley. University of California Press, 1994.

Gilpin, William. *Observations on the River Wye 1782.* Oxford, England: Woodstock Books, 1991.

Hartman, Geoffrey. *The Unmediated Vision: An Interpretation of Wordsworth, Hopkins, Rilke, and Valéry.* New Haven: Yale University Press, 1954.

———. *Wordsworth's Poetry, 1787–1814.* New Haven: Yale University Press, 1964.

Levinson, Marjorie. *Wordsworth's Great Period Poems.* Cambridge: Cambridge University Press, 1986.

Mahoney, John L. *William Wordsworth: A Poetic Life.* New York: Fordham University Press, 1997.

Taylor, Dennis. "The Need for a Religious Literary Criticism." *Religion and the Arts* 1 (1996): 124–150.

Watson, J.R. "A Note on the Date in the Title of 'Tintern Abbey'." *The Wordsworth Circle* 10 (1979): 379–380.

Wordsworth, William. *The Poems.* 2 Vols. Ed. John O. Hayden. New Haven: Yale University Press, 1977, 1981.

———. *The Prelude 1799, 1805, 1850.* Ed. Jonathan Wordsworth, M.H. Abrams, and Stephen Gill. Norton Critical Edition. New York: Norton, 1979.

SALLY BUSHELL

The Excursion:
Dramatic Composition, Dramatic Definition

DEFINING THE DRAMATIC POEM

A full defence of Wordsworth's dramatic tendencies in his earlier poetry has already been given by Stephen Parrish in *The Art of the Lyrical Ballads*, a work which has been seminal in arguing for a 'dramatic' Wordsworth and to which this study is indebted. Parrish argues convincingly for the importance of the dramatic mode in *Lyrical Ballads* and that Coleridge's refusal to see the importance of this for Wordsworth is a major cause of his dissatisfaction with the other man's principles.[1] However, Parrish concludes that Coleridge's discontent had a powerfully negative effect:

> Long before these strictures appeared in print, Wordsworth had abandoned his experiments with dramatic method. We can only guess how large a part Coleridge may have played, in the early years, in turning his partner away from the dramatic monologue and towards the philosophic mode. (147)

In many ways this study picks up the argument where Parrish leaves off and tries to show that what has been successfully argued for the earlier poems may also be true of *The Excursion* and that, in fact, as the gap between Wordsworth and Coleridge grew wider, Wordsworth returned to the dramatic and tried to explore problems of dramatic voice in new ways.

From *Re-Reading* The Excursion: *Narrative, Response and the Wordsworthian Dramatic Voice*, pp. 42–59. © 2002 by Sally Bushell.

225

One critic who has given considerable time to defining the dramatic poem in more general terms is, of course, T. S. Eliot. In his essay 'The Three Voices of Poetry' he defines the first two voices as 'the voice of the poet talking to himself' (89) and 'the voice of the poet addressing an audience' (89) before moving on to the third voice:

> The third is the voice of the poet when he attempts to create a dramatic character speaking in verse; when he is saying, not what he would say in his own person, but only what he can say within the limits of one imaginary character addressing another imaginary character. (89)

As a critic and poet-dramatist himself Eliot is able to give an interesting perspective upon the question of voice by openly assessing his own plays and the extent to which they fail to be fully dramatic:

> This chorus of *The Rock* was not a dramatic voice; though many lines were distributed, the personages were unindividuated. Its members were speaking *for me*, not uttering words that really represented any supposed characters of their own. (91)

Such comments help us to see that *The Excursion* may, to some extent, bear similar characteristics and similarly fail to be 'fully' dramatised. At the simplest level, the dramatic poem must be defined as the poet speaking in voices not his own—as Eliot defines it—and it is certainly in relation to this (central) definition that Wordsworth is least successful in *The Excursion*, since there are times when characters' voices are not absolutely distinct from each other, or from the poet's own. Speaking of his own limitations as a dramatist, Eliot states that 'When the poetry comes, the personage on the stage must not give the impression of being merely a mouthpiece for the author' ('Three Voices', 93). Just such a response to Wordsworth's dramatic limitations in *The Excursion* is given by Hazlitt who, as we have seen, states in his review of the poem that 'The recluse, the pastor, and the pedlar, are three persons in one poet' (542), and by Coleridge for whom Wordsworth's utterances should always be 'told of a poet in the character of a poet' (CW, 7 ii: 135).

The question of character definition, and the emergence of different voices, will be further discussed below in relation to the manuscripts. Nonetheless, it seems to me that this is only *one* aspect of the dramatic poem. I still want to try to consider what other characteristics might positively define dramatic poetry in its own right. The limitation of T.S. Eliot's approach, for the purposes of this chapter and this kind of text, lies in the fact that he is primarily interested in defining the extent to which a drama on the stage can be poetic whereas my concern is with the extent to which a poem can be dramatic. To do him justice, Eliot does note this assumption on his part in his discussion of the dramatic monologue:

> It would seem without further examination from Browning's mastery of the dramatic monologue, and his very moderate achievement in the drama, that the two forms must be essentially different. Is there, perhaps, another voice which I have failed to hear, the voice of the dramatic poet whose dramatic gifts are best exercised outside of the theatre? (94)

There are many ways in which Wordsworth's thinking about the dramatic, and the articulation of such ideas in *The Excursion*, directly anticipates the Victorian dramatic monologue, a form which is important for this argument in as much as it successfully articulates a dramatic voice in a poetic form which is not intended for stage production.[2] (Indeed, this is why Eliot has to address it.) It defines for us a distinct 'dramatic poetry' which has as its focus not audience-directed features of stage performance but the adaptation of these for a particular land of poetry with particular intentions towards the reader. Eliot here acknowledges the possible existence of a dramatic poem written to be read, not acted, but the second category into which he finally places the dramatic monologue—'the voice of the poet addressing an audience' (89)—is not fully appropriate for a form in which boundaries and distinctions between the voice of poet and character are constantly and consciously crossed and re-crossed. In other words, the category which Eliot continually passes by or edges around is that of the dramatic poem written in voices but written to be read, not acted.[3] This still leaves us with the question of what, exactly, this kind of dramatic poem is.

J.L. Styan in his discussion of stage drama offers a general definition of the dramatic:

> dramatic meaning cannot lie in words alone, but in voices and the tone of voices, in the pace of the speaking and the silences between; and not alone in this, but also in the gesture and expression of the actor, the physical distinctions between him and others ... (*Drama, Stage and Audience*, 26)

This is useful in supplying a broad definition of what it means for a work to be dramatic in ways which we can apply to a poetic text written to be read. Using this as a base, fundamental characteristics (shared with the stage drama) could be defined as: the expression of thoughts and ideas through voice and character; dialogue between characters; the distinction of different voices through various means; the use of silence for particular effect; the incorporation of various 'stage' effects (such as gesture). Styan also writes of the stage play that:

> we ought not only to be thinking of the variety of contributors to the finished production, author, actor, producer, designer.... We ought to recognize instead that, essentially, the words which stand for a production must make for a synthesis of the elements of drama; that the complexity of drama lies in this; that this kind of complexity and this kind of synthesis is unique and peculiar to drama. (*The Elements of Drama*, 4)

It seems to me equally possible that a dramatic poem, written to be read, might be an attempt to create a poetic locus where this 'unique synthesis' can occur. Such synthesis is now directed at the reader rather than an audience and has a particular literary and poetic intention. What emerges is a kind of poetic text which places emphasis on its own reception and has a heightened desire to establish some kind of dialogue with the reader.

A second major reason for choosing to make a poem dramatic, and one related to that outlined above, is the attempt to employ some kind of active dynamic of sympathy or alienation with the reader. The ways in which this may be manipulated will vary considerably. Robert Langbaum, discussing Browning, for example, highlights the way in which he uses the dramatic monologue to manipulate the reader's identification with the 'speaking' voice. Thus, a poem such as 'My Last Duchess' plays upon the reader's divided response to the Duke by using 'an effect peculiarly the genius of the dramatic monologue—[I mean] the effect created by the tension between sympathy and moral judgment' (*The Poetry of Experience*, 85). This occurs both at a general level in response to the portrait(s) painted in the poem, but also at a local level in the act of reading through the unfolding ironies and subtleties of tone in the poem itself. The full potential of such a form is later summed up by Langbaum after discussion of Browning's monologues in defence of Christianity:

> Not only can the speaker of the dramatic monologue dramatize a position to which the poet is not ready to commit himself intellectually, but the sympathy which we give the speaker for the sake of the poem and apart from judgment makes it possible for the reader to participate in a position, to see what

it feels like to believe that way, without having finally to agree.
(105)

In *The Excursion*—an earlier and less sophisticated dramatic poem—such
ideas certainly exist in embryo. For example, the reader is encouraged both
to sympathise with, and be distanced from, the Solitary at different points in
the text and to see a single character from different directions. For
Wordsworth, however, these ideas are expressed largely in a tension between
an emotional and rational response to be elicited from the reader, a tension
that emerges in his work in different ways over time. In his early 'Essay on
Morals' (1798) (as in *The Borderers*) Wordsworth adopts an anti-Godwinian
position, arguing against an 'undue value set upon that faculty which we call
reason' (*Prose*, 1: 103), and the emphasis in the 1800 'Preface' on the
'essential passions of the heart' (*Prose*, 1: 124) is, in part at least, a further
reaction to this. By 1815, however, rejection of 'reasoning' in favour of
feelings is far less absolute, and in relation to the reader a combination of
rational and emotional response is implied, as when in the 1815 'Preface' he
talks of 'a sadness that has its seat in the depths of reason, to which the mind
cannot sink gently of itself but to which it must descend by treading the steps
of thought' (*Prose*, 3: 82). It seems possible, then, that by the time of writing
The Excursion, Wordsworth was attempting to articulate a dramatic voice
which looks back not simply to a tradition of Aristotelian 'empathy' but to
one of Socratic (or Platonic) engagement through dialogue which is mental
as well as emotional.[4]

INTERNALISED DRAMATIC CONVENTIONS

Wordsworth's only play, *The Borderers*, was written in 1796–97 but not
published until 1842 when Wordsworth declared in a note added to the text
that:

> as it was at first written, and is now published, without any view
> to its exhibition upon the stage, not the slightest alteration has
> been made in the conduct of the story, or the composition of the
> characters; above all, in respect to the two leading Persons of the
> Drama... (Osborn, 813)

The claim that it was never intended for dramatic production is partly
disingenuous since Wordsworth was eager to pursue the possibility in 1797
when he used Coleridge's connections with Sheridan and Harris (the
manager of Covent Garden) to submit the play for consideration.[5]

Nonetheless, Wordsworth's statement is an interesting one with implications for his concept of the dramatic. In a comment given in the *Fenwick Notes* of 1843 he elaborated on changes that he would have made to the text if he had written it later in life:

> The plot would have been something more complex & a greater variety of characters introduced to relieve the mind from the pressure of incidents so mournful. The manners also wd. have been more attended to—my care was almost exclusively given to the passions & the characters, & the position in which the persons in the Drama stood relatively to each other that the reader (for I had then no thought of the Stage) might be moved & to a degree instructed by lights penetrating somewhat into the depths of our nature. (FN, 77)

The comment reveals those elements which Wordsworth later considers to be unsuitable for a purely dramatic work: lack of plot; too few characters; too intense a focus on particular emotions. Equally interesting is the sense of audience—or rather the total lack of such a sense—which exists even in this retrospective justification.[6] Emphasis is on the dynamic between characters, and the reader's engagement with such a dynamic. This sounds more like a blueprint for *The Excursion* than an account of *The Borderers*.

In his work on *Shakespeare and the English Romantic Imagination*, Jonathan Bate draws our attention to Wordsworth's lack of interest in performance. He refers to a letter of 1805 in which Wordsworth states:

> I never saw Hamlet acted my self nor do I know what kind of play they make of it. I think I have heard that some parts which I consider as among the finest are omitted ... The Players have taken intolerable Liberties with Shakespear's Plays. (EY, 587)

Bate concludes from this that 'any conclusions about Wordsworth's Shakespeare must be based firmly on his reading of the plays' (77). Again, later he returns to this point:

> The effect of what Wordsworth calls "incarnation" was the major difficulty faced by Romantics on seeing Shakespeare in the theatre. Certain plays were of such importance to their conceptions of imagination and the "spirit" of poetry that stage representation was limiting. Wordsworth's response to

> Shakespeare is private, meditative, rich and many-layered ... by its
> very nature far removed from public performance ... (112)

Wordsworth's personal privileging of reading over dramatic performance in
his response to drama is typical of his time, and some sense of context is
helpful here. We can compare his comment on *Hamlet* to Hazlitt's
articulation of similar ideas in 'Mr Kean's Richard II' in which he states that
'Those parts of the play on which the reader dwells the longest, and with the
highest relish in the perusal, are hurried through in the performance' (HW,
5: 222), and that 'all that affects us most deeply in our closets .... is little else
than an interruption, and a drag on the business of the stage' (222). The idea
of 'closet drama' as the Romantic response to drama—a privileging of the
play as text to be read alone rather than performed—has been looked at in
detail by a number of critics.[7] To some extent such a response can be
explained by the nature of early nineteenth-century theatre itself. The Drury
Lane theatre, for example, had been rebuilt in 1794 to house 3,611 people.[8]
Janet Heller outlines the consequences of this:

> Because so many spectators were far from the stage, actors were
> forced to speak more loudly and to exaggerate their gestures and
> movements. Another solution to this problem was to introduce
> the latest technological marvels to change scenes, to make ghosts
> fly, and otherwise to entertain even those spectators in the back
> rows. (13)

Charles Lamb, in 'On the Tragedies of Shakespeare, Considered with
Reference to Their Fitness for Stage Representation' clearly articulates
contemporary dissatisfaction with such characteristics of the theatre when he
states that:

> the Lear of Shakespeare cannot be acted. The contemptible
> machinery by which they mimic the storm which he goes out in,
> is not more inadequate to represent the horrors of the real
> elements, than any actor can be to represent Lear.... The
> greatness of Lear is not in corporal dimension, but in intellectual
> ... (*The Works of Charles and Mary Lamb*, 1: 107)

Lamb reacts against the nature of contemporary performance by
distinguishing between text as text, and text as words, written to be translated
into performance: 'I am not arguing that Hamlet should not be acted, but
how much Hamlet is made another thing by being acted' (101). Nonetheless,

he does of course side in favour of the text 'The sublime images, the poetry alone, is that which is present to our minds in the reading' (106). Later Lamb sums up his own (and what we might call the Romantic) position:

> What we see upon a stage is body and bodily action; what we are conscious of in reading is almost exclusively the mind, and its movements: and this I think may sufficiently account for the very different sort of delight with which the same play so often affects us in the reading and the seeing. (108)

This explanation helps us to understand the reasons why stage presentation made the Romantics so uneasy. What Lamb responds negatively to is the rapid gratification of the senses which occurs in performance because this allows no space for thought on the part of the audience.[9] When he says that 'what we are conscious of in reading is almost exclusively the mind, and its movement' he suggests that the real value of such reading is not only that it demands a more thoughtful response to a text, but that it also, essentially, allows for an awareness of that response on the part of the reader and a self-conscious examination of it once such an awareness has been recognised. The dramatic reading experience, then, contains stages of analysis and a multiplicity of potential responses within the individual which cannot exist in the context of seeing the play performed, or at least cannot exist contemporaneously with the seeing of the play. In contrast then, the reading of a dramatic work—and perhaps of a dramatic poem—allows and even encourages this kind of self-consciousness in a way that the play performed cannot. It brings along with it a different awareness of the text as a dramatic and literary work. Indeed, it could be argued that whilst the successful performance must show no consciousness of its audience, and of the falseness of its construction, the text of that play clearly has to show such awareness at a practical level. So, for example, when we read a play the very existence of stage directions, character's names, scene divisions and so on makes the reader aware of its artifice, its literariness, in ways that performance necessarily elides. One of the strengths of a dramatic poem over a purely dramatic work then, might be its ability to self-consciously explore the nature of dramatic representation, and to encourage the reader to respond in this way also. Such an emphasis on self-conscious examination is, I think, very important in relation to the land of 'dramatic' poem which Wordsworth was trying to create.

We can explore this question further by looking at the use of dramatic conventions by Wordsworth, firstly in *The Borderers* (which in spite of Wordsworth's denials is clearly written to be staged) and secondly in *The*

Excursion which is *not* intended for dramatic performance but nonetheless responds in interesting ways to such consideration. All references to *The Borderers* are from the Cornell edition. I have taken as my base text that of the Early Version (1797–99).

The most visually apparent of such dramatic characteristics in Wordsworth's play is the layout of text upon the page. For example:

> Rivers
> You are safe as in a sanctuary
> Speak
> > Mortimer
> > > Speak
> > > Beggar
> > He is a most hard hearted man
> (Osborn, 326–27 [31v]).[10]

Speech is clearly attributed to a particular character, with names consistently written in the centre of the page, and dialogue spaced in terms of an exchange between characters.[11]

Surviving early fragments of the play are also interesting in revealing drafts in prose which Wordsworth later turned into blank verse, a technique very untypical of him. Such material is sometimes clearly a prose synopsis, and Osborn suggests that there may have been a series of these 'covering more or less the whole play, drafted at the outset of composition' (45) as in this example:

> Matilda having executed her commission comes to a church yard—meets a pilgrim whom she discovers to be her mother. Her joy at the thought of meeting her father. (Osborn, 48)

At other times characters speak in prose in an earlier version of a passage which is later turned into verse or translated in various ways. An excellent example of this can be seen in the account of Ferdinand's despair in scenes i and ii of Act V. In early drafts for the play the second scene opened with a soliloquy, originally written in prose:

> Scene the edge of a heath—Enter Ferdinand,
> > dress
> his hair loose and ^ disordered, his looks betraying
> extreme horror.
> > How many hours have I wandered night and

day through every comer of this dreary heath—
My eyes have been strained, my voice has
called incessantly but in vain
(Osborn, 422–23 [55v])

Wordsworth reworks these lines elsewhere in the notebook, still keeping
them in prose but then at the end of the scene he attempts to turn them into
verse, the change in the length of line clearly visible on the manuscript page
(412–13 [53r]). The scene which follows the shift into verse in the
manuscript involves a verse dialogue between Margaret and the peasant in
which a third person, eye witness account of Ferdinand on the bridge is
given:

I heard these words the whole of what he spoke
"The dust doth move and eddy at my feet"
            Most
This was ^ strange the air being dead
                                    and still
(Osborn, 416–17 [54r])

The scene ends with Ferdinand's entry at which point, Osborn suggests, the
soliloquy was to follow. In the final version of the play these two distinct
representations—of Ferdinand (now Mortimer) by himself and of Mortimer
by another—are conflated in Rivers' eager, morbid, desire to gather a
description of him from the two woodsmen. All three characters are placed
in the position of eavesdroppers as 'MORTIMER appears crossing the stage at
some distance' (254) and the scene continues as follows:

            Mortimer
The dust doth move and eddy at my feet.
            Second Woodman
This is most strange; the air is dead and still.
            First Woodman
Look there, how he spreads out his arms as 'twere
To save himself from falling!
(Osborn, 256)

Here we are given an example of Wordsworth translating the presentation of
the scene in a number of ways as well as moving speech from one mouth to
another. The early drafts work by establishing contrasting perspectives, with
the distinct vision of Ferdinand/Mortimer hanging over the chasm being

retold through the eyes of the peasant. This works quite powerfully but it is, nonetheless, only given indirectly so that such a moment has a largely narrative power and is only visual in so far as the audience is individually capable of visualising it. In the later version Wordsworth changes this to make of it a dramatic and (unusually for him) a quite theatrical moment as the audience now directly witnesses the physical manifestations of the character's despair. Having conflated the two perspectives, and made his audience into complicit eavesdroppers alongside the characters, he then removes the soliloquy altogether from the play. At first sight this kind of direct translation of lines or sections of the text as part of the act of composition seems particularly characteristic of this work, and, superficially, of Wordsworth's own distinction between writing a 'dramatic' work (drama in verse) as opposed to a 'poetic' one (a dramatic poem).

One final example of dramatic conventions in the manuscripts of *The Borderers* occurs with the use of stage directions. Again, these are laid out very clearly on the page, usually with the aid of brackets:

> (Rivers conducts Herbert into the house—) (to Mortimer)
>   Host
>   Good Master
> (Osborn, 336–37 [34r])[12]

Exits are also often indicated:

> —fare well farewell
> Exit Matilda
> (Osborn, 342–43 [35v])

To sum up, then, we can say that in writing *The Borderers* Wordsworth closely adheres to dramatic conventions on the page and, whether he is writing the play only to be read or not, he uses these conventions to make clear distinctions between voice and character and to describe movement and action. Whilst there are ways in which the content may be 'undramatic' (which will be discussed below) the composition and layout of the text conform to what we would expect of a playscript.

A direct comparison of the physical appearance of the play manuscript with that of *The Excursion* is illuminating. At first glance, the pages of the notebooks look very different. In the manuscripts of the poem—in contrast to the layout of *The Borderers*—there is little sense of which character is speaking at any one time. This is partly due to the fact that speeches last considerably longer without interruption than in the play, but there is also no labelling of speech to character as there is in *The Borderers*. Instead, such signposts occur within the text itself to indicate a change of speaker as, for example, in the line: 'Our Nature, said the Priest in mild reply' (Bushell, Butler, Jaye, MS 74 [28r]).[13] In fact at times this is confusing in reading the poem because when such labels are not incorporated, particularly in sections of lengthy debate, it is not always immediately apparent which character is speaking.

As this example suggests, many of the obvious dramatic conventions so immediately identifiable in the manuscripts of *The Borderers* have been assimilated into *The Excursion*. One could consider, for example, the prose synopses which Osborn suggested were the starting points of the play. The 'Arguments' at the start of each book of *The Excursion* can certainly be equated with prose synopses. Indeed, they often suggest connections and emphases not made explicit within the text itself, as in the summary of Book VI:

> an Instance of Perseverance, which leads by contrast to an Example of abused talents, irresolution, and weakness—Solitary, applying this covertly to his own case, asks for an Instance of some Stranger ... (xviii) (p.186)

In the poem, however, it seems unlikely that these exist as starting points for composition, and far more likely (as in the example above) that they are written afterwards as clarifications to reading.[14] They therefore perform a different function in the poetic text. In the play they exist as part of the process of composition for the poet, and, if they do remain, it is only as stage directions unheard by the audience. In the poem they are part of a process of contraction and clarification for the reader.

A further comparison, in terms of the translation of prose into poetry which occurred in the composition of the play, is less immediately apparent but also present in *The Excursion*. The reason we fail to consider it is because it often involves the translation of another text entirely into this one. An obvious example occurs in Book VI when the poem directly echoes Wordsworth's second 'Essay on Epitaphs'. The texts placed alongside each other read as follows:

> It is such a happiness to have, in an unkind World, one Enclosure where the voice of detraction is not heard; where the traces of evil inclinations are unknown; where contentment prevails, and there is no japing tone in the peaceful Concert of amity and gratitude. (*Prose*, 2: 63–64)

>   " 'twas no momentary happiness
> To have one enclosure where the voice that speaks
> In envy or detraction is not heard;
> Which malice may not enter; where the traces
> Of evil inclinations are unknown;
> Where love and pity tenderly unite
> With resignation; and no jarring tone
> Intrudes; the peaceful concert to disturb
> Of amity and gratitude."
> (278–79) (VI 637–44)

These kind of translations—or transpositions—of other and earlier texts into the final poem will be considered in detail later in this chapter. For the present it is worth noting that such moments exist within the poem as they did in the play and that the act of translating them may be part of a personalised 'dramatic' dialogue essential to the act of composition for the poet.

When we look closely, it is even possible to discern 'stage directions' embedded within the poetic text. The account of the Solitary before he begins to tell his story in Book III is introduced thus:

> But, while he spake, look, gesture, tone of voice,
> Though discomposed and vehement, were such
> As skill and graceful Nature might suggest
> To a Proficient of the tragic scene,
> Standing before the multitude, beset
> With sorrowful events; and we, who heard
> And saw, were moved.
> (116) (III 463–68)

In a sense, the Poet here is voicing for us the 'stage directions' which are immediately to be followed by the character's direct speech. He draws attention to the dramatic nature of the Solitary's self-presentation ('look, gesture, tone of voice') in a way which prepares us to receive his words. Furthermore, the Poet also directly articulates and affirms that the desired affect has been achieved to some extent even before giving the tale. The assimilation of such dramatic instructions into the fabric of the poem allows him to do this.

Finally, it is worth noting that the use of landscape in *The Excursion* at times seems to suggest the appearance of a stage. This may look back to the picturesque movement, and the viewing of landscape as a scene, as much as to the dramatic, but certainly the actual journey is repeatedly halted as characters stop before a particular backdrop: the four bare walls of the cottage; the Solitary's retreat; the country churchyard. At certain points such use of scenery and stage is almost explicitly dramatic as in the description of the Wanderer's response to the Solitary's story:

> near that lonely House we paced
> A plot of green-sward . . . .
> . . . .
> Small space but for reiterated steps
> Smooth and commodious; as a stately deck
> Which to and fro the Mariner is used
> To tread for pastime ...
> (152) (IV 241–42, 245–48)

The Wanderer, also, 'treads the boards' as he articulates his response to the Solitary's tale.

The extent to which conventions and techniques used in the purely dramatic work exist at a level not immediately apparent within the poem is surprising. We still need to consider, however, what the function of such features in a dramatic poem might be. The most obvious point is that the text now anticipates the nature of its own reception. The sense of it as a work to be read aloud is partly built into the poem, as the example of internalised labelling of speech to character suggests. The internalisation of dramatic signposts directly anticipates a semi-dramatic presentation of the final work.[15]

To consider fully the function of internalised conventions, however, it is necessary to reconsider the implications of Wordsworth's interest in a play written 'without any view to its exhibition upon the stage' (Osborn, 813), and intended for 'the reader' (FN, 77). In *The Excursion*, Wordsworth is able to write dramatically for the reader in a way that he could not in *The Borderers* where he was always *supposed* to be writing for an audience before whom his text would have to be translated into performance. In watching a performance the audience has no access to the kinds of features examined above. Only by reading the playscript do various directions and framing devices—devices intended to aid the translation of that text into spoken word—become apparent, and in a playscript they remain extra-dramatic, not intrinsic to the text itself. Wordsworth wants the response to his play to be a 'read' rather than a 'viewed' one, or at least he accepts that this is the ideal response for the kind of play he has written. It seems, then, that the structures of interpretation provided by the format of a playscript are part of the ideal response to be elicited from the reader, or are essential to the promotion of it. The effect of placing these signposts within the poem is that the text constantly draws attention to its own false construction and to the fact that it is *presented* as being dramatic rather than simply being so. With the 'stage directions' given above, for example, such comments operate as a frame which does not simply introduce the speech but *reminds* us of its indirectness, of the fact that we are not actually hearing the voice from the Solitary's own mouth but only the Poet's reformulation of that voice. In other words, the use of dramatic elements in the poem—and inevitably in any dramatic poem that is not written in the form of a play—can only operate to draw attention to the fact that speech is *not* really speech. It constantly draws attention to its own limitations. I think Wordsworth is content for this to be the case and, indeed, that it is an essential defining characteristic of the dramatic poem as opposed to the play. It is able to play upon and draw attention to its dramatic representation. Equally too, it can exploit to the full the flexible temporality of its reading—the ability to pause, discuss, compare, re-read, which a dramatic work seen in performance must deny.

INDIRECTNESS

Wordsworth often seems to be interested in dramatising acts such as recalling, retelling and responding to retelling in such a way as to remove dramatic action from the present into the past. In *The Borderers* the indirect narrative—with its sense that one is hearing something second-hand, and often that what one hears is not being told only once or for the first time— gives us an example of such a structure at work within a purely dramatic work, which Wordsworth then goes on to make central to his dramatic poem. *The Borderers* provides us with a handling of the dramatic which is only partially successful in the play but which directly anticipates its centrality to *The Excursion*.

In *The Fenwick Notes* Wordsworth draws attention to his essay 'On The Character of Rivers' written 'while I was composing this play' (FN, 78).[16] Whilst Wordsworth explores Rivers' motivations at length in the essay, for the most part this character does not appear to stand at the centre of the play itself where it is the replaying of such stages by the unwitting Mortimer that is the focus of the action. The significant exception to this is the point at which Rivers gives the story of his own life in Act IV. Wordsworth places great weight upon this part of the play in his essay commenting that 'when dormant associations are awakened tracing the revolutions through which his character has passed, in painting his former self he really is great' (65). The means by which this 'greatness' is achieved is through the act of retelling, or as Wordsworth puts it 'painting' (65). Elsewhere in the essay he comments of Rivers that 'His imagination is powerful, being strengthened by the habit of picturing possible forms of society where his crimes would be no longer crimes' (Osborn, 64) and 'He looks at society through an optical glass of a peculiar tint' (Osborn, 65). Above all Rivers is an onlooker, a person standing outside the action, one who paints, pictures, gazes. There is something innately and dangerously passive about him in relation to his own fallen self, which translates only negatively into the urge to lure others into a similar state.[17] It is unsurprising, then, that, at the point at which he does become the focus of the play, the effect of this is to make the play itself lose focus around him.

The dramatic purpose of Rivers' autobiography is to reveal to Mortimer that he has deliberately deceived him, and the retelling is thus punctuated throughout by Mortimer's responses and own changing reactions from sympathy and understanding to horror and rejection, culminating in the realisation that 'Monster, you have betray'd me' (Osborn, 242). Within the context of the play, it performs a central and decisive dramatic function in relation to its auditor, since it compels him to reinterpret all the events so far, and his own participation in them. However, the focus is upon motive rather than event and to slow the action of the present down at this point in order for another character to give his autobiography remains a basically 'undramatic' act in terms of the requirements of the stage production. When we look at this section of the play the passage is introduced quite awkwardly without there being any real stimulus for Rivers to give an extended account of himself.[18] The telling of Rivers' own story from the distant past then becomes a rewriting of Mortimer's in the recent past of the play. It works to remove the audience from the immediate context and it establishes a parallel narrative which allows us to see all that has happened in the play from fresh perspectives. Alan Richardson describes the effect of this very well in his discussion of *The Borderers* as 'a work of mental theater':

> The borders of time grow as unstable as those in space. The pressure of Oswald's past crime is so great that it loses its anteriority and takes place again in the present; its original effects included the incursion of the future ... (29)

Where previously we had the double vision of watching Mortimer act in the belief that he was driven by right principles whilst he was really being manipulated, now we can also clearly see events from Rivers' perspective with his full motives and the parallels between his story and Mortimer's made clear. Finally, we can also share Mortimer's retrospective re-reading of his own actions in the immediate past in the light of this knowledge.[19] This sudden wholeness of vision after partial understanding is something which Wordsworth deliberately intends and recognises as an absolute characteristic of a literary work as he sees it at this time: 'In works of imagination we see the motive and the end. In real life we rarely see either the one or the other' (Osborn, 67). However, the significance of these changes of perspective within the play remains far greater for Mortimer than for the audience, to whom the tale does not come as a complete revelation. The result of this is that it is easier to respond to the material in terms of narratives which rewrite each other, than as a drama unfolding.

The retold tale has a tendency to slow the action of a play. The emphasis on retelling, the deliberate embodiment of a past history within the play, works as a static force within the necessarily active linear movement of the stage drama. Immediate events are to be viewed through a wider context of psychological layering and comparison, a context for which the dramatic form, in this case at least, is hardly suited. The writer wants to compel the audience and characters to look back on and reinterpret what has gone before. However, if this kind of Wordsworthian dramatic structure, clearly illustrated by Rivers' narrative, is uneasily present in his purely dramatic work, it becomes absolutely fundamental to *The Excursion* where, as part of a text written to be read, it is both more justifiable and more powerfully operative. A comparable example in terms of the effect of Rivers' tale on the work as a whole, can immediately be seen in the Solitary's autobiography of Book III where the telling of his own life compels a reassessment of the first narrative told by the Wanderer in Book II.[20] In *The Borderers* the limitations (for Wordsworth) of the dramatic and its demands are evaded by an opening backward into the past so that any dramatic impetus is redirected out of the base-narrative into the contained one. The core of the 'action' then is not about action at all, and in a sense the play itself becomes a frame for what it contains. In a purely dramatic work this has the danger of weakening the momentum of the play, but in the dramatic poem it can become a strength. Also of great importance to the telling of a tale in *The Excursion* is the sense that the poem is able to communicate that this is only one of many tellings, that it has been told before, that it will be told again. Thus, the narrative is not only multi-layered in terms of its presentation within the poem as we read it, but it presents the act of narrative itself as multi-layered. The emphasis provided by 'indirectness' which makes clear the importance of changing perspectives, of seeing the same events in different ways through a series of filters, is made to become a central concern of the Wordsworthian dramatic poem.

I have used a comparison of *The Borderers* and *The Excursion* to try to develop a tighter definition of the Wordsworthian dramatic poem. Such a comparison also raises for us the question of whether *The Excursion* needed *The Borderers* to exist, of whether Wordsworth's one attempt at writing a play is in fact essential to his later dramatic writing. This question is not directly answerable, but it reminds us, I think, of the importance of viewing his dramatic long poem not just as a poetic work in comparison with *The Prelude* or with earlier dramatic poems such as *Paradise Lost*, but as a text which explores and reconsiders Wordsworthian dramatic concerns through poetry.

NOTES

1. See *The Art of the Lyrical Ballads* (Cambridge, Massachusetts: Harvard University Press, 1973), 137–48.

2. I have not gone on to explore this in detail here since it will be the subject of future study (focusing in particular on a comparison between *The Excursion* and *The Ring and the Book*).

3. At the same time Eliot does state later in the essay that his three voices are often all to be found in one work: 'I think that in every poem, from the private meditation to the epic or the drama, there is more than one voice to be heard' On *Poetry and Poets* (London: Faber and Faber Ltd., 1987), 100.

4. The use of philosophical dialogue as an informing principle in the poem will be further discussed in the following chapter. See also Don H. Bialostosky who sees Wordsworth as developing a 'poetics of speech' (11) looking back to Plato rather than Aristotle (*Making Tales*, Chapter 1).

5. See *The Borderers by William Wordsworth*, ed. Robert Osborn (Cornell University Press: Ithaca and London, 1982), 45.

6. Alan Richardson states that 'his description touches on the essentials of Romantic mental theater: the mental states or "passions" of the central characters, the psychic effect of the characters upon one another, and the appeal to the reader's engagement with a text that can illuminate hidden aspects of the mind'. *A Mental Theater: Poetic Drama and Consciousness In the Romantic Age* (University Park: Pennsylvania State University Press, 1988), 20. See also discussion of this below.

7. See particularly: Catherine B. Burroughs, *Closet Stages: Joanna Baillie and the Theater Theory of British Romantic Women Writers* (Philadelphia: University of Pennsylvania Press, 1997); Janet Ruth Heller, *Coleridge, Lamb, Hazlitt and the Reader of Drama* (Columbia and London: University of Missouri Press, 1990); Tim Webb, 'The Romantic Poet and the Stage: A Short, Sad History,' *The Romantic Theatre: An International Symposium*, ed. R.A. Dave (Colin Smythe: Gerrards Cross, 1986), 9–46; Alan Richardson, *A Mental Theater*, Terry Otten, *The Deserted Stage: The Search for Dramatic Form in Nineteenth Century England* (Athens: Ohio University Press, 1972).

8. See Tim Webb, 34–35.

9. A wider tradition for this distrust of the appeal to the senses in drama, looking back to Plato's *Phaedo* and Aristotle's *Poetics*, is given in the first chapter of Janet Ruth Heller's book: *Coleridge Lamb, Hazlitt and the Reader of Drama*.

10. In referencing to *The Borderers* I have given fast the page number and then the MS page reference where applicable. The changing names in different versions of the play are

confusing and require brief clarification. Ferdinand (in the 'Ur-Borderers') becomes Mortimer and then Marmaduke; Danby becomes Rivers then Oswald; Matilda remains as Matilda in the first two versions and then becomes Idonia in the last. See also Osborn (8).

11. There are occasional points where different voices are not distinguished. See for example the prose fragment on page 315 [19v] where, as Osborn points out, the first six lines are spoken by Matilda, the seventh by Herbert, but this distinction is only marked by a long dash.

12. The initial bracket before Rivers is not marked on the transcription on page 337 but is clearly visible on the manuscript facsimile on page 336. I have therefore included it.

13. All quotations from *The Excursion* in manuscript form should be accurate to transcriptions made for the forthcoming Cornell edition of this poem. Some errors may result from this work being published before the edition is complete. I am very grateful to the editors of the Cornell Series for allowing access to such materials which has greatly facilitated work on the manuscripts. Page references for the edition were not available at the time of writing so I have referenced according to manuscript page only.

14. There is no evidence of drafting for the 'Arguments' present in the surviving manuscripts of the poem.

15. Wordsworth's expectations for the text being read aloud will be discussed in more detail in Chapter 4.

16. In fact Osborn states that 'The essay must have been composed after the play had been largely completed, since it is obviously an apology for an already created character' (15).

17. In this he anticipates, in an extreme way, the Solitary of *The Excursion*. In the later poem too the relationship between the central character and the text as a whole is dangerously static, the nature of the Solitary's mental state bringing the poem in one sense—as a journey at least—shaking and shuddering around a point which it is slow to move on from.

18. I am working from the 1797–99 version of the play. In the later version a slightly more plausible reason for telling is given 'This day's event has laid on me the duty / Of opening out my story; you must hear it' (Osborn, 229).

19. This use of repetition as a kind of psychological plot device is discussed by Geoffrey Hartman for whom Wordsworth at this point 'came close to formulating the principle of "repetition-compulsion ..."' *Wordsworth's Poetry* (130). See also Alan Richardson, *Mental Theater* (33–34).

20. This will be explored in detail in Chapter 4.

Chronology

1770   William Wordsworth is born on April 7 at Cockermouth in Cumberland into a comfortable family with roots in the Lake Country. His father, John Wordsworth, is a legal agent to wealthy landowners, the Lowthers. Though often away on business, John Wordsworth introduces his children to English poetry as well as such classics as *Don Quixote* and the *Arabian Nights*. His mother, Ann Cookson Wordsworth, is from a respectable merchant family in Penrith.

1776   Begins grammar school near Cockermouth Church.

1778   Ann Wordsworth dies suddenly.

1779   In June, Wordsworth begins his education at Hawkshead Grammar School, known for its excellent instruction in mathematics and the classics, and boards with Ann Tyson, a very kind elderly lady of whom he is very fond.

1782   The appointment of a young schoolmaster, William Taylor, who will encourage Wordsworth to share his love of poetry, especially that of the eighteenth-century poets of sensibility.

1783   During the Christmas holiday, John Wordsworth dies, leaving a substantial and unresolved debt to the Lowthers. This financial burden will weigh heavily for many years upon the Wordsworth children. At the time of his death, the Wordsworth household is dispersed, the boys being sent back to school and Dorothy sent to live with relatives.

1784–1785   Wordsworth writes "Lines Written as a School Exercise at Hawkshead," which indicate how much his religious attitude to the universe owed to the Newtonian enlightenment of William Taylor.

1786–1787   Wordsworth's last academic year at Hawkshead, during which time he composes most of "The Vale of Esthwaite," a descriptive poem with Gothic and supernatural elements.

1787   In March, his first published poem, "Sonnet, On Seeing Miss Helen Maria Williams Weep at a Tale of Distress," appears in *European Magazine*. In the fall, Wordsworth begins his studies at St. John's College, Cambridge University, as a sizar, a designation applied to students who pay reduced fees. Having received an excellent background in mathematics, Wordsworth is well prepared for the curriculum, though he decides early in his career at Cambridge not to pursue the prescribed path towards honors. He studies modern languages, particularly Italian, under the tutelage of Agostino Isola, where he acquires a deep appreciation for Italian poetry which, in turn, enhances his reading of Milton and Spenser.

1790   In July, Wordsworth decides to leave Cambridge to the dismay of his family who deem his behavior both mad and reckless. From July to October, he is on a walking tour of the Alps with his Welsh friend, Robert Jones and ascends Mount Snowdon. His relatives consider his decision especially dangerous in light of the political climate of revolutionary France. In the autumn, Wordsworth returns to Cambridge.

1791   In January, Wordsworth receives his B.A. from Cambridge followed by a visit to London and Wales. Sometime before Christmas, he returns to France, ostensibly to learn to speak French. Although in *The Prelude* he claims to be fairly aloof, he sympathizes with the Girondins' values and their intellectual connection with the English republican tradition.

1792   Wordsworth befriends Michael Beaupuy, a highborn Frenchman who supports the revolution. He also becomes involved with Annette Vallon, a young woman from Blois who will give birth to their daughter, Anne-Caroline, on December 15, following Wordsworth's "escape" back to

England amidst his own inner conflicts. He continues work on *Descriptive Sketches*.

1793   In January, Wordsworth publishes *An Evening Walk*, and the poem written during his year-long stay in France, *Descriptive Sketches*, both under the imprint of the radical bookseller Joseph Johnson. He spends time in London with his brother Richard, a lawyer and then travels to the Isle of Wight and back to England on foot from Salisbury to Robert Jones's home in Wales. While wandering across Sarum Plain, Wordsworth begins his early versions of the Salisbury Plain poems, later published as part of the very grim tale, "The Female Vagrant," in the *Lyrical Ballads* (1798) and in 1842 as "Guilt and Sorrow." It is also quite probable that Wordsworth makes a brief and dangerous third trip to France in October, after England and France are at war.

1794–1795   During this time, Wordsworth writes, but does not publish, "A Letter to the Bishop of Llandaff," an attack on the conservative values of the monarchy and the aristocracy associated with Edmund Burke. He is drawn to William Godwin's *An Enquiry Concerning Political Justice* (1793), which asserts that independent intellect can be severed from familial feelings and affections. There is also evidence that Wordsworth helped in the planning of the Godwinian newspaper, *The Philanthropist*, which runs for several months in 1795. Wordsworth inherits nine hundred pounds from Raisley Calvert, a Lake District friend whom he nursed during his final illness. In September, Dorothy and he establish their household, rent-free, at Racedown Lodge, Dorset. His reunion with Dorothy will prove to be critical to his "recuperation" from his experiences in France. It is here, also, that Dorothy and William will cultivate their relationship with Coleridge, whom Wordsworth met in Bristol in the late summer or early fall of 1795.

1796   Wordsworth begins composing his first major work, a tragedy in five acts, *The Borderer*. He will try unsuccessfully to stage this play in London, but it would not be published until 1841 where it would appear in revised form in his volume, *Poems, Chiefly of Early and Late Years*. *The Borderers* would also lead directly to the composition of his first major poem, *The Recluse*.

1797–1798   In order to be closer to Coleridge, the Wordsworths move to Alfoxden House, four miles from the Coleridges in the little village of Nether Stowey in Somerset. Neighbors gossip about their unconventional habits and their association with Coleridge's radical friend, John Thelwall. Here, Wordsworth composes more poems, including additions to *The Recluse*, as well as his projected poem on "Man, Nature and Society" that will never be completed.

1798   During the Alfoxden residency, Wordsworth will also write the varied poems, renditions of folk-ballads, ballad debates and blank verse, that would be published anonymously in September with selections from Coleridge as the *Lyrical Ballads*. Wordsworth and Coleridge have planned this volume in order to finance a trip to Germany. The volume sells well enough, and will be followed by further editions in the following years, and includes such artistically acclaimed poems as "Tintern Abbey," and "Michael."

1798–1799   In September, the Wordsworths accompany Coleridge to Goslar, Germany. Though Coleridge is successful in his intellectual pursuits, Wordsworth retreats into himself, suffering from nervous headaches. The German winter of 1798–1799 is bitter cold, and the Wordsworths return to England in May of 1799, settling in with old Penrith friends for seven months. It is here that Wordsworth establishes his ties with his future wife, Mary Hutchinson. Happy to be back in England, Wordsworth continues to be plagued by financial burdens. In December, Dorothy and William move to Grasmere, where they rent a cottage at Town End (later known as Dove Cottage). Continuing his work on *The Recluse*, Wordsworth celebrates his domestic contentment with what will become the first book, *Home at Grasmere*.

1800   Wordsworth publishes another edition of the *Lyrical Ballads*, adding his now-famous Preface, in which he seeks to clarify his poetic theory and rhetorical strategy.

1802   In the spring, Wordsworth writes "The Leech-Gatherer," (later known as "Resolution and Independence"), the beginnings of the Intimations Ode, many lyrics inspired by sixteenth and seventeenth poetry, and a revised preface to the *Lyrical Ballads*. He also begins to receive letters from Annette Vallon. With the Peace of Amiens in place, Wordsworth decides to go to France, with Dorothy accompanying him.

He spends the month of August in Calais with Annette and Caroline, and writes a group of sonnets that exhibit his anxiety, and departs France on friendly terms. Wordsworth and Mary Hutchinson are married on October 2, and his finances improve, with Lowther heirs agreeing to repay the debt to John Wordsworth's estate.

1803   John Wordsworth is born on June 18. In August, Wordsworth, Dorothy and Coleridge tour Scotland, where they visit Sir Walter Scott. However, the tour is not entirely happy as Coleridge has fallen in love with Sara Hutchinson and, suffering from ill health and drug dependency, decides to go to the Mediterranean.

1804   At the beginning of the year, Wordsworth begins working in earnest on *The Prelude* and, by March, has completed a five-book version covering his life through his days at Cambridge University. Dorothy (Dora) Wordsworth born on August 16.

1805   On February 5, Wordsworth's beloved younger brother, John, drowns with many of his crew when his ship is wrecked by a storm near Weymouth Bay. Wordsworth is so distraught he cannot write tributes to his deceased brother. By May, he has completed the thirteen-book *Prelude*. However, only members of Wordsworth's circle can provide a response to the text as *The Prelude* would not be published until 1850.

1806   In May or June, with his brother in mind as well as his own trip to Piel Castle in 1794, Wordsworth writes "Elegaic Stanzas Suggested by a Picture of Peele Castle, in a Storm, by Sir George Beaumont." Thomas Wordsworth is born on June 16. During this period, Wordsworth becomes a regular churchgoer, reveals his skill as a landscape gardener and makes frequent trips to London in late summer and early fall. He is also concerned about Coleridge, and is shocked by his friend's bad health and broken spirit when the two meet again in the fall. In October, the Wordsworths take up residence at Coleorton where they will live until June of 1807.

1807   During the spring at Coleorton, Wordsworth is busy preparing copy for his new publication to appear in May as *Poems, in two Volumes*, which include many of his finest works, such as the Intimations Ode, "Resolution and

Independence," "The Solitary Reaper," and "I wandered lonely as a cloud." Nevertheless, the volumes receive terrible reviews, chief among them Francis Jeffrey's indictment in the *Edinburgh Review* in the October 7 issue.

1808   *The White Doe of Rylstone*, a poem in seven cantos, is completed in January, but will take seven years before it is published in 1815. In May, the family moves across Grasmere Vale from Town End to Allan Bank, a larger house to accommodate the growing family. Wordsworth will live here for three years, working intermittently on what will become *The Excursion* (1814) as well as writing a good deal of prose. Catharine Wordsworth is born September 6.

1809   *The Convention of Cintra* is published. The first of Wordsworth's *Essays Upon Epitaphs* appears in Coleridge's publication *The Friend* (February 22, 1809)

1810   The beginning of Wordsworth's long and painful disagreement with Coleridge. *A Guide to the Lakes*, published as an introduction to *Select Views in Cumberland, Westmoreland, and Lancashire* and three *Essays Upon Epitaphs*.

1811   In June, the Wordsworths move to Grasmere Vicarage.

1812   In the spring, Wordsworth and Coleridge are reconciled, although their friendship will never be as intimate as it was in their earlier years. Wordsworth's four-year-old daughter, Catherine, dies in June, followed by the six-year-old, Thomas, in December. Both Wordsworth and Mary go through a long period of mourning. Wordsworth becomes even more solicitous of his remaining children, especially Dora.

1813   In March, Sir William Lowther, Earl of Lonsdale, appoints Wordsworth as Distributor of Stamps for Westmorland and part of Cumberland. The position suits Wordsworth well by providing a supplement to his income and allowing him to travel several times a year around the counties to collect revenue. Shortly thereafter the Wordsworths move to their final home, Rydal Mount, about two miles from Grasmere.

1814   Wordsworth publishes *The Excursion*, which he dedicates to Lord Lonsdale and advertises as a portion of his work in the progress, *The Recluse*. *The Excursion* is a long poem in nine books and begins with the oft-revised version of *The Ruined*

Cottage as its first book. The poem consists of four main characters or dramatic voices: the Wanderer (the Pedlar of *The Ruined Cottage*), the Poet, the Solitary, and the Pastor. Jeffrey writes a scathing review, objecting above all to Wordsworth's lack of decorum in making pedlars and ploughmen his heroes.

1815   *The White Dove of Rylstone* is published in an expensive quarto volume with an engraving of the doe after Sir George Beaumont's painting. Wordsworth intended his quarto to rival the presentation of Byron's more popular tales. Reviews were generally mixed. In the October issue of the *Edinburgh Review*, Jeffrey complains about the poem's "metaphysical sensibility" and "mystical wordiness." Wordsworth also publishes two additional volumes of poems.

1816   Percy Bysshe Shelley attacks *The Excursion* as reactionary, seeing betrayal and apostasy in Wordsworth. Wordsworth writes "A little onward lend they guiding hand," a poem which links his need for Dora's guidance to his increasing affliction from an inflammation of the eyes.

1818   Wordsworth's campaigns for the Lowthers in Parliamentary elections and *Two Addresses to the Freeholders of Westmoreland*, arguing for "mellowed feudality" rather than democracy. Keats stops at Rydal Mount and is disappointed with Wordsworth's politics.

1819   Wordsworth publishes *Peter Bell* (written in 1798) and *The Waggoner* (probably written in 1806).

1820   Wordsworth begins to find a new audience. His first collected edition of poems appears (four volumes excluding *The Excursion*). Wordsworth also publishes a well-received collection of sonnets in *The River Duddon, Vaudracour and Julia, and Other Poems.*

1821   Wordsworth is busy working on *Ecclesiastical Sonnets.*

1822   Wordsworth publishes *Memorials of a Tour on the Continent, 1820*, the result of one of his many trips to Europe, and *Ecclesiastical Sketches*, sonnets influenced by his brother Christopher Wordsworth and his work in Church history.

1824   Byron dies. Wordsworth begins to enjoy a growing popularity. In the late 1820s he is admired and promoted by the Apostles at Cambridge, a group of poets including

Tennyson, Arthur Henry Hallam, and Richard Monckton Milnes.

1827   Wordsworth publishes a five-volume collection of poems.

1828   A pirated edition of his complete works comes out in Paris. In the Christmas issue of *The Keepsake* Wordsworth publishes "The Promise" (later "The Triad"), praising the domestic and nurturing virtues of Edith Southey, Dora Wordsworth, and Sara Coleridge, daughters of the poets.

1832   Sir Walter Scott dies.

1834   Samuel Taylor Coleridge dies.

1835   While in the Lake District, Tennyson composes his most Wordsworthian poem, "Dora." Wordsworth's *Yarrow Revisited, and Other Poems*, including poems from the most recent tour of Scotland and other works of the 1820s and 1830s, is published. His reputation is now firmly established and his literary influence will eventually go beyond the genre of poetry: novelists such as Charles Dickens, George Eliot, and Elizabeth Gaskell are indebted to Wordsworth.

1837   Wordsworth tours Italy with Crabb Robinson and writes *Memorials of a Tour in Italy, 1837*.

1839   Shelley writes *Peter Bell the Third*, the most serious attack on Wordsworth's poem and amounts to a critique of Wordsworth's career and political views.

1842   Wordsworth finishes *The Borderers* and *Guilt and Sorrow in Poems, Chiefly of Early and Late Years*. Memorials of a Tour in Italy, 1837 is also published in this volume.

1842–1843   Between the winter of 1842 and the spring of 1843, Wordsworth dictates notes on his poems to his friend Isabella Fenwick that provide insight into his poetry.

1843   Wordsworth becomes Poet Laureate.

1847   Dora Wordsworth dies of consumption; Wordsworth will never fully emerge from his grief to compose again.

1850   In March, Wordsworth develops his final illness. In his enjoyment of walking out of doors in all weather, he develops pleurisy, and he never regains his strength. Wordsworth dies at Rydal Mount on April 23, Shakespeare's birthday and sixteen days after his own eightieth birthday. Three months after her husband's death, Mary Wordsworth brings out *The Prelude*.

1879   Matthew Arnold rehabilitates Wordsworth's poetry.

1909   A.C. Bradley claims, in the *Oxford Lectures on Poetry*, that "Wordsworth is indisputably the most sublime of our poets since Milton."

Contributors

HAROLD BLOOM is Sterling Professor of the Humanities at Yale University. He is the author of 30 books, including *Shelley's Mythmaking* (1959), *The Visionary Company* (1961), *Blake's Apocalypse* (1963), *Yeats* (1970), *A Map of Misreading* (1975), *Kabbalah and Criticism* (1975), *Agon: Toward a Theory of Revisionism* (1982), *The American Religion* (1992), *The Western Canon* (1994), and *Omens of Millennium: The Gnosis of Angels, Dreams, and Resurrection* (1996). *The Anxiety of Influence* (1973) sets forth Professor Bloom's provocative theory of the literary relationships between the great writers and their predecessors. His most recent books include *Shakespeare: The Invention of the Human* (1998), a 1998 National Book Award finalist, *How to Read and Why* (2000), *Genius: A Mosaic of One Hundred Exemplary Creative Minds* (2002), *Hamlet: Poem Unlimited* (2003), *Where Shall Wisdom Be Found?* (2004), and *Jesus and Yahweh: The Names Divine* (2005). In 1999, Professor Bloom received the prestigious American Academy of Arts and Letters Gold Medal for Criticism. He has also received the International Prize of Catalonia, the Alfonso Reyes Prize of Mexico, and the Hans Christian Andersen Bicentennial Prize of Denmark.

M.H. ABRAMS is Class of 1916 Professor of English Emeritus at Cornell University. He is general editor of the *Norton Anthology of English Literature*; and the author of *The Mirror and the Lamp: Romantic Theory and the Critical Tradition* (1953); *Natural Supernaturalism: Tradition and Revolution in Romantic Literature* (1971); and *The Correspondent Breeze: Essays on English Romanticism* (1984).

FRANCES FERGUSON has been a professor of English at Johns Hopkins University. She is the author of *Solitude and the Sublime: Romanticism and the Aesthetics of Individuation* (1992); an editor of *The Wordsworthian Enlightenment: Romantic Poetry and the Ecology of Reading: Essays in Honor of Geoffrey Hartman* (2005), and editor of *Jane Austen's "Emma"* (2006) .

PAUL H. FRY has been a professor of English at Yale University. He is the author of *The Reach of Criticism: Method and Perception in Literary Theory* (1983), *William Empson: Prophet Against Sacrifice* (1991), and *A Defense of Poetry: Reflections on the Occasion of Writing* (1995).

THOMAS WEISKEL, who died in a tragic accident at the age of twenty-nine, was a professor of English at Yale University. He is the author of *The Romantic Sublime: Studies in the Structure and Psychology of Transcendence* (1976).

GEOFFREY HARTMAN is Sterling Professor Emeritus of English and Comparative Literature at Yale University. He is the author of *Wordsworth's Poetry, 1787–1814* (1964), *The Unmediated Vision: An Interpretation of Wordsworth, Hopkins, Rilke, and Valery* (1954), *A Critic's Journey: Literary reflections, 1958–1998* (1999) and *Beyond Formalism: Literary Essays, 1958–1970* (1975).

DAVID BROMWICH is Sterling Professor of English at Yale University. He is the author of *Hazlitt: The Mind of a Critic* (1983), *A Choice of Inheritance: Self and Community from Edmund Burke to Robert Frost* (1989); *Disowned by Memory: Wordsworth's Poetry of the 1790s* (1998), and *Skeptical Music: Essays on Modern Poetry* (2001).

KENNETH R. JOHNSTON has been a professor of English at Indiana University. He is the author of *Wordsworth and The Recluse* (1984), *The Hidden Wordsworth: Poet-Lover-Rebel-Spy* (1998) and an editor of *The Age of William Wordsworth: Critical Essays on the Romantic Tradition* (1987).

JONATHAN WORDSWORTH has been a professor of English literature at Oxford University. He is the author of *The Music of Humanity: A Critical Study of Wordsworth's "Ruined Cottage"* (1969), *William Wordsworth: The Borders of Vision* (1983), *New Penguin Book of Romantic Poetry* (2003) and editor of *The Prelude: The Four Texts (1798, 1799, 1805, 1850)* (1995).

DENNIS TAYLOR has been a professor of English at Boston College. He is the author of *Hardy's Poetry, 1860-1928* (1981), *Hardy's Literary Language and Victorian Philology* (1993), and an editor of *Shakespeare and the Culture of Christianity in Early Modern England* (2003).

SALLY BUSHELL is a professor in the English Department at Lancaster University. She is currently completing working on a book entitled *A Compositional Method: Wordsworth, Tennyson, Dickinson* which will be published by the University Press of Virginia and is co-editor of the forthcoming Cornell Edition of *The Excursion* with James Butler and Michael Jaye.

Bibliography

Abrams, Meyer Howard, ed. *The Mirror and the Lamp: Romantic Theory and the Critical Tradition*. New York: Oxford University Press, 1953.

———. *English Romantic Poets: Modern Essays in Criticism*. New York: Oxford University Press, 1960.

———. *Natural Supernaturalism: Tradition and Revolution in Romantic Literature*. London: Oxford University Press, 1971.

Averill, James. *Wordsworth and the Poetry of Human Suffering*. Ithaca, N.Y.: Cornell University Press, 1980.

Baker, Jeffrey. *Time and Mind in Wordsworth's Poetry*. Detroit, MI: Wayne State University Press, 1980.

Barker, Juliet R.V. *Wordsworth: A Life*. New York: Ecco, 2005.

Beer, John B. *Wordsworth and the Human Heart*. New York: Columbia University Press, 1978.

Bernhardt-Kabisch, Ernest, "The Stone and the Shell: Wordsworth, Cataclysm, and the Myth of Glaucus." *Studies in Romanticism* vol. 23, no. 4 (Winter 1984): 455– 490.

Bewell, Alan J. Wordsworth and the Enlightenment: Nature, Man, and Society in the Experimental Poetry. New Haven: Yale University Press, 1989.

Bialostosky, Don H. *Making Tales: The Poetics of Wordsworth's Narrative Experiments*. Chicago: The University of Chicago Press, 1984.

Blades, John. *Wordsworth and Coleridge: Lyrical Ballads*. Houndmills, Basingstoke, Hampshire; New York: Palgrave Macmillan, 2004.

Blank, G. Kim. *Wordsworth and Feeling: The Poetry of an Adult Child.* Madison, N.J.: Fairleigh Dickinson University Press; London: Associated University Presses, 1995.

——. *Wordsworth's Influence on Shelley: A Study of Poetic Authority.* New York: St. Martin's Press, 1988.

Bloom, Harold (ed.). *William Wordsworth's "The Prelude."* New York: Chelsea House, 1986.

——. *The Visionary Company: A Reading of English Romantic Poetry.* Ithaca: Cornell University Press, 1971.

——. *Romanticism and Consciousness: Essays in Criticism.* New York: Norton, 1970.

Brennan, Matthew, "The Light of Wordsworth's Desire for Darkness in *The Prelude*." *Romanticism Past and Present* vol. 7, no. 2 (Summer 1983): 27-40.

Brett, R.L. and A.R. Jones, eds. *Lyrical Ballads, 1798 and 1800.* London: Methuen, 1978.

Chase, Cynthia, "The Ring of Gyges and the Coat of Darkness: Reading Rousseau with Wordsworth." In *Romanticism and Language.* Edited by Reed Arden. Ithaca: Cornell University Press (1984): 50–85.

Clancey, Richard W. *Wordsworth's Classical Undersong: Education, Rhetoric and Poetic Truth.* New York: St. Martin's Press, 2000.

Davis, James P. "The 'Spots of Time': Wordsworth's Poetic Debt to Coleridge." In *Colby Quarterly* vol. 28, no. 2 (June, 1992): 65–84.

De Man, Paul. "Time and History in Wordsworth." *Diacritics*, vol. 17, no. 4 (Winter 1987): 4-17.

——. "Wordsworth and the Victorians." In *The Rhetoric of Romanticism.* New York: Columbia University Press, 1984.

Devlin, David Douglas. *Wordsworth and the Poetry of Epitaphs.* London: Macmillan Press, 1980.

——. *Wordsworth and the Art of Prose.* London: Macmillan Press, 1983.

Durrant, Geoffrey H. *Wordsworth and the Great System: A Study of Wordsworth's Poetic Universe.* Cambridge: Cambridge University Press, 1970.

Edmundson, Mark. *Towards Reading Freud: Self Creation in Milton, Wordsworth, Emerson, and Sigmund Freud.* Princeton: Princeton University Press, 1990.

Eilenberg, Susan. *Strange Power of Speech: Wordsworth, Coleridge and Literary Possession.* New York: Oxford University Press, 1992.

Erskine Hill, Howard. "The Satirical Game at Cards in Pope and Wordsworth." *English Satire and the Satiric Tradition*, edited by Claude Rawson. Oxford: Blackwell, (1984): 183–195.

Ferris, David. "Where Three Paths Meet: History, Wordsworth, and the Simplon Pass." *Studies in Romanticism* vol. 30, no. 3 (Fall 1991): 391–438.

———. *The Limits of Mortality: An Essay on Wordsworth's Major Poems.* Middletown, Conn.: Wesleyan University Press, 1959.

Gérard, Albert S. *English Romantic Poetry: Ethos, Structure and Symbol in Coleridge, Wordsworth, Shelley and Keats.* Berkeley: University of California Press, 1968.

Gill, Stephen, ed. *The Salisbury Plain Poems of William Wordsworth.* Ithaca: Cornell University Press, 1975.

Graver, Bruce E. "'Honorable Toile': The Georgic Ethic of Prelude 1." In *Studies in Philology* vol. 92, no. 3 (Summer 1995): 346–360.

Gravil, Richard. *Wordsworth's Bardic Vocation: 1787–1842.* New York: Palgrave Macmillan, 2003.

Griffin, Robert J. *Wordsworth's Pope: A Study in Literary Historiography.* Cambridge; New York: Cambridge University Press, 1996.

Grob, Alan. *The Philosophic Mind: A Study of Wordsworth's Poetry and Thought, 1797–1805.* Columbus: Ohio University Press, 1973.

Haney, David P. *William Wordsworth and the Hermeneutics of Incarnation.* University Park: Pennsylvania State University Press, 1993.

———. *Wordsworth: A Poet's History.* Basingstoke, Hampshire; New York: Palgrave, 2001.

———. Haney, David P. "Catachresis and the Romantic Will: The Imagination's Usurpation in Wordsworth's *Prelude*, Book 6." *Style*, vol. 23, no. 1 (Spring 1989): 16–31.

———. "The Emergence of the Autobiographical Figure in *The Prelude*, Book I." *Studies in Romanticism* vol. 20, no. 1 (Spring 1981) 33–63.

Havens, Raymond Dexter. *The Mind of a Poet.* Baltimore: Johns Hopkins University Press, 1972.

Hartman, Geoffrey. *Wordsworth's Poetry: 1787–1814.* New Haven and London: Yale University Press, 1971.

———, ed. *The Selected Poetry and Prose of Wordsworth.* New York: New American Library, 1980.

———. *The Unremarkable Wordsworth.* Minneapolis: University of Minnesota Press, 1987.

Heath, William Webster. *Wordsworth and Coleridge: A Study of their Literary Relations in 1801–1802.* Oxford: Clarendon Press, 1970.

Heffernan, James A.W., "The Presence of the Absent Mother in Wordsworth's *Prelude*." *Studies in Romanticism* vol. 27, no. 2 (Summer 1988): 253–272.

Hodgson, John A. *Wordsworth's Philosophical Poetry, 1797–1814*. Lincoln: University of Nebraska Press, 1980.

———. "'Was It for This...?': Wordsworth's Virgilian Questionings." *Texas Studies in Literature and Language* vol. 33, no. 2 (Summer 1991): 125–136.

———. "Tidings: Revolution in The Prelude." *Studies in* Romanticism vol. 31, no. 1 (Spring 1992): 45–70.

Jacobus, Mary. *Tradition and Experiment in Wordsworth's Lyrical Ballads (1798)*. Oxford: Clarendon Press, 1976.

Johnston, Kenneth R. *Wordsworth and "The Recluse."* New Haven: Yale University Press, 1984.

Jones, John. *The Egotistical Sublime: A History of Wordsworth's Imagination*. London: Chatto & Windus, 1954.

Kelly, Theresa M. "Spirit and Geometric Form: The Stone and the Shell in Wordsworth's Arab Dream." *Studies in English Literature, 1500–1900* vol. 22, no. 4 (Autumn 1982): 563–582.

Kneale, J. Douglas. "Romantic Aversions: Apostrophe Reconsidered." In *Rhetorical Traditions and British Romantic Literature*. Edited by Don H.. Bialostosky and Lawrence D. Needham. Bloomington: Indiana University Press (1995): 149–166.

———. "Milton, Wordsworth, and the 'Joint Labourers' of *The Prelude*." *English Studies in Canada* vol 12, no.1 (Mar 1986): 37–54.

———. "The Rhetoric of Imagination in *The Prelude*," *ARIEL* vol. 15, no. 4 (October 1984): 111–127.

Kramer, Lawrence. "The 'Intimations Ode' and Victorian Romanticism. *Victorian Poetry* 18 (1980): 315–335.

Lindenberger, Herbert. *On Wordsworth's Prelude*. Princeton, N.J.: Princeton University Press, 1963.

Liu, Alan. *Wordsworth: The Sense of History*. Stanford, Calif.: Stanford University Press, 1989.

Lyon, Judson Stanley. *The Excursion: A Study*. New Haven: Yale University Press, 1950.

Magnuson, Paul. *Coleridge and Wordsworth: A Lyrical Dialogue*. Princeton, N.J.: Princeton University Press, 1988.

Manning, Peter J. "Reading Wordsworth's Revisions: Othello and the Drowned Man." *Studies in Romanticism* vol. 22, no. 2 (Spring 1983): 3–28.

Matlak, Richard E. *The Poetry of Relationship: The Wordsworths and Coleridge, 1797–1800*. New York: St. Martin's, 1997.

———. "Wordsworth's Lucy Poems in Psychobiographical Context." *PMLA* 93 (January 1978): 46–65.

McConnell, Frank D. *The Confessional Imagination: A Reading of Wordsworth's "Prelude."* Baltimore: Johns Hopkins University Press, 1974.

McFarland, Thomas. *Romanticism and the Forms of Ruin: Wordsworth, Coleridge and the Modalities of Fragmentation*. Princeton: Princeton University Press, 1981.

McGhee, Richard D. *Guilty Pleasures: William Wordsworth's Poetry of Psychoanalysis*. Troy, New York: The Whitston Publishing Company (1993).

Miall, David S. "Wordsworth and *The Prelude*: The Problematics of Feeling." *Studies in Romanticism* vol. 31, no. 2 (Summer 1992): 233–253.

Mitchell, W. J. T. "Influence, Autobiography, and Literary History: Rousseau's Confessions and Wordsworth's *The Prelude*." *English Literary History* vol. 57, no. 3 (Fall 1990): 643–664.

Morton, Lionel. "Books and Drowned Men: Unconscious Mourning in Book V of *The Prelude*." *English Studies in Canada* vol. 8, no. 1 (March 1982): 23–37.

Mudge, Bradford K. "Song of Himself: Crisis and Selection in *The Prelude*, Books 1 and 7." *Texas Studies in Literature and Language* vol. 27, no. 1 (Spring 1985): 1–24.

Noyes, Russell. *Wordsworth and the Art of Landscape*. Bloomington: Indiana University Press, 1968.

Onorato, Richard. *The Character of the Poet: Wordsworth in The "Prelude."* Princeton: Princeton University Press, 1971.

Owen, W. J. B., "Such Structures as the Mind Builds." In *The Mind in Creation: Essays on English Romantic Literature in Honor of Ross G. Woodman*. Edited by Douglas J. Kneale. Montreal: McGill-Queen's University Press (1992): 27–43.

Pace, Joel and Matthew Scott, eds. *Wordsworth in American Literary Culture*. New York: Palgrave Macmillan, 2005.

Page, Judith W. *Wordsworth and the Cultivation of Women*. Berkeley: University of California Press, 1994.

Parrish, Stephen Maxfield. *The Art of the Lyrical Ballads*. Cambridge: Harvard University Press, 1973.

Patterson, Annabel. *Pastoral and Ideology: Virgil to Valéry*. Berkeley: University of California Press (1987): 193–262.

Perkins, David. *The Quest for Permanence*. Cambridge: Harvard University Press, 1965.

———. *Wordsworth and the Poetry of Sincerity*. Cambridge, Belknap Press of Harvard University Press, 1964.

Pfau, Thomas. *Wordsworth's Profession*. Stanford: Stanford University Press, 1997.

Philmus, Robert M., "Wordsworth and the Interpretation of Dreams." In *Papers on Language and Literature* vol. 31, no. 2 (Spring 1995): 184–205.

Pinion, F.B. *A Wordsworth Companion: Survey and Assessment*. New York: Macmillan, 1984.

Pirie, David. *William Wordsworth: The Poetry of Grandeur and of Tenderness*. London and New York: Methuen, 1982.

Potkay, Adam, "'A Satire on Myself': Wordsworth and the Infant Prodigy." *Nineteenth Century Literature* vol. 49, no. 2 (September 1994): 149–166.

Reed, Mark L. *Wordsworth: The Chronology of the Early Years, 1770–1799*. Cambridge: Harvard University Press, 1967.

———. *Wordsworth: The Chronology of the Middle Years, 1800–1815*. Cambridge: Harvard University Press, 1975.

Regueiro, Helen. *The Limits of Imagination: Wordsworth, Yeats, and Stevens*. Ithaca: Cornell University Press, 1976.

Rehder, Robert. *Wordsworth and the Beginnings of Modern Poetry*. Totowa, New Jersey: Barnes and Noble, 1981.

Roe, Nicholas. *Wordsworth and Coleridge: The Radical Years*. Oxford: Clarendon Press; New York: Oxford University Press, 1988.

———. "Wordsworth, Milton and the Politics of Poetic Influence." *Yearbook of English Studies* vol. 19 (1989): 112–126.

Ross, Marlon. *The Contours of Masculine Desire: Romanticism and the Rise of Women's Poetry*. New York: Oxford University Press, 1989.

Ruoff, Gene W. *Wordsworth and Coleridge: The Making of the Major Lyrics, 1802–1804*. New Brunswick, N.J.: Rutgers University Press, 1989.

——— and Kenneth R. Johnston, eds. *The Age of William Wordsworth: Critical Essays on the Romantic Tradition*. New Brunswick, N.J.: Rutgers University Press, 1987.

Setzer, Sharon M. "Sicilian Daydreams and Parisian Nightmares: Wordsworth's Representations of Plutarch's *Dion*." *Studies in English Literature, 1500–1900*, vol. 32, no. 4 (Autumn 1992): 607–624.

Sheats, Paul D., ed. *The Poetical Words of Wordsworth*. Boston: Houghton Mifflin Co., 1982.

Sherry, Charles. *Wordsworth's Poetry of the Imagination*. Oxford: Clarendon Press, 1980.

Simpson, David. *Wordsworth and the Figurings of the Real*. London: Macmillan Press, 1982.

Sitterson, Joseph C., Jr. "Oedipus in the Stolen Boat: Psychoanalysis and Subjectivity in *The Prelude*." *Studies in Philology* vol. 86, no. 1 (Winter 1989): 96–115.

Simpson, David. *Wordsworth and the Figurings of the Real*. Atlantic Highlands, N.J.: Humanities Press, 1982.

———. *Wordsworth's Historical Imagination: The Poetry of Displacement*. New York: Methuen, 1987.

Stein, Edwin. *Wordsworth's Art of Allusion*. University Park: Pennsylvania State University Press, 1988.

Stoddard, E.W. "'All freaks of nature': The Human Grotesque in Wordsworth's City." *Philological Quarterly* vol. 67, no. 1 (Winter 1988): 37–61.

Waldoff, Leon. *Wordsworth in His Major Lyrics: The Art and Psychology of Self-Representation*. Columbia: University of Missouri Press, 2001.

Warminski, Andrzej. "Missed Crossing: Wordsworth's Apocalypses." *MLN* vol. 99, no. 5 (December 1984): 983–1006.

Watson, J.R. *Wordsworth's Vital Soul: The Sacred and the Profane in Wordsworth's Poetry*. London: Macmillan, 1982.

Wedd, Mary R. "Wordsworth's 'Spots of Time.'" *Literature and Belief*, vol. 10 (1990): 43–65.

Wolfson, Susan J. *The Questioning Presence: Wordsworth, Keats, and the Interrogative Mode in Romantic Poetry*. Ithaca: Cornell University Press, 1986.

———. "The Illusion of Mastery: Wordsworth's Revisions of 'The Drowned Man of Esthwaite': 1799, 1805, 1850." *PMLA* vol. 99, no. 5 (October 1984): 917–935.

Woodman, Ross. "Milton's Satan in Wordsworth's 'Vale of Soul-Making.'" *Studies in Romanticism* vol. 23, no. 1 (Spring 1984): 3–30.

———. "Wordsworth's Crazed Bedouin: *The Prelude* and the Fate of Madness." *Studies in Romanticism* vol. 27, no. 1 (Spring 1988): 3–29.

Woolford, John, "Wordsworth Agonistes." *Essays in Criticism* vol. 31, no. 1 (January 1981): 27–40.

Wordsworth, Jonathan. "Revision As Making: *The Prelude* and Its Peers." *Bucknell Review* vol. 36, no. 1 (1992): 85–109.

———. *William Wordsworth: The Borders of Vision*. Oxford: Clarendon Press; New York: Oxford University Press, 1983.

Wu, Duncan. *Wordsworth: An Inner Life*. Oxford, UK; Malden, MA: Blackwell Publishers, 2002.

Acknowledgments

"Two Roads to Wordsworth" by M.H. Abrams. From *Wordsworth: A Collection of Critical Essays*. Englewood Cliffs, N.J.: Prentice Hall (1972): 81–91. © 1972 by Prentice Hall. Reprinted by permission.

"The Scene of Instruction: 'Tintern Abbey'" by Harold Bloom. From *Poetry and Repression: Revisionism from Blake to Stevens*. New Haven: Yale University Press (1976): 52–82. © 1976 by Yale University Press. Reprinted by permission.

The Prelude and the Love of Man" by Frances Ferguson. From *Wordsworth: Language as Counter-Spirit*. New Haven: Yale University Press (1977): 126–154. © 1977 by Yale University. Reprinted by permission.

"Wordsworth's Severe Intimations" by Paul H. Fry. From *The Poet's Calling in the English Ode*. New Haven and London: Yale University Press (1980): 136–157. © 1980 by Yale University Press. Reprinted by permission.

"Wordsworth and the Defile of the Word" by Thomas Weiskel. From *The Romantic Sublime: Studies in the Structure and Psychology of Transcendence*. Baltimore and London: Johns Hopkins University Press (1976): 167–204. © 1976 and 1986 by The Johns Hopkins University Press. Reprinted by permission.

" ' Was it for this...?': Wordsworth and the Birth of the Gods" by Geoffrey Hartman. From *Romantic Revolutions: Criticism and Theory*. Edited by Kenneth R. Johnston, Gilbert Chaitin, Karen Hanson, and Herbert Marks. Bloomington and Indianapolis: Indiana University Press (1990): 8–25. © 1990 by Indiana University Press. Reprinted by permission.

"Wordsworth to Emerson" by David Bromwich. From *Romantic Revolutions: Criticism and Theory*. Edited by Kenneth R. Johnston, Gilbert Chaitin, Karen Hanson, and Herbert Marks. Bloomington and Indianapolis: Indiana University Press (1990): 202–218. © 1990 by Indiana University Press. Reprinted by permission.

" 'While We Were Schoolboys': Hawkshead Education and Reading" by Kenneth R. Johnston. From *The Hidden Wordsworth: Poet, Lover, Rebel, Spy*. New York and London: W.W. Norton & Company (1998): 69–92. © 1998 by Kenneth Richard Johnston. Reprinted by permission.

"William Wordsworth, *The Prelude*" by Jonathan Wordsworth. From *A Companion to Romanticism*. Edited by Duncan Wu. Oxford, UK and Malden, Mass.: Blackwell Publishers Ltd. © 1998 by Blackwell Publishers Ltd. Reprinted by permission.

"Wordsworth's Abbey Ruins" by Dennis Taylor. From *The Fountain Light: Studies in Romanticism and Religion*. Edited by J. Robert Barth, S.J. New York: Fordham University Press (2002): 37–53. © 2002 by Fordham University Press. Reprinted by permission.

"Dramatic Composition, Dramatic Definition" by Sally Bushell. From *Re-Reading* The Excursion: *Narrative, Response and the Wordsworthian Dramatic Voice*. Hampshire, England and Burlington, VT: Ashgate Publishing Company (2002): 42–59. © 2002 by Sally Bushell. Reprinted by permission.

Every effort has been made to contact the owners of copyrighted material and secure copyright permission. Articles appearing in this volume generally appear much as they did in their original publication—in some cases Greek text has been removed from the original article. Those interested in locating the original source will find bibliographic information in the bibliography and acknowledgments sections of this volume.

Index